West Virginia

A History for Beginners

WEST VIRGINIA: A History for Beginners
Copyright © 1997 John Alexander Williams

Text layout by Rita Damous Kee
Cover by Bruce Appelgren
First Hardcover Edition
Printed in USA

ISBN 0-9627486-6-8

Published by
Appalachian Editions
Topper Sherwood, Editor
Martinsburg, West Virginia

Support materials available
at the
West Virginia: A History for Beginners website:
http://www.westvirginia.com/history

Cover art: "Harpers Ferry by Moonlight," 1874, R. Hinshelwood; Library of Congress

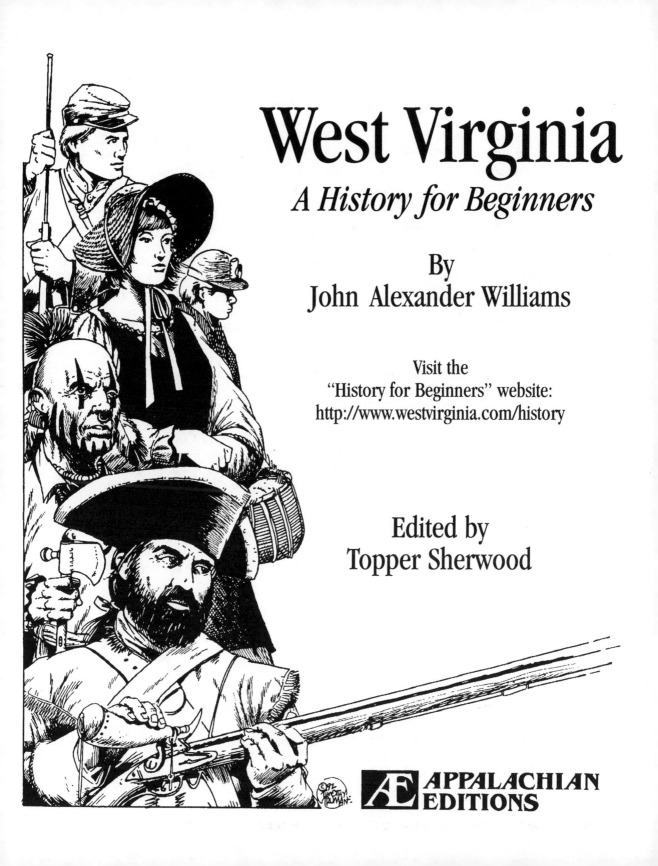

West Virginia
A History for Beginners

By
John Alexander Williams

Visit the
"History for Beginners" website:
http://www.westvirginia.com/history

Edited by
Topper Sherwood

**APPALACHIAN
EDITIONS**

Author's Acknowledgments

My first debt is to certain young people whose experience studying West Virginia history first suggested to me the need I've attempted to meet: namely, the need for a book that good teachers can use creatively to introduce ideas that students can use as adult citizens. I'm thinking in particular of Sander, Jared and Matthew Williams and Claudia and Wallace Colyer.

Without the support of Merle Moore, formerly librarian of the Clarksburg-Harrison Public Library and now of the National Mine Health and Safety Academy in Beckley, I might never have taken the project beyond the bright-idea stage. Helen Jones-formerly a teacher in Salem, West Virginia, and now on the faculty of Fairmont State College-taught me most of what I know about writing effectively for a beginning audience.

Jared Williams talked me out of shelving the project at a crucial stage, and Topper Sherwood and Gordon Simmons provided the encouragement that finally brought it to fruition. Topper also served as a model editor and occasionally too as a research assistant.

Along the way, we relied-as historians must-on the work of archivists and librarians, particularly the Kanawha County Public Library, West Virginia University, the West Virginia Division of Culture and History, the Library of Congress, the National Parks Service, the National Archives, and the Appalachian Collection at Appalachian State University.

George Parkinson, Harold Forbes, Fred Armstrong, John Cuthbert, Martha Neville and Dean Williams were especially supportive. I am grateful for the encouragement and help of all these good people and I exempt each of them from blame for any defects that remain in the book despite their care.

John Alexander Williams

* * *

The publisher would like to thank Christine M. Kreiser and Latelle LaFollette IV for their valuable assistance in preparing this book. Also, credit should be given to the West Virginia and Regional History Collections, West Virginia University Libraries for the photos labeled "West Virginia Collection - WVU Library."

TABLE OF CONTENTS

INTRODUCTION

People are the same, everywhere you find them. They have to eat. They need fresh water, food, clothing, and shelter. If they are very young - or, sometimes, very old - they need someone to care for them. These are basic human needs. They are the same for someone living in West Virginia, in Oregon, or Delaware. They are the same today as they were twenty years ago, or two centuries.

People are the same, yet they are different. Our differences exist in the ways we act to meet our basic needs. Some people hunt for their food; others grow it. Most people you know likely get it from a store. All of these are differences in human behavior, and they exist in the ways we buy and sell, work and play - the ways in which we live. Differences exist in languages, customs, housing, styles of art, as well as in the institutions we establish to express our hopes and meet our goals - our governments, schools, and religious organizations.

The list can be as long as you make it. But the point here is that the differences and similarities we find among people are important. They are important to understand because learning about them is an essential part of learning about ourselves and the world in which we live.

You are about to study the differences and similarities among the people of West Virginia as they have acted as individuals and in groups - in families, communities, societies, corporations and government. Understanding the group - or social - behavior of human beings is what social studies is all about.

Studying history helps us understand the social behavior of people who lived in the past. By observing the changes which affected their lives, we can also observe the ways in which our society came to be the way it is today. Thus, studying history is how we learn to observe and understand social change.

West Virginia is a relatively large place that has nurtured a diverse population for a long time. The varieties of human behavior occurring in its history make it well worth studying. This is easier than it sounds. The state is not so large, nor the historical figures so far-removed in time as to make it hard for us to imagine what life was like for them, the people who lived here years ago.

Even today, we can still observe the interaction of a variety of cultures, each within its own distinctive natural environment. In studying the history of our own state, we can develop skills for observing social behavior. With practice, we can learn to organize our observations into general explanations of how societies change over time. Studying a society "close to home" gives us a command of skills, methods and concepts that we can apply later to other, broader areas.

There is still another reason for studying West Virginia history - a more philosophical reason. It was nicely summed-up by an old mountain man, whose granddaughter questioned the value of learning the family history: "Why, girl," he said, "how can we know where we're going, if we don't know where we've been?"

You, the student reading this book, are likely to spend at least part of your adult life in West Virginia. As a citizen of the state, you will be called upon to make judgments and choices for the future, no doubt involving others who live here. A knowledge of West Virginia's resources - including its institutions and cultural values - will help you make more intelligent decisions about our future. Simply put, you should be better able to decide where your state should go if you know where it's been.

- John Alexander Williams

PART I:
Becoming A
Settled
Frontier

Chapter 1:
The Prehistory of West Virginia

One of West Virginia's most famous landmarks lies in the center of Moundsville - the **Grave Creek Indian Mound**. The Grave Creek Mound was already very old - more than 2,000 years old - when it was discovered by the first European explorers, traveling along the banks of the Ohio River during the 1700s. The mound was also very large - 69 feet (21 meters) high and 295 feet (90 meters) in diameter. In fact, for many decades after Europeans first noticed it, the Grave Creek Mound remained the largest object made by humans in this part of North America.

From investigations of smaller mounds, eighteenth-century Europeans realized that mounds were used for Indian burials. A small number of skeletons found in shallow graves near the top of the Grave Creek Mound seemed to confirm this. From the size of the mound, it seemed logical to assume that it contained thousands of Indian skeletons.

Thus, before the mound was first excavated in 1838, the mystery focused not on its contents but on the question of why so many bodies had been buried in one place. One theory supposedly came from a Native American leader who was questioned about the origin of the mound. He suggested that it was built in honor of thousands of warriors who had died in an ancient battle nearby. Another theory held that the mound had served as sort of a national cemetery for its prehistoric builders, who simply piled graves on top of one another until there was no more room at the top.

Because the mound is so large, it could not have been constructed in a casual manner. It had to have

1.1 The Mystery of the Mounds

Topper Sherwood

The Grave Creek Mound, in Marshall County

been built by a large number of people working together over a short time, or by the persistent efforts of a small group working for a very long time. Either way, the mound implies a fairly high level of social organization among the people who built it.

Some early white people assumed that such a task was beyond the capabilities of native societies. Thus, they theorized that the Mound Builders were actually Europeans who came across the Atlantic in pre-Columbian times (that is, before Christopher Columbus's voyage from Spain to America in 1492). Some theories even linked the Mound Builders to the civilization that constructed the ancient pyramids of Egypt.

Most of these theories collapsed in 1838, when the Grave Creek Mound was finally opened. Excavations that year showed that only three people were buried inside the mound. A man's remains were found in a wooden tomb, located about halfway between the top and the bottom. The skeletons of another man and a woman were found in another log tomb in the center of the mound, at its base. No mass grave was discovered, nor were there any golden treasures, as had been the case in some of the pyramids of Egypt. In addition to the remains, however, a small number of simple objects - flint spear points, copper ornaments and shell beads - were discovered near the two male skeletons.

Cross-section diagram of the Grave Creek Mound

On the basis of the new evidence, investigators concluded that earlier theories about the mound had been wrong. They inferred that the shallow graves near the top of the mound came from relatively recent Native American burials. They concluded that these burials were not associated with the ancient tombs inside.

From the way it was constructed, nineteenth-century researchers also concluded that the mound had been built in two stages from materials gathered nearby. The bottom tomb was constructed and then covered by a smaller mound. Then, much later, the second tomb was built on top of the first and covered in exactly the same way. It seemed reasonable to conclude that both tombs were intended to honor the people who were buried there, especially the two males, who were probably chieftains or religious leaders in the societies of their times.

The interpretation of this evidence solved the mystery about the function of the mound. But it did not settle all the questions the ancient monument inspired. For most of the nineteenth century, people continued to speculate about the age of the mound and the society that built it.

In 1839, the owners of the land took advantage of people's natural curiosity, and opened up a small museum in the lower tomb, hoping to make money from tourists. One of the skeletons was hung upon the museum wall, and a stone tablet - supposedly found when the mound was opened - was displayed.

Few visitors were drawn by this gloomy attraction, however, and the museum soon went out of business. The skeletal remains found in the Indian mound became scattered, and much of them have since been lost. Also lost was the tablet, whose markings were thought to be some kind of writing. (Later, the marks were "translated" into English and French. Various "experts" suggested that the writing, if it was such, was Old Norse, the language spoken in medieval Scandinavia. Others thought it was ancient Egyptian.)

Ideas and Issues: Evidence, Inference and Interpretation

The mystery of the Mound Builders is a good place to introduce you to some useful concepts for studying history. These concepts are **evidence**, **inference**, and **interpretation**. Two other important concepts are **prehistoric** and **historic**. It will be helpful to read more about all of these concepts before we return to the mystery of the Grave Creek Mound.

Like police detectives, historians search for **evidence**, which consists of facts about some kind of human activity or values that existed in the past. But gathering evidence is only the first thing historians do. The evidence must next be processed. This involves two different steps. You must sort out (*classify*) the evidence so that you can see what types of facts you have gathered, how much of each different type, and so on. And you must **evaluate** it, which means to make a judgment about its quality. Evaluation nearly always involves some sort of comparison. You can compare the facts gathered from one source to facts gathered from another. (Is source A better than source B?) Or you can compare them with some ideal level of quality. (Is the evidence enough or too little? Is it solid or is it shaky?)

The final step in the historian's job is to **interpret** the evidence. This is a complicated step because of the need to make **inferences**. Like detectives, historians rarely find enough evidence to form a complete explanation of what happened (or when it happened, or why it happened, or who did what to whom). Instead they have to piece the evidence together with inferences. A television cop might call these inferences "hunches." An historian calls them "theories." In either case, the inferences amount to the same thing.

Inferences are formed when historians use their imaginations to fill in the blank spaces between the pieces of evidence they have gathered. The theories must be based on the evidence, but they stretch it further than it will go by itself. They are like bridges which cover the gaps in the evidence. If there is a lot of evidence, the gaps are small and the bridges will be strong, able to support a very solid explanation of the historical behavior involved. The less evidence there is, the greater the need for inferences, and the greater the need for imagination. In this case, the theories which fill in the gaps are likely to be numerous and will be too weak to bear the weight of a very strong explanation.

If the evidence is hard to find, then sometimes theories about past behavior or events can get pretty far off base. It is easy for your imagination to run wild if it is not held down by some facts. This is what happened when people tried to explain the mystery of the Mound Builders. Before the mound was opened, they guessed that there were thousands of graves there. This was a logical inference, but a wrong one. Then, when excavating the mound proved this wrong, they made other, even wilder guesses to explain other parts of the mystery.

Thus it is important to learn to distinguish between evidence and inference, between facts and theories. As a producer of history, you will need to do this in order to develop the most accurate possible explanations of past behavior and events. As a consumer of history, this will help you judge the accuracy of someone else's explanations. You will be able to tell how much of a particular explanation is based on evidence and how much on interpretation.

In its simplest terms, the historian's interpretation clears up the mystery that he or she has investigated. It identifies the most important evidence and inferences and tells, in the simplest possible terms, exactly what happened (or when, where, why or to whom). Think again about some detective stories you have seen or read. Wasn't there usually a scene at the end of the story in which the detective explains to a friend or a client or a boss exactly how the mystery was solved? This scene identifies the clue or clues which gave the criminal away and ties up loose ends. This scene is the interpretation.

Historians interpret their evidence a little more formally, but the process is the same. Historical interpretations can be found in museum exhibits and historical films, as well as in history books. Even when there is no formal passage in which the historian speaks directly to the reader or viewer and tells how the problem was solved, there is an interpretation. When historians decide which evidence to base an explanation on and which evidence to exclude, they are making an interpretation. The same thing is happening when the evidence is arranged in a certain order in an explanation, or a story, or a display. Some historians have an ideal of "letting the facts speak for themselves," but facts rarely do this. No matter how many facts an investigator collects, some form of interpretation will be needed to explain which facts are important and which are merely interesting.

One other important idea is the difference between **prehistoric** and **historic** societies. A related idea is the difference between **history** and **archeology**. The Mound Builders were prehistoric. That is, their society left no written records. We can observe their past behavior only by interpreting objects, such as tools or weapons or the entire array of objects found in the Grave Creek Mound.

Historic peoples are those societies which left written records, such as letters, diaries, journals, account books, government records, and many other forms of written or printed documents. Historic peoples also created objects as well as written records, so historians can use both type of evidence in studying them.

Today historians also gather evidence from oral sources. These include the memories of individuals and the traditions of groups. The oral type of evidence may not actually be written down, but it provides a record which can be compared against and added to written sources. But there is no one left alive today to relate the memories and traditions of the Mound Builders. Thus, our knowledge of them or of other prehistoric native societies is completely dependent upon finding and interpreting objects.

Archeology is the system of methods and concepts that are used to study the history of societies that disappeared and left few or no written records behind. Archeologists classify and evaluate evidence that comes in the form of objects. This evidence includes the physical remains of things which were once alive, such as human skeletons or food refuse. Archeology is also used for analyzing **material culture**, that is, the objects made by humans. Burial mounds, pottery fragments, and spear points are all examples of material culture.

As you will see when you read further, archeologists have come up with interpretations that clear up many of the mysteries of the Grave Creek Mound. These interpretations are partly based on comparisons with other prehistoric societies. Thus, before we return to the Mound Builders, it will be helpful to see how archeologists classify them in comparison to other pre-historic peoples who lived in the region that became West Virginia.

1.2 Prehistoric Peoples of West Virginia

Today, we call the first known people of our region **early hunters** or **Paleo-Indians**. The early hunters left little to tell us about their culture, other than stone projectile points, presumably from spears. But we know they hunted mastodons and other large animals, now extinct, by following the herds from place to place.

Only a small amount of material evidence of early hunters has been found in West Virginia. However, one campsite was discovered in western Pennsylvania, near West Virginia's Northern Panhandle. Evidence at this Paleo-Indian camp suggests that it was used, off and on, between 13,000 and 16,000 years ago. The hunters who left this evidence probably can be counted as West Virginia's first visitors.

Next came the **Archaic Peoples**, who discovered permanent sources of food in the shoals of the larger rivers. The large refuse heaps left along the Ohio River in the Northern Panhandle tell us that these people were gatherers, as well as hunters. They pulled fish and shellfish from the rivers and harvested wild fruits, nuts and berries from the surrounding forests.

An Archaic site on the Kanawha River, in St. Albans, was more or less continuously occupied or visited between 8,000 and

ARCHEOLOGICAL PERIODS AND CULTURES
IN WEST VIRGINIA

Time and Period	Culture & Area	Period Description
Historic 1675 -	Cherokee, Shawnee, Delaware, Seneca	Few settlements in WV
Late Woodland (Late Prehistoric) 1000 - 1675 AD	Monongahela Valley, Potomac Valley, Big Sandy Valley, Ohio County, Kanawha County, Putnam County	Settled stockaded village farmers; corn, beans and squash; many material remains. Rise of village life; decline of mound building.
Middle Woodland 500 BC - 1000 AD	Kanawha Valley, Brooke County, Nicholas County, Fayette County, Hancock County, Marshall County, Randolph County	Hopewell; burial mounds still important. Hunting and gathering economic base.
Early Woodland (Adena) 1000 BC - 500 BC	Kanawha County, Cabell County, Moundsville, Beech Bottom, Mason County	Burial mounds very important; hunting and gathering economy supplemented by minor horticulture (sunflower).
Archaic 9000 BC - 4000 BC	Putnam County, Ohio County, Brooke County, Hancock County, Kanawha County	Specialized food gathering/hunting; beginning of polished stone tools.
Paleo-Indian 11000 BC +	Around Parkersburg	Big game hunters of now-extinct mammals. Fluted projectile points.

11,000 years ago. This could be the place where West Virginia's first real "settlers" lived.

Then came what experts call the **Early Woodland** culture, the people who built the mounds. Another name for these people is the "Adena" culture. The Adena hunted and gathered food, but also grew food crops - especially sunflowers, which they cultivated for the seeds. The Adena culture flourished between 2,000 and 3,000 years ago.

After the Early Woodland period came the **Middle Woodland** societies, which practiced simpler burial rituals but grew better crops. The Middle Woodland peoples are thought to have introduced corn to our region. The best-known evidence of Middle Woodland peoples is called the Hopewell culture. Like "Adena," the name "Hopewell" comes from the site in southern Ohio where most of the culture's identifying traits were first discovered.

The Hopewell culture likely penetrated West Virginia about 2,500 years ago. Most of the mounds in the Kanawha Valley were apparently influenced by this group, as well as by the Adena culture. One example is the Murad Mound, near St. Albans, the only Kanawha Valley mound to be investigated using scientific means. The culture's influence persisted into the **Late Woodland** period, beginning about 1,000 years ago.

The Late Woodland period is also called the **Late Prehistoric** period. The people of this time appear to have been strongly influenced by the **Mississippian** culture, originating in Illinois and Missouri around 1,200 years ago. Late prehistoric people lived in villages surrounded by log stockades. They grew corn, beans and squash, and hunted deer and small animals. As many as 1,500 people may have lived in some of these settlements. Two late prehistoric cultures are known to have flourished in West Virginia. These were the **Fort Ancient** culture, along the Kanawha and lower Ohio rivers, and the **Monongahela Woodland** culture, in the Monongahela and upper Ohio valleys. Smaller groups whose cultural traits resembled the older Hopewell culture lived on in the surrounding hills.

In most respects, the late prehistoric peoples can be recognized as the ancestors of the Native Americans (Indians) who were living near West Virginia when Europeans first appeared in the region. Archeologists, however, classify Indians as historic peoples because they are mentioned in the written records that European explorers and settlers left behind.

The people whom nineteenth-century West Virginians called the "Mound Builders" are known today as the Early Woodland or Adena people. Using evidence gathered from the Adena and other Early Woodland sites, archeologists have been able to make reliable generalizations about the builders of the Grave Creek Mound, even though most of the evidence gathered from this site has been lost or destroyed.

Archeologists have also been able to evaluate some of the theories which the mound inspired during the nineteenth century. For example, since no other inscribed tablets turned up at any other Adena site, it seems reasonable to assume that the "writing" found at the Grave Creek Mound was a fraud. It may have been created by pranksters, or by someone who hoped to drum up tourist traffic at the mound.

Another theory made popular by an early, not-so-careful examination of the Moundsville skeletons was that the Adena people were unusually tall. Careful measurement of adult male skeletons at other sites, however, puts the average Adena height at five-and-a-half feet. This is three inches shorter than the average adult American male today. It seems unlikely that the Grave Creek skeletons were larger than this. The story of "giant" Mound Builders might be attributed to the fact that bones lying underground for centuries can spread apart. This can create a false impression of the skeleton's original size. The skeleton at Grave Creek also may have been mishandled when it was hung up for tourists to see.

Of course, there will always be people who prefer to believe that the Mound Builders were an ancient race of giants who spoke fluent Egyptian. Such theories are more fun to believe than facts sometimes. The lack of evidence often makes it easier for people to create such theories about prehistoric societies.

The truth is that we've been able to extract a fair amount of information about

1.3 Intrepreting the Mound Builders

Grave Creek Mound State Park

A drawing of the Grave Creek Mound as it appeared around 1850.

West Virginia's earliest cultures. Still, we know less about them than we would like. Skeletons and other objects tell us little or nothing, for example, about the languages the people spoke or the songs they sang. We know nothing about their personalities, and we can form only crude ideas about their religions, governments, or their economies. Unfortunately, historical judgments that are based on archeological bits and pieces often leave gaps for the imagination to fill.

The more clearly an interpretation identifies the evidence on which it is based, and the more clearly it separates fact from theory (that is, evidence from inference), the more accurate it is likely to be. You can see how this works by evaluating the following interpretation of the Mound Builders' culture, written by an archeologist in 1953:

> The Adena people lived in hamlets near a special burial place which was characterized by one or more earth mounds. Hunting and gathering wild foods were important aspects of Adena economy but these people were probably experimenting with farming, and they cultivated various plants, especially the sunflower. There was evidently some kind of class structure in the society, since certain individuals were buried with special honors and rites, while others received only simple burial.

How can we tell whether this interpretation is any good? It was written more than a century after the mound was first opened. But how do we really know whether the writer's understanding of the Mound Builders' culture is any better than the erroneous theories of the nineteenth-century "experts"?

It is important to ask questions like this, because most readers of history don't get a first-hand look at the evidence supporting the interpretation. That is, they will be consumers of the written history, not producers. Even when we do get a look at the evidence - as we do in museums, for example - we can't know as much about it as the people who gathered and processed it. So the question stands: How can people who are not experts tell whether a particular interpretation is accurate?

As with any other product, we begin assessing an historical interpretation by looking at its "label." The Mound Builders analysis quoted above is from a book, titled *Prehistory of the Upper Ohio Valley*, sponsored and published by the Carnegie

Museum of Pittsburgh. Major educational institutions such as universities and museums often fund historical publications and exhibits, and they usually try to make sure that the interpretations they sponsor are accurate. This means that our historical interpretation above has a pretty good "label."

Writers for newspapers and television also produce historical interpretations, but accuracy is often not the main consideration there. Too often, journalists must work quickly to produce a story that will interest their readers or viewers. For this reason, a newspaper or TV label isn't usually as reliable as one from a university or museum.

But, as you know, the label isn't everything. Although they are more reliable, the historical interpretations produced by museums and universities are very technical. They are often hard to read and, unlike newspapers, they are sometimes hard to find in the average library. (These highly technical interpretations are one of the reasons that history has the reputation of being dull.) Aside from the "label," there are two other tests you can apply to judge whether an historical interpretation is any good.

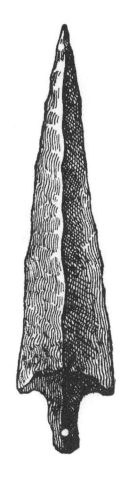

First, it should identify the evidence upon which it is based. In other words, it should describe the clues the author considered to be most important. To see how this rule works, go back to the interpretation of the Adena people quoted above. Each sentence contains one or more statements of fact. In the first sentence, *hamlets* and *earth mounds* are mentioned. In the second sentence, there is reference to *hunting and gathering* and also to the *cultivation* of plants. Each of these activities can be inferred from tools, weapons and food refuse that have been discovered frequently at Adena sites - and they are described in other parts of the author's book. Thus, these parts of the interpretation are clearly based on well-documented evidence. The author passes our first test.

Second, the interpretation should distinguish clearly between what is evidence and what is theory. In other words, you should be able to tell the difference between clues that were actually gathered or deduced, and the "bridges" the author built to cover gaps in the evidence. Look at the quotation's second and third sentences, for example. Can you find the theories they contain? Look for the words "probably" and "evidently" - words that imply a conditional statement. The second sentence says the Adena *probably* experimented with farming. Experimentation implies an attitude. We really can never know exactly *why*

Adena farmers grew plants even while they depended on hunting and gathering as the main source of their food. The author *supposes* that they were doing this in an experimental manner. But by using the conditional term "probably," he warns us that this part of his interpretation is a theory, not a fact.

The third, or last, sentence is similar. Most Adena skeletons have been found in simple burial places and only a few in large mounds. We *might* assume that there was a class structure that distinguished some Adenas as being worthy of fancy burials while many more were buried in simpler graves. But the evidence itself says only that the Adenas' cultural values produced different styles of burial, and that the simplest styles were much more common than the grandest. Thus, the suggestion that there was a "class structure" is based on theory, not on fact. Once again, the writer's language warns us that the "class structure" idea is only an assumption. In this case, he uses the word "evidently" to tell us he is theorizing. Again, this is an indicator of good historical interpretation.

1.4 Native Societies, Environment and Culture

The story of the Mound Builders shows how people living in past societies have used their natural environment to create their culture. The concept **environment** refers to all the things that influence people's lives - all their external circumstances. **Natural environment** includes all the resources and influences that originate in nature. Climate is a part of the natural environment; so are the plants, animals and minerals found on or in the earth.

Culture includes all those resources and influences that originate with people. This concept includes the material culture of a society - those objects which the society's members create for their use and enjoyment. Culture also includes the **cultural values** of the society - the customs, beliefs and attitudes that people express in their lives and pass on to their children.

Our natural environment influences our culture, and vice versa. A brief discussion of housing provides a good example of this two-way (or reciprocal) influence.

The dwellings a society builds are usually adapted to its climate. The Indian societies of West Virginia built dwellings of wood, using the region's abundant supply of trees. But in other parts of North America, a dry climate and a scarcity of trees prompted Native Americans to build houses made of earth shaped into bricks. In both cases, people adapted their material culture - in this case, their houses - to their natural environment.

At the same time, they utilized their environment to create their culture.

Two archeological concepts, in particular, help us to interpret the material culture left behind by the Mound Builders. The first is **sequence**, which derives from the fact that most of the objects remaining from prehistoric societies are found buried in the ground. Thus, archeologists have to dig for most of their evidence. Sequence is a theory that all the objects found at a particular level of an archeological "dig" were created by the same people at roughly the same time. Thus, archeologists classify the evidence they find according to the level at which it was unearthed. By comparing newer objects (found at higher levels) with older objects (found at lower levels), they can get an idea of how the material culture of a society changed. Such comparisons also show whether different societies with different cultures occupied the same site at different times.

Also important is the concept of **cultural traits**. A group that made long narrow spear points, for example, is distinguished from one that made short triangular points. Pipes that were carved into simple tubes are distinguished from pipes that were made into human or animal shapes. Similarly, the wood dwellings of West Virginia's native peoples are distinguished from the longer-lasting brick "apartment buildings" that were typical among desert natives of the American Southwest.

Archeologists at a dig in St. Albans, in Kanawha County.

Indicators of cultural traits are a society's "footprints." Cultural traits are seen in the layout of villages (as indicated by the marks that house poles left in the ground), and the types of food refuse - shells, bones, or seeds, for example - discovered at archeological sites. Traits are also defined in pottery-making techniques, tools, and burial practices. Cultural traits often become the primary basis for classifying prehistoric societies. "Mound Builders" is an example of an archeological classification based on a cultural trait - the building of mounds.

The cultural traits of ancient societies changed over time, of course. But they changed very slowly. By comparing similar objects found at different levels of a site, archeologists are able to "track" such changes. In this way, they can make a record of a particular society's evolving cultural traits.

The growth of archeology and its concepts helped twentieth-century investigators identify several different native societies in West Virginia - largely through the material cultures they left behind. Concepts such as sequence and cultural traits are specially designed to study peoples who did not leave written records. Archeologists use evidence and inference in much the same way that historians do when they study and interpret written documents.

The task of investigating and interpreting history changes when we enter the era of written documents. West Virginia history can be based on written records from the middle of the seventeenth century onward. From this point, the historian's job becomes both easier and harder. It is easier because written evidence is easier to find and interpret. It is harder because written evidence is so much more abundant.

There are still many historical mysteries for which even written evidence is scarce. But often the job of gathering written evidence is not just hunting out clues. Rather it is the task of sorting out the facts you need from documents which are crammed with facts.

As you read further, you will see that historical methods are not especially difficult to master. Whether you use them as a producer or as a consumer of history, a better knowledge of historical methods will help you make better judgments about history. Making better judgments about history is a way of learning to make judgments about your own society, the one in which you live today.

Adena artifacts discovered near the Grave Creek Mound. They include (from top) a projectile point, a pottery bowl, a deer-bone awl decorative sea shell and a stone tobacco pipe.

Study Questions - Chapter 1

1. If you were looking for "clues" to the culture of West Virginia's prehistoric people, what evidence can you find in Sections 1.1 and 1.2 that show examples of their *material culture*?

2. How did the builders of the Grave Creek Mound use their environment to create culture?

3. What do the artifacts pictured on page 14 tell us about the Adena people and their culture?

Chapter 2:
The First Historic West Virginia Societies

Ideas and Issues:
Dividing West
Virginia History
into Periods

None of the societies in West Virginia before the year 1650 created any written account of their members' activities. We call these societies "prehistoric" because they left no written records for historical study.

In the middle of the seventeenth century, European explorers came into the region, followed by the first settlers roughly one hundred years later. The arrival of these people marks the beginning of West Virginia's "historic period," because written records of human activity here begin to exist.

The historic period of West Virginia, then, is the period roughly since 1650. In order to make the interpretation of this long stretch of time easier to understand, this book divides the historic period into four shorter periods. These shorter periods include:

1. **The Frontier Period**, beginning with the first seventeenth-century explorations and extending to around 1800. The Frontier Period featured contact and conflict between the Native American peoples of the Ohio Valley and the Europeans and Euro-Americans, who arrived there after 1650. There was also conflict among different European nations over who would control the region. Such conflict often involved Indian allies of rival European groups. In spite of these conflicts, thousands of Euro-Americans, along with smaller numbers of African-Americans, moved into Western Virginia, establishing homes in a territory that previously had been controlled entirely by Native Americans. (Part I of this book explains the cultural encounters and conflicts of the Frontier Period with the help of concepts used in the discipline of anthropology.)

2. **The Statehood Period,** extending roughly from 1800 to 1880. This was the period when farming was the dominant form of economic activity in West Virginia. From the standpoint of the state's future development, however, the most important events of this

time were political. A sequence of events occurring during the Statehood Period led to the creation of the political jurisdiction called the state of West Virginia. If these events had not occurred, there would be no reason for studying West Virginia history except as a way of understanding the western part of Virginia. (Part II of this book analyzes the history of the Statehood Period using concepts from law and political science.)

3. The Industrial Period, extending roughly from 1850 to 1930. This period gets its name for economic reasons. Industrial activity was not the only form of economic activity during this period, but it was the most important one. The process of industrialization introduced important changes into the state's political, cultural and social life as well. This was particularly true of the mineral and timber industries. (Part III describes the history of the Industrial Period and introduces concepts from the discipline of economics to help you understand the changes it brought about.)

4. The Bureaucratic Period, extending roughly from 1920 to the present. The economic activities of West Virginians grew more diversified during this period. In terms of their social and cultural lives, however, people tended to become more alike. Nearly every area of the state's life was affected in some way or other by large organizations - business corporations, labor unions, government agencies and the like. Thus, the technical name for these organizations, "bureaucracies," provides an appropriate name for the period. (Part IV analyzes this period with the help of concepts drawn from the discipline of sociology.)

There were very few Indians in West Virginia when white people first began to explore and settle here. There were no permanent Indian settlements like the ones encountered by whites earlier in Eastern Virginia, Pennsylvania and New England. There were some hunting camps and a few villages that were occupied for only a few years, but there were no natives who could look back across generations and call the land of West

2.1 Native Peoples of the Frontier Period

Virginia "home."

    Explorers and settlers, however, found a lot of evidence that Indians had lived here earlier. There were, for example, "old fields" and "old towns," human-made clearings, not yet overgrown by the forest. These clearings indicated recently aban-

Location of major Native American tribes of the Eastern United States.

doned Indian settlements. One party, led by Thomas Batts and Robert Fallam, explored what is now part of southern West Virginia in September 1671. They found cultivated corn, still growing in an old field near a river. But the explorers found no people living there, and neither did the whites who came later.

What had happened to the people who made these clearings and planted the corn? This is one of the mysteries of our state's history. There are two theories about this mystery. The first is that the late-prehistoric population was wiped out by disease. Indians had no immunity to most common European diseases, such as measles or smallpox. After the first Europeans arrived on the Eastern seaboard, these diseases spread rapidly inland and they killed thousands - perhaps hundreds of thousands - of native people. Europeans thought they had found a virgin wilderness in North America. Actually, they were invading a graveyard.

Still, unless the Indians of West Virginia were more vulnerable to disease than native people elsewhere, epidemics alone do not explain their absence here. Another explanation involves the way Europeans may have affected the Indians' relations among each other. All Indian societies were weakened by disease. But some of their societies were still able to benefit more than others from the weapons and tools made by the Europeans.

In the Great Lakes region, the arrival of the whites set off a series of wars among the native societies. In these wars, the stronger tribes attacked and sometimes destroyed the weaker ones. Apparently, this also happened to many of the Indian peoples living in West Virginia. The powerful Iroquois Confederacy boasted to Virginia officials in 1744 that it had conquered "the several nations" living on the Susquehanna and Potomac rivers and "on the back of the great mountains of Virginia." Among these conquered societies were the last of the Canawese or Conoy people, who were incorporated into some Iroquois communities in New York. (The name of the Conoy survives in the names of two West Virginia rivers, the Little Kanahwa and the Great Kanawha.)

Whatever the reason for the absence of Native Americans, West Virginia was almost vacant territory when white settlement began. This led to peaceful settlement in some parts of the territory. The first settlers moved into the Shenandoah Valley in the 1730s. In the 1740s, settlers established homes along the South Branch and other tributaries of the Upper Potomac. But when the settlers made the journey across the highest mountains, and into the Ohio Valley, things began to change. They found that several Indian groups had claims to the Ohio Valley section of West Virginia. Even though none of them lived here, they considered it to be part of their hunting territory.

2.2 Iroquois, Seneca and Mingo

The struggle between Indians and whites for control of the Ohio Valley began around 1750. It continued until 1795, and involved at least four Indian societies with significant claims to West Virginia land. The largest and most powerful claimant was the Iroquois Confederacy. The Iroquois' claim to West Virginia grew out of its conquest of earlier inhabitants. The respect and fear which the Iroquois commanded from other Indians rein-

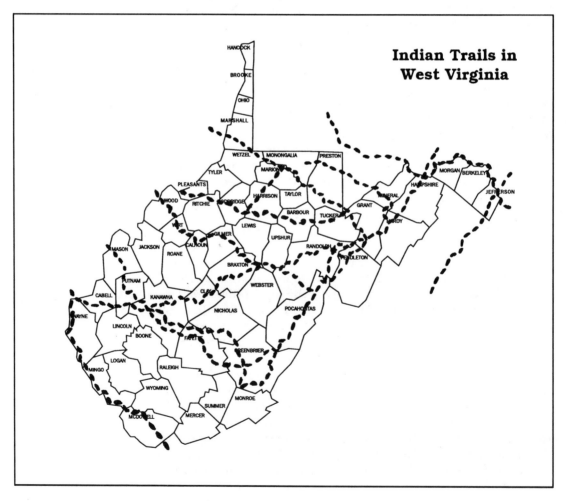

Indian Trails in West Virginia

forced their claim. Europeans also respected and feared the Iroquois. In fact, if the Iroquois had decided to resist white occupation of West Virginia, the whites might not have tried to settle here when they did.

The Iroquois had three advantages in dealing with Europeans when whites began to settle the region. First, the Iroquois had already formed an ethnic confederacy. (A confederacy is a loose political grouping of different societies.) The Iroquois Confederacy consisted of five tribes: the Mohawk, the Oneida, the Onondaga, the Cayuga and the Seneca. These tribes were connected by ethnic features, such as culture and language. They were able to form a common council in which each tribe was represented. The council discussed the serious business involving the confederacy and tried to arrive at a common policy on matters such as trade, warfare and dealings with the whites. This organization increased the Iroquois' unity and strength in dealing with outsiders.

Secondly, the Iroquois enjoyed a good strategic location. Their original territory extended from the Hudson River across central and western New York to the Genessee Valley, where Rochester, New York, is now located. This meant that the Iroquois occupied the fastest and easiest route between the Atlantic Coast and the Great Lakes region.

Some evidence suggests that the Iroquois were weaker than their neighbors before 1600. But their land holdings created a real advantage for them after the Europeans arrived. In 1608 the French established a settlement in Canada. In 1609 the Dutch explored the Hudson Valley, and began settling there in 1623. Soon, both the French and the Dutch were trying to move inland, and both of these European powers encountered the Iroquois, who were able to play them against one another.

First, the Iroquois played the French against the Dutch. Then, in 1664, the Dutch in the Hudson Valley were conquered by the English, and the Iroquois played the French against the English. Later they played the English against Americans. Thus, the Iroquois exploited their good location through skillful diplomacy. They were able to retain their independence and to hold onto their home territory for almost two hundred years after the Europeans arrived. Among the other Native American societies, only the Cherokees (whose original territory is now part of the states of Tennessee, North and South Carolina and Georgia) compiled such a good record.

Finally, the Iroquois societies shared a cultural tradition

Colorful, "turban"-style cap of silk or expensive cotton, usually decorated with the feather of a native turkey or, often, with peacock feathers acquired from traders.

Face and eyebrows plucked free of hair. Hair commonly cut short or completely shorn except for a single patch or braid. Face painted or, often, tattooed, nose pierced with silver ring. Ears slit to lobes and decorated with silver.

Silver "gorgets" and venetian "trade beads" around neck. Silver bands and bracelets on arms.

Linen or cotton muslin pullover "trade shirt" - a popular item also acquired from European traders, (sometimes white but usually made of colorful cloth).

A "pipe tomahawk" acquired from traders.

Multi-colored woven sash around waist to secure wool or heavy linen breech cloth.

Heavy blanket-wool or animal-hide "leggings" worn over bare legs with decorated flaps.

Cloth or leather "garters" to secure leggings.

Eastern native "center-seam" moccasins, made of heavy animal hide.

Typical Dress of 1700s Native American of the Ohio Valley Area

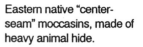

© Timothy Truman

that valued fierceness in war and a double-edged policy toward enemies. In the mid-seventeenth century, the Iroquois launched a series of wars against other Indians. In one way or another, these wars affected nearly all tribes in the eastern part of North America.

Some tribes avoided dissolution and incorporation into the Iroquois communities. Instead they became a kind of junior partner in the confederacy. As the Iroquois explained it, these tribes became "women" as far as fighting was concerned. They were not supposed to take up weapons without Iroquois permission. Politically, they became "nephews" of the Iroquois, since they could talk in Iroquois councils only by special arrangements. These tribes were supposed to let their Iroquois "uncles" speak for them in dealings with the whites.

The Tuscarora, who lived in eastern West Virginia briefly during the early eighteenth century, migrated northward to New York. In 1712, they became the sixth Indian society formally admitted to the Iroquois Confederacy. Thus, the whites sometimes referred to the Iroquois as the "Five Nations" before 1712. After 1712, the confederacy became known as the "Six Nations." The later title is somewhat misleading, for the Tuscarora never acquired full voting rights in the Iroquois council. Their status in the confederacy was somewhere between full membership and simply being "nephews."

Two Iroquois groups were particularly interested in West Virginia. One was the Seneca. This was the largest and strongest Iroquois tribe. It was also the tribe whose home territory was closest to West Virginia. Presumably, it had been Seneca warriors who had conquered the original inhabitants of the upper Ohio Valley. Many Seneca still came here to hunt in the mid-eighteenth century. Seneca and other Iroquois war parties also traveled through West Virginia on their way to attack Cherokee enemies in the South.

Tanacharison was a Seneca leader who lived in the upper Ohio Valley in the mid-eighteenth century. The English knew him as "Half-King." Although there was no such thing as royalty in Indian society, the title Half-King was not a bad translation of Tanacharison's duties. His job was to watch over the conquered peoples and territories of the upper Ohio Valley on behalf of the Seneca and other Iroquois tribes. Thus, when French influence began to grow strong in the region, he encouraged the English to come into the region too. He tried to make the English a counterweight to the French. George Washington was one of the

Virginians whom Tanacharison befriended in the process.

Another Iroquois group in the Ohio Valley was called Mingo or Minqua. The Mingos were not actually a tribe. Rather they were a multi-ethnic group. Their communities lay outside the original Iroquois territory. Different Mingo communities might have branched off from different tribes within the Iroquois Confederacy or from some of the confederacy's "nephews." Mingos had no central authority other than the Iroquois Confederacy council back in New York.

The most famous Mingo in West Virginia history was known to white people as Logan. His original name was Talgayeeta. His father, named Shikellamy, was a Cayuga leader who lived in and watched over territory that the Iroquois had conquered in central Pennsylvania. There, Talgayeeta adopted the name "Logan" after a white Pennsylvania official, James Logan. In 1763, the Iroquois gave up the territory to white settlers and Logan moved west to the Ohio River. He established a small settlement there consisting of members of his own family.

In April 1774, a group of white settlers murdered all but one of Logan's family, including the women and children. The murders took place on the West Virginia side of the river, within the present limits of Hancock County. Logan was away from home and so escaped the murderers. The brutal revenge that he took against the settlers, and the eloquent answer he gave when he was sent for by Virginia authorities, made this one of the most famous incidents on the Virginia frontier.

The Iroquois claimed the right to dispose of most of West

> I appeal to any white man to say if ever he entered Logan's cabin hungry, and he gave him not meat; if ever he came cold and naked, and he clothed him not. During the course of the long and bloody war Logan remained idle in his cabin, an advocate for peace. Such was my love for the whites, that my countrymen pointed as they passed and said, "Logan is the friend of white men." I had even thought to have lived with you but for the injuries of one man. Colonel Cresap, the last spring, in cold blood and unprovoked, murdered all the relations of Logan, not even sparing my women and children.
>
> There runs not a drop of my blood in the veins of any living creature. This called on me for revenge. I have sought it. I have killed many. I have fully glutted my vengeance. For my country I rejoice at the beams of peace. But do not harbor a thought that mine is the joy of fear. Logan never felt fear. He will not turn on his heel to save his life. Who is there to mourn for Logan? Not one.

Virginia's territory. Generally, they were happy to part with it. In a way, they were West Virginia's first "absentee landlords." The Seneca in particular exploited West Virginia resources on hunting trips. But, except for a small number of Mingos, none of the Iroquois peoples lived here. Since the Iroquois were willing to sell this territory, the whites were happy to accept the Iroquois claim of ownership. (Whenever they could, Europeans liked to deal with a central authority when they were purchasing Indian land. That is why so many minor Indian leaders turn up in European records as chieftains or kings.)

Virginia officials purchased the Iroquois title of ownership to West Virginia at the Treaty of Lancaster in 1744. This was the signal for various groups of Virginians to make preparations to move into the Ohio Valley.

Other treaties in 1768 and 1772 canceled Cherokee claims to southern West Virginia. The Iroquois and Cherokee, the largest and most powerful Indian forces in eastern North America, were willing to turn West Virginia over to the Europeans by the mid-eighteenth century. There were, however, smaller groups of Indians living nearby who were not willing to give up this territory. These included the Delawares, Wyandots and, most of all, the Shawnees.

2.3 Cherokee and Delaware

The Delawares were an important group of Indians in West Virginia. Unlike the Iroquois, the Delawares did not have centralized political institutions. They lived in small communities, which were independent of one another. They did not have overall tribal leaders or councils. Thus, it is impossible to say accurately that the Delawares did this or that. Some Delawares did one thing; other Delawares did something else. This lack of unity is one reason why the whites pushed them so quickly and easily out of their original territory. In the mid-eighteenth century, some Delawares remained in eastern Pennsylvania as "nephews" of the Iroquois. Others moved west to get away from the whites. They settled in the upper Ohio Valley in communities as small as five or six families.

One such community was established in West Virginia. This was Bulltown, located in Braxton County near the falls of the Little Kanawha. Bulltown was named for the leader of the community, a warrior whom the whites called Captain Bull.

Captain Bull's career was similar to Logan's. His father had been Teedyuscung, a spokesman whom Pennsylvania officials referred to as "the Delaware King." Teedyuscung, like Shikellamy, worked to create good relations between Indians and whites in Pennsylvania. Presumably Captain Bull assisted in and supported these efforts. In 1763, however, Teedyuscung was murdered by whites and Captain Bull sought revenge by going to war.

Before it was finished, Captain Bull claimed to have killed twenty-six people with his own hands. Ten of the victims, whom he found living on his father's land, were tortured to death - although torture was not an ordinary Delaware practice. In 1764, white officials forced Captain Bull to move west and he established his Bulltown settlement.

The Delawares lived peacefully at Bulltown for several years. They manufactured salt from a salt spring near the Little Kanawha and sold the product to whites who were starting to settle nearby. In 1772, the entire community was attacked and destroyed by a small group of settlers. This time there were no Indian survivors left.

Other Delawares settled on the western tributaries of the Ohio River. Their villages were located on territory which is now part of the state of Ohio, but these Indians used West Virginia territory as a hunting ground. Intermingled with these settlements were small groups of Shawnees.

2.4 The Shawnee

The Shawnee Indians - unlike the Iroquois, Delawares and Wyandots - did not encounter Europeans until fairly late in the seventeenth century. No European missionaries or diplomats came among them to record their customs and beliefs. Thus, we know less about them than we do many other Eastern tribes.

It is known that, at one time, the Shawnees inhabited the Ohio Valley. Sometime in the 1600s, they began moving out of the valley, apparently in an attempt to avoid the Iroquois, or white explorers, or both. These migrations divided the Shawnees. Segments of the tribe were recorded as far apart as eastern Pennsylvania and Georgia.

By the mid-eighteenth century, the majority of Shawnees were again living in the Ohio Valley, although their numbers had been reduced by warfare and disease. First they settled in villages along the Ohio River. Then, after British authorities established Fort Pitt in 1758, the tribe fell back from the big river and built a series of villages along the Scioto River, in southern Ohio. These villages, collectively known as "Chilicothe," were well-located for hunting and fighting in West Virginia. The Scioto villages were not purely Shawnee settlements, however. They included Delawares, Wyandots and other Indians who had been driven from their original homes.

Some historians believe the Shawnees descended from the "Fort Ancient" peoples - a late-prehistoric culture, found in southern Ohio, central Kentucky and the Kanawha Valley of West Virginia. Supporters of this theory believe that the Shawnees returned to the Ohio Valley in the mid-1700s, but did not mean to give up their other territories along the Kanawha River and in central Kentucky. Instead, they continued to claim these lands as the homes of their Fort Ancient ancestors.

There is a certain logic to the theory, for while there were no Shawnees actually living in Western Virginia when the white settlers came, they were extremely fierce defenders of that territory and Kentucky in the eighteenth century. The tribe's fierceness might be explained by the fact that they were defending their ancestral homes, as well as their hunting ground.

For their part, the Iroquois considered the Shawnees to be "nephews," just like Delawares and Wyandots. In fact, the Shawnee was one of the conquered tribes overseen by the Iroquois Half-King in the 1750s. The Shawnees respected the Iroquois, but they did not always follow Iroquois wishes. They did not believe, for example, that the confederacy had the right to sell Shawnee land. Thus, they did not honor the bargain the Iroquois made to sell West Virginia to Virginia officials in 1744. They did not feel bound by Iroquois promises not to attack whites who moved into the Shawnee hunting grounds.

After the American Revolution, Iroquois power declined and the Shawnees gradually replaced them as the leading Indian tribe in dealings with the whites. During the 1790s, the Shawnees organized a Western Confederacy to defend the lower Ohio Valley from the whites. Between 1795 and 1815, they played the British in Canada against the Americans just as the Iroquois had once played the French against the British. By that time, however, the Shawnee hunting grounds in West Virginia were already lost.

The Cornstalk, known among his people as Colesquo, was a famous Shawnee war chief. He led numerous successful raids against pioneer West Virginia settlements. In 1774, he organized and led a force of about one thousand Shawnee, Wyandot and Delaware warriors in the Battle of Point Pleasant. The Battle of Point Pleasant was the most important Indian battle ever to take place on West Virginia soil. The Cornstalk took a prominent role in the fighting and showed that Indians could be much better generals than whites had ever believed.

Later, the Cornstalk became a spokesman for peace between Indians and whites. In 1777, while on a peaceful mission to Fort Randolph, on the site of the old Point Pleasant battlefield, the Indian chief was taken and held. Later that year, white soldiers - angry over murders committed by other Indians - killed the Cornstalk at the fort. The Cornstalk's murder was one of the incidents that triggered a new outbreak of Indian warfare in West Virginia during the American Revolution.

A popular local legend says that the Cornstalk placed a curse upon Point Pleasant at the time of his death. Few people really believe this, but the Point Pleasant area does seem to have had more than its share of disappointments and disasters. During the twentieth century, some white West Virginians sought to make amends by erecting a monument to the Cornstalk near the site of the old battlefield.

Tecumseh was another famous Shawnee military leader. He was too young to have taken part in his people's defense of their West Virginia territory. But his father, Pucksinwah, was killed in the battle of Point Pleasant.

The conflict between the Indians and settlers of West Virginia, then, was mixed up with the struggle between France, Britain and the United States for control of the Ohio Valley. More about Indian warfare in the West Virginia frontier will be described in the next chapter.

> ...He [the Cornstalk] displayed the skill of a statesman, joined to powers of oratory, rarely, if ever, surpassed... Sketching in lively colours, the once happy and powerful condition of the Indians, he placed in striking contrast their present fallen fortunes and unhappy destiny. Exclaiming against the ...dishonesty of the traders, he proposed as the basis of a treaty, that no persons should be permitted to carry on a commerce with the Natives, for individual profit; but that their white brother should send them such articles as they needed, by the hands of honest men, who were to exchange them at a fair price, for their skins and furs; and that no spirit of any kind should be sent among them, as from the "fire water" of the whites, proceeded evil to the Indians.
>
> *From* Chronicles of Border Warfare

Study Questions - Chapter 2

1. Give several probable reasons that some Indian societies were willing to give up land in West Virginia to the white settlers, while other Indian societies were not.

2. Some Indian societies were more successful than others in dealing with the white settlers.

    (a.) What special strengths did the more successful Indians possess?

    (b.) What tactics did the more successful Indians use?

3. If you had been Logan or some other Native American leader in the Ohio Valley during the mid-eighteenth century, what tactics would you suggest to strengthen your society against the white settlers' advances?

4. Compare the diplomacy of the Iroquois to that of small nations in the world today. Can you think of examples of recent world events in which leaders practiced similar acts of diplomacy?

Chapter 3:
Cultural Encounters

The following sections will introduce you to some concepts which are useful in explaining the relationship between Indians and whites during West Virginia's Frontier Period.

Every society has a way of identifying itself. Every society has a way of choosing and naming leaders, and of organizing itself for warfare and diplomacy. The ways in which different societies accomplish these things often vary considerably. One of the objectives of social studies is to teach you how to identify cultural differences such as these. The concept of cultural differences helps to explain why there is so much cultural conflict between different societies. But differences don't necessarily mean conflict. Cultural differences can also lead to cultural exchange. Both events - cultural conflict and cultural exchange - are likely to occur on a frontier, which is a kind of border zone between different societies.

After you finish reading this chapter, you should be able to define the concepts of **cultural differences**, **cultural conflict** and **cultural exchange**. You should also be able to identify examples of all three concepts in the relations between European and Indian societies. You should also be able to explain how **frontier** situations, such as those that occurred between West Virginia's Indians and whites, can bring about cultural conflict and cultural exchange.

3.1 Cultural Differences

Beginning with Christopher Columbus, Europeans called the natives of North America "Indians." This is not what the natives called themselves, however. (Today many Indians prefer to be called "Native Americans," but even this term is a recent one.) Originally, each Indian society had a name for itself in its own language. Usually this name meant something like "the people." English settlers, for example, called the Lenai Lenape people "Delawares," after the river near which these people originally lived. The Delawares called themseleves " Lenai Lenape," or "the original people."

Interestingly, the British had named the Delaware River itself in honor of one of their own people, Lord De la Warr. The Dutch colonists, however, had a different name for it and a different name for the Lenni Lenape. So did the French and so did other Indian societies who lived near the Lenai Lenape. Any particular Indian group, in fact, can show up in the historical records under five or six names. There was the group's name for itself (which was usually flattering), the names by which it was known to its neighbors (usually unflattering), and the names by which it was known to European nations who explored or settled in its neighborhood.

It isn't surprising, then, that Europeans often got confused by all these names. Indians would have been just as confused if they had invaded Europe and tried to sort out the distinctions between the English, the Irish and the Scots, or the French, the Dutch and Germans. The point is that it wasn't always easy for Europeans to know exactly which group of Indians they were dealing with. This was particularly true if they got their information about Indian activities secondhand, from other Europeans or other Indians.

Because it was so hard to distinguish the different Indian societies from each other, it was hard for whites to separate rumors from facts - or to tell hostile Indians from friendly ones. Under these circumstances, some whites decided that it was easier to shoot first and ask questions later. The settlers who wiped out Captain Bull's Delaware settlement in West Virginia, for example, were apparently seeking revenge for misdeeds committed by another Delaware group or by Shawnees.

> ## "Indian" or "Native American"?
>
> Euro-Americans are white people whose ancestors came from Europe. African-Americans are black people whose ancestors came from Africa. Native Americans are the aboriginal peoples of North America. The European term for the native peoples is "Indian," and that term will be used frequently in this book. We should understand, however, that many native leaders today think of "Indian" as an alien term. They prefer to be called Native Americans or "indigenous peoples."

The Europeans were also confused by the ways in which Indian societies were organized. Europeans called the Indian societies "tribes" or "nations." They called Indian leaders "chieftains" or "kings." These terms reflected the Europeans' own cultural traditions, not those of the Indians. Europeans learned about tribes and chiefs from the Bible and from the histories of ancient Greece and Rome. During the Frontier Period, European kings had wide decision-making powers over their civil governments and armies. But Indian societies were not organized this way at all.

Indians did not have strong central authorities, and they did not place civil and military leadership in one person. Even the central council of the Iroquois did not have the authority to make binding decisions for all the Iroquois tribes. The council could discuss, advise and persuade. But it could not force anyone to obey.

In fact, this seeming weakness is what made the Iroquois such skillful diplomats. The Mohawks, in the eastern end of the confederacy, were friendly toward the Dutch and later toward the English. The Seneca, in the western end, were friendly toward the French. The other three members of the confederacy leaned first one way and then the other, trying to balance the Seneca and Mohawk views. But the council could never force a tribe to go along with its decisions if that tribe disagreed.

Most Indian societies divided their military and civil authorities. The civil leader was usually a man, often chosen by a council of the tribe's older women. If he did not do a good job, the women who elected him could choose someone else to take his place.

The Conoy called their leaders "wizoes." They could be either women or men. Leaders in war were younger men who had demonstrated their skill and courage in battle. All a man needed to do to become a war leader was to gather some followers and organize a successful raid. A society's civil authorities could not prevent this from happening, except by persuasion. This was why Indian societies sent such large delegations to take part in negotiations with the whites. Each important leader of the group had some power to persuade, and had to decide on matters of war and peace for himself.

Indians relied heavily on persuasion to make their societies work. This is why they held lengthy discussions when making decisions. It is also why they set such high value on speaking skills. Indian oratory was elaborate and subtle, full of rich images. Men who were noted for their speaking abilities were sometimes given the task of speaking for entire communities or tribes in negotiations with the whites. Faced by such an impressive orator, whites might believe that they were dealing with a "chief" or a "king." Frequently, however, the Indian orator was only a spokesman - not a chief or even a counsellor. He was someone who could put into beautiful language the message that other leaders had agreed upon "behind the scenes."

The Indians did not have any written language. Instead, they had a highly developed system for memorizing speeches and describing events. This system created an oral record for them - and an oral tradition. Individuals were assigned specific sections of the record to memorize, which they did with the help of "wampum." These shell beads, strung together in strings and belts, served as a memory aid, or mnemonic. The color or the pattern of a particular belt served as the key to a particular oral record. The whites thought the Indian wampum was some kind of money, because native societies valued it so much. Actually it was a kind of historical document. The function of wampum was similar to the written documents that recorded white societies' decisions and laws.

All of the whites - the English, Spanish, Dutch, French or Americans - valued strong leaders and quick decisions. On the frontiers, the Europeans combined civil and military authorities. They negotiated with the Indians through a specific individual who was, in theory, the representative of a particular European king. They expected the Indians to refer to the white kings as "father," as mark of highest respect. The Europeans wrote down their decisions and treaties on paper, which the Indians didn't know how to read.

Compare this to the Indian societies. Indians preferred more than one leader. They divided military and civil authorities. They spent days making decisions and recorded them in wampum, which the whites didn't know how to use. The highest title of respect among Indians was "uncle," since an Indian child was brought up to seek guidance and authority from his or her mother's brother, not from the father.

> "We know that you esteem highly the kind of learning taught in those Colleges, and that the Maintenance of our young Men while with you, would be very expensive to you. We are convinced that you mean to do us Good by your Proposal; and we thank you heartily. But you who are wise, must know that different Nations have different Conceptions of things and you will therefore not take it amiss, if our Ideas of this kind of Education happen not to be the same as yours. We have had some Experience of it. Several of our young People were formerly brought up at the Colleges of the Northern Provinces: they were instructed in all your Sciences; but, when they came back to us, they were bad Runners; ignorant of every means of living in the woods ... neither fit for Hunters, Warriors, nor Counsellors, they were totally good for nothing.
>
> We are, however, not the less obliged by your kind offer, though we decline in accepting it; and, to show our grateful Sense of it, if the Gentlemen of Virginia will send us a Dozen of their Sons, we will take Care of their Education, instruct them in all we know, and make Men of them."
>
> — *The Chiefs of Indians of the Six Nations at Lancaster, Pa., in response to an offer from the commissioners of Maryland and Virginia to educate twelve young Indian men at William and Mary College. June 17, 1744.*

All these cultural differences made for trouble between Indian and European societies. Neither side was able to make itself clearly understood by the other. Neither was able to make promises that were clearly understood and respected by both sides. This was especially true on the frontier, the zone of transition between European and Indian settlements.

The frontier steadily moved to the west; the white settlements advancing, the Indians in retreat. The whites who lived on the frontier were the most likely to get into trouble with Indians -but they were also the hardest for their own governments to control. Frontier settlers lived far from white governments. Thus, a European government had no way of forcing the frontiersmen to abide by any agreements the king's representatives had made with the Indians. In other words, the *theory* of European government broke down in *practice* on the frontier.

This was especially true of the British colonies. In 1774, the royal governor of Virginia confessed to the king's government in London that he could not control the settlers on the West Virginia frontier. These people were wild and "ungovernable," the governor said, and they could not be counted upon to respect any agreements the British had made with the Indians.

The frontier presented similar problems for the Indians. The native communities that were closest to the whites were the most difficult for Indian leaders to control. Such communities were likely to be full of strangers: There were refugees who had lost their lands in the east, various kinds of captives and adoptees from other tribes, as well as white traders, hunters and missionaries. All of these strangers in some way posed a challenge to the authority of a community's traditional leadership.

More than the others, frontier Indian villages were likely to lose members to battles and disease. When the hunters of an Indian household disappeared, that household went hungry. A shortage of game animals also contributed to Indian hunger. As white settlers grew nearer, game always grew scarcer and harder to find.

Thus, frontier conditions presented many temptations for young Indian men to get into trouble by attacking isolated whites, or by stealing food, horses and cattle. This was why periods of peace between Indian and white societies were never really peaceful. Instead, the periods between wars were punctuated by occasional murders and other crimes. The culprits included both Indians and white settlers. The "quiet times" were actually times that grievances built up and, in both societies, violent young men looked forward to the next outbreak of full-scale warfare. War gave people on both sides the opportunity to avenge grievances, both real and imagined, that had grown during times of relative peace.

Cultural differences gave Indians and whites plenty of reasons for conflict, while conditions on the frontier gave them plenty of opportunities. As we have learned, however, cultural differences do not necessarily lead only to cultural conflicts. When different cultures come together, there can also be cultural exchange.

3.2 Cultural Exchange

This is particularly true of material culture. It is usually easier to adopt new technologies and products than it is to adopt new values. People can learn to use new products very quickly, whereas learning new values often takes a good deal of time.

The Indians' use of the white peoples' drug, alcohol, is an example of cultural exchange. It is not a very attractive example, but alcohol was a European product that was one of the most rapidly and most widely adopted by Indians after the two cultures came into contact. In return, they gave the whites a drug which was used in the Indian culture - tobacco. The whites adopted tobacco as rapidly and as widely as the Indians did alcohol. As you can see from this example, cultural exchange, like cultural conflict, is a two-way process.

No one knows for sure who were the first Europeans to give the Indians alcohol. The Dutch in New York accused the French in Canada of being the culprits. The French accused the Dutch and both accused the English and Spanish. The fact is, all European colonies regularly supplied the Indians with the drug during the Frontier Period. In the Ohio Valley for example, English authorities regularly dispensed casks of rum to Indians who came to Fort Pitt.

Regardless of whether the first alcohol supplied was French brandy, English rum or American whiskey, its impact on Native American culture was devastating. Native American societies had not learned how to manufacture alcohol before the Europeans came. Alcohol was therefore completely foreign to them, and they had no cultural values that could guide them toward moderate and controlled use of this powerful drug. Thus, from the time of their first exposure to it, alcohol formed a destructive force in Indian culture. Drunkenness became a common problem wherever Indians had access to a supply of the drug. This was especially true on the frontier.

During the Frontier Period, many white people became

concerned about the problem of alcohol addiction among the Indians. They knew how badly drunkenness disrupted native communities. They also believed that Indians under the influence of alcohol were more likely to commit assaults on white settlers. Many Indian leaders were also concerned about the problem and complained bitterly to white authorities about the sale of the drug to their people.

White authorities occasionally did prohibit alcohol sales to the Indians. Such measures might have been effective if they were enforced. Since the Indians never acquired the tools for manufacturing alcohol, they always had to get it from the whites. But alcohol remained available to the Indians. It was sometimes used by European or American government agencies to weaken Indian resistance to demands for more land. It was almost always on hand from white traders, who exchanged it for furs or skins. Alcohol addiction remained a problem for Indian societies long after the end of the Frontier Period, and it is still a problem among Native Americans today.

But, again, cultural exchange is not a one-way street. Just as the Indians overdid it with the Europeans' drug, alcohol, the whites overdid it with the Indian drug, tobacco. The use of tobacco in Native American culture was in many ways similar to the use of alcohol in European culture. Just as wine was used in some European religious services, a pinch of tobacco was tossed into the air to invoke spirits to whom Indians prayed. Offering alcohol to guests was a sign of hospitality in white society; offering tobacco to a visitor was the Indians' symbol of welcome.

The same comparison applies to material cultures. Chalices and other drinking vessels became prized possessions for white people. In Europe, craftsmen made such vessels of gold and silver and decorated them with jewels. Similarly, Indian tobacco pipes were prized by their owners and Indian craftsmen made these pipes to show off their skills in carving and ornamentation.

Soon after the discovery of tobacco in the New World - and its initial export from Virginia to England - tobacco use became a craze in Europe. Tobacco addiction spread among European populations and became a common trait of European and Euro-American cultures. Government authorities, such as King James I of England, protested this development; but they could not stop it.

However, there is no evidence to suggest that many Indians became tobacco addicts. When they used the drugs with which they were familiar, Indians usually did so under strict rules that were part of their religious observances. It was only the new drug, alcohol, that got out of control. Indians adopted alcohol as readily and as recklessly as the whites adopted tobacco. Whites did not use tobacco moderately and ceremonially as the Indians did. Nor did they adopt social controls to regulate its use.

There are many other examples of exchanges between the European and the Native American cultures. You have probably read about how Indians taught the first English settlers in Virginia and New England how to grow corn. They also taught the uses of medicinal herbs, found in the forest. White woodsmen learned many of their hunting and tracking skills by imitating the Indians. There were also exchanges of population. The white explorers and traders who first ventured into Indian communities often took Indian wives and became the fathers of mixed Indian-white children. For example, the baby girl who was the sole survivor of the Logan massacre was a mixed Indian-European child. She was the daughter of Logan's sister and a white trader. After her mother was murdered, the child was taken to a white settlement and placed in her father's care.

White captives of the Indians also contributed to this genetic exchange. Many captives were adopted into Indian households and lived happily in their new homes. Some white men, particularly younger and poorer men, liked the free-ranging life of the Indian men in the forest. They preferred this to a life of drudgery, which many poor men faced in white society. Some women captives also preferred to remain with the Indians. Indian women worked hard, but they worked cooperatively without interference or supervision by males. This was a reason given by one Seneca captive when she refused to go back to the white settlements. Most women had to work just as hard among the whites, she explained, and they might have to put up with bossy husbands or fathers as well.

Black captives had special reasons for wanting to live among the Indians. African-Americans usually came to the West Virginia frontier as the slaves or servants of whites. Being captured by Indians often meant an escape from slavery for blacks. In fact, many blacks did not wait to be captured but escaped into the forest, hoping to find freedom in the Indian country. White authorities sometimes accused Indians of stealing slaves. It is just as likely, however, that these black captives "stole" themselves.

Each time they were defeated in wars, Indian leaders promised to return all their white and black captives. Each time,

Jaeger Rifles were brought to settlements in Virginia and eastern Pennsylvania in the mid-1700s.

however, there were some captives who refused to return to the white settlements. Sometimes the Indians had to force them to return there anyway. Sometimes the Indians balked at returning them. In 1775, for example, the Shawnees agreed to turn over a black woman who had escaped from slavery in Western Virginia. They refused to give up her child, whose father was an Indian. They did not wish to see the child taken from them and made to be some white person's slave.

The "Indian trade" was another form of exchange which took place on a regular basis during the Frontier Period. Indian societies seemed primitive, even "savage" to most European and Euro-American observers. Yet Indians readily adopted many European tools. They did so whenever an available European tool could be fitted into their culture. In the areas of hunting and warfare, for example, the Indians quickly recognized the superiority of European weapons. They made it a point to acquire as many guns, knives and hatchets as possible. They were eager to give up their stone weapons for metal ones, and earthen pottery in favor of brass kettles for cooking. The Indians also gave up wearing animal skins in favor of blankets and woven cloth.

As Native Americans grew accustomed to European weapons, clothing and tools, they became dependent on them. In other words, they lost the skills they once used in supplying their own needs. The Indians readily used European tools for practices that were already well-established in their culture. But they did not learn new practices. They learned how to shoot guns, but not how to make or repair them. Thus, they remained dependent on the whites for repairs and spare parts, such as the flints used to fire muskets. It did not take very long for trade with the whites to break down Indian societies' self-sufficiency.

As early as 1762, an Iroquois war party of eighteen men passed through West Virginia on its way to attack Cherokee enemies in the South. The warriors had to have their guns repaired at Fort Pitt before they could carry out their mission. At least five other Indian war parties stopped at Fort Pitt to ask for ammunition that year.

In the same way that many Indians became addicted to alcohol, their societies became more dependent on European trade goods. This increased the power that white traders exerted over Indian communities. For example, at the start of the French and Indian War, the Seneca ordered their Shawnee "nephews" to remain neutral between the French and the British. The Shawnee could not afford to do this. They were too dependent on European goods. The French pushed the English back from the Ohio in 1754, leaving the Shawnee no way to trade with the English. The Indians were forced to turn to the French to acquire the tools, weapons and clothing that they needed to live.

While many Indians depended upon trading with whites, some whites depended on trading with Indians. Virginia leaders hoped to secure more Indian trade for their colony in the seventeeth century, when they sent the first exploring parties into western Virginia. A similar desire led the Ohio Company, a business organization of Virginia politicians and merchants, to seek control of the Upper Ohio Valley around 1750.

The French established trading posts and forts at strategic points along the Great Lakes and the Mississippi River in order to channel most of the regional Indian trade toward Canada or New Orleans. A desire to keep control of this trade led France to oppose the Virginian move into the Ohio Valley. Britain won control of the French outposts in 1763, and the same desire for Indian trade caused King George I to order American settlers to stay out of the region.

So, France competed with Great Britain for the Indian trade. In our immediate region, Virginia competed with Pennsylvania for the trade. And individual traders and groups of traders competed among themselves. What was the prize for all this competition? What did the Indians offer in return for weapons, tools, clothing and alcohol?

The answer is furs - specifically the pelts of beaver, bear and deer. The Indians offered all these, along with the occasional buffalo robes and skins of smaller animals. To us, animal furs might seem to be a minor currency. For white authorities during the seventeenth and eighteenth centuries, however, the Indian fur trade was a big gold mine. Animal furs were well worth fighting for - and everybody did.

Beaver pelts were the most valuable. During the Frontier Period, beaver hats became very fashionable among European men. These hats were made from the soft inner hairs of the beaver's coat, matted together in dense, warm fabrics called "felts." Even more valuable than fresh pelts were the old pelts that had been conditioned by being worn as Indians' clothing. This may have seemed strange to the Indians, but they readily took advantage of the opportunities the fur trade offered them.

Indian tribes that were most exposed to the temptations of trading spent more and more time trapping beaver and hunting other fur-trade animals. When settlers moved into a particular

Huntington Museums

An American-made rifle of the 1770s.

region, however, the game became scarce and the hunting more difficult. This is one reason why Indians defended territories where they did not live, such as West Virginia, against white encroachment.

By 1750, the Native American societies of the Ohio Valley were caught in a vicious circle. The whites came closer and raised more opportunities for valuable trade. The more the Indians traded, the more they needed to hunt, because the prices of goods they wanted always rose and those prices were always expressed in terms of pelts. The more the Indians hunted, the more they needed to trade, because they spent less time making tools and weapons in their own traditional way. But behind white traders came white settlers. Settlers, as a Shawnee delegation complained at Fort Pitt in 1762, "drove away the Game and Spoiled the Indians Hunting."

It is no wonder that, in such circumstances, peaceful exchange often gave way to violent conflict. Indian-white relations in Western Virginia during the Frontier Period were much more likely to take the form of cultural conflict than cultural exchange. This was true for a very simple reason. Indians did not live in significant numbers in West Virginia when the whites began settling there. At first glance, it might seem that the absence of Indian residents would make for peaceful occupation by the whites. This was not the case. West Virginia was a hunting territory, which the Indians were prepared to defend. Also, the earliest white settlements were separated from Eastern Virginia by the Blue Ridge and Allegheny Mountains. This made the western settlements isolated and vulnerable to attack.

Thus, during the Frontier Period, West Virginia was a border territory. It was a land claimed and contested by Indians and whites, by British and French, by Americans and English, and by Virginians and Pennsylvanians. To a large extent, the nature of the early history of this territory is nicely summed up in the title of one of the first books written about it: *Chronicles of Border Warfare.*

3.3 First
Explorations

The first permanent English colony in the New World was started at Jamestown, Virginia, in 1607. The French established their fortress of Quebec in Canada in 1608. In 1609 the Dutch began exploring the Hudson River. Their settlement of Nieuw Amsterdam was started in 1624. The Spanish founded the city of Santa Fe in New Mexico in 1610, but their fortress at St. Augustine in Florida was even older. It had been founded in 1565.

The creation of these settlements and fortresses were the first steps in a race to decide which of the nations of Western Europe would control the eastern half of North America. This race had a strong influence on West Virginia's Frontier Period.

The Dutch were the first to drop out of the race. In 1664 the English attacked and conquered Nieuw Amsterdam and its surrounding colony of Nieuw Nederland. The British renamed both the city and the colony "New York." The contest between the French and English went on for another 99 years. In the American colonies, between 1689 and 1745, they fought three wars. These wars affected the English colonies in New England and New York, but they did not affect Virginia. The English in Virginia and the French in Canada remained far apart during this period. They were kept away from each other partly by geographic conditions. They were also kept apart by the Iroquois.

In the interior of the Virginia colony, great mountain ranges were found. These kept the English pinned to the Atlantic coastal region. The mountain ranges were the Blue Ridge and the Alleghenies. Two explorers, Thomas Batts and Robert Fallam, tried to cross these mountains in September 1671. They got as far as the New River, and may even have gone as far as the Tug Fork of the Big Sandy River.

Fallam looked upon the mountains stretching westward from where he stood and called them a "pleasing tho' dreadful" sight. The mountains were "pleasing," of course, because they were so beautiful. They were "dreadful" because crossing them required dreary and difficult travel.

About one-fifth of West Virginia's territory - the Eastern Panhandle - stretches

West Virginia Collection, WVU Library

West Virginia's mountains posed an awesome challenge to early explorers. One called the landscape a "pleasing tho' dreadful" sight.

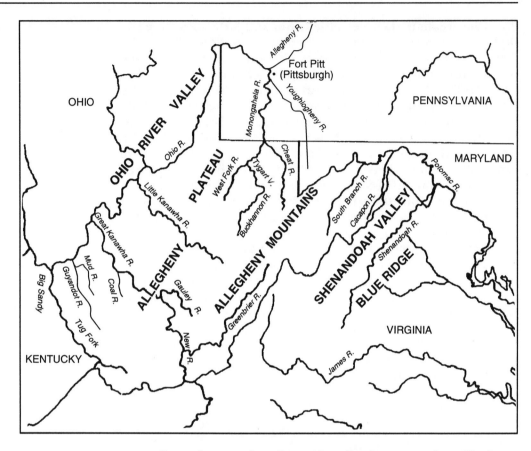

over the ridges and valleys that lie between the Allegheny Mountains and the Blue Ridge. The largest of these valleys is the Shenandoah. In Virginia and West Virginia history, the Shenandoah Valley is known as The Valley. The rest of West Virginia - four-fifths of its territory - lies in another valley, the Ohio Valley. The Ohio Valley, like the Shenandoah Valley, actually consists of many valleys. These are drained by many different rivers, such as the Monongahela, Greenbrier, Big Sandy, New, Great Kanawha, plus, of course, the Ohio River itself.

Batts and Fallam did not know it, but their expedition had crossed the eastern part of the Ohio Valley. Not long after they turned away from the mountains, a group of French explorers came within eighty miles - maybe much closer - of the Ohio Valley's northern edge. No mountains divided the French colony in Canada from the Ohio Valley. In fact, there was only one serious geographic obstacle between Quebec and the center of North America. This was the great waterfall at Niagara, where water from the four upper Great Lakes tumbles over cliffs 167 feet high. From there, it churns north through a narrow canyon, down to the level of the fifth Great Lake, Lake Ontario. (See map on page 49.)

Apart from this one obstacle, French explorers could travel entirely by water for a thousand miles into the North American interior. Niagara itself could be bypassed by a portage. A portage was a place where voyagers could carry their supplies and canoes from one body of water to another.

The portage at Niagara was called the Carrying Place. This portage was steep, but it was only fourteen miles long. Eighty miles south, another portage - shorter and less steep - brought travelers from Lake Erie to the northernmost waters of the Ohio Valley. Some historians think that the French explorer Robert Cavelier de LaSalle came south from Niagara into the Ohio Valley as early as 1669. There is no proof of this, however. It is certain that LaSalle was at Niagara ten years later. In 1679 he built a small fort there. He also constructed a sailing ship which could be used to conduct the Indian fur trade throughout the Great Lakes. Nothing came of this, however. Soon LaSalle's fort was dismantled. His sailing ship mysteriously vanished. France, like Virginia, fell back from the Ohio country. The French did not return there for another seventy years.

The French problem was not geography. There was a human barrier between their Canadian settlements and the Ohio. This barrier was the Iroquois Confederacy, particularly the Seneca, the largest and fiercest of the Iroquois tribes. Both the Niagara Carrying Place and the streams of the northern Ohio Valley lay in territory that had been conquered and occupied by the Senecas. These Indians were "the keepers of the western door" of the Iroquois, according to the poetic Indian language. During the seventeenth century, the Seneca were not at all willing to open this door to the French.

At first, the French could not accept this. In 1687, they invaded the Senecas' home territory, but they were badly defeated. This defeat temporarily halted the French attempts at southward expansion. While Virginians busied themselves building up their settlements along the Atlantic Coast, the French extended their trading networks westward, across the upper Great Lakes.

The years between 1671 and 1730 are thus a shadowy period in West Virginia's history. Among the mountains, out of the Europeans' sight, a great drama was probably taking place. Iroquois war parties were traveling along the trails that crossed the territory to strike at distant Indian enemies. During this period, the destruction or flight of West Virginia's original Indian population was completed. This may have been one of the most interesting periods of our history, but we will never know much about it. From the standpoint of both the French in Canada and the English in Virginia, West Virginia remained an unknown and unsettled land.

3.4 Frontier Wars

Things began to change in the second decade of the eighteenth century, thanks in part to two individuals. One was Alexander Spotswood. He was a royal governor of Virginia, the top representative in the colony of the English king. In 1716, Governor Spotswood organized and led an exploring party which traveled across the Blue Ridge Mountains into the Shenandoah Valley.

This journey drew attention to the idea of settlement in Virginia's interior. In 1722, the Virginia government signed a treaty with the Iroquois. It granted Virginians permission to settle in the valleys between the Blue Ridge and the high ridge of the Alleghenies. During the next few years, several individuals visited the Shenandoah and upper Potomac regions, looking for good land. There may have been settlers there as early as 1719. But there is no solid evidence of any settlement within West Virginia's Eastern Panhandle before the 1730s. Then the settlers came in with a rush.

One reason for the rush was that the Virginia government started making large amounts of land available to a type of businessman called a land **speculator**. During the 1730s the government granted speculators huge amounts of property in eastern West Virginia - along the Shenandoah, Potomac, South Branch and Cacapon rivers. The size of these grants ranged from 20,000 to 100,000 acres.

This land was not exactly given away. The speculators paid little or no money for it, but they did have to meet certain conditions. Usually the speculators had to agree to bring a certain number of families to settle on their land grant. They had to do this within a stated period of time, usually five or ten years. If they failed to meet these conditions, the speculators lost the grant.

These early grants of wilderness land in eastern West Virginia led to conflicts with another land owner, Lord Fairfax. Fairfax was an English nobleman. His seventeenth-century

ancestors had acquired a huge grant of
land along the Potomac River from King
Charles II. This grant covered some five
million acres. The Fairfax family, however, had done little to develop it before
the Virginia government began making
its own grants there. The British government upheld Lord Fairfax's right to this
land. But, for some time afterward, Virginia speculators quarreled with Fairfax's
representatives. Eventually, a compromise was worked out. In 1745, the British government confirmed the smaller
grants already made by Virginia. It
awarded the rest of the disputed land to
Lord Fairfax.

West Virginia Collection, WVU Library

In 1746, an exploring party surveyed the western limits of Lord Fairfax's
land. This party placed a famous land-
mark, the **Fairfax Stone**, at the head-
spring of the Potomac River. This river
marked the north edge of the Fairfax
Grant. The south edge was a line drawn from the Fairfax Stone
to the Rappahannock River, which was east of the Blue Ridge.
Lord Fairfax owned most of the land between the river and the
line. This means that he owned most of what is now Hardy,
Hampshire, Mineral and Morgan counties and parts of Berkeley,
Jefferson, Tucker and Grant counties in West Virginia.

The second reason for the rush of new settlers after 1730
was a rush of immigrants from northern Ireland and Germany.
Immigrants from these places poured into the American colonies
during the mid-eighteenth century. There were also smaller
numbers of Scottish and Welsh immigrants. Many of these
immigrants arrived at the port of Philadelphia, which was located
within quick and easy reach of the newly-opened Virginia lands.
Also, English and Anglo-American settlers were moving west
from Eastern Virginia through gaps in the Blue Ridge. This added
another group to the new settlements. This westward movement
of Virginians also included a small number of African-American
servants or slaves.

The population in West Virginia's eastern counties was
drawn from all of these groups. Jefferson County, for example,
was about thirty percent English, thirty percent German and
thirty percent Scotch-Irish (that is, Irish immigrants of Scottish

*In 1746, an exploring
party marked off
land for Lord Fairfax
with a stone at the
head of the Potomac
River (at the corner of
Preston, Tucker and
Grant counties). This
photograph was
taken at the Fairfax
Stone in 1905.*

descent.) The remaining ten percent was drawn from other British and European ethnic groups and from African-Americans.

By 1750, The Valley had been pretty well scouted and occupied by land speculators and settlers. In addition, there were over two thousand people living in the smaller valleys along the upper Potomac. Both speculators and settlers were taking the first steps toward occupying the nearest portions of the Ohio Valley. These were the Greenbrier and New River valleys, near the present southeastern border of West Virginia, and the branches of the Monongahela River in the northern part of the state.

During the late 1740s, the Virginia government began getting ready for a move into the Ohio Valley. It made another treaty with the Iroquois in 1744. According to Virginia, this treaty gave Virginians the right to make settlements between the high ridge of the Alleghenies and the Ohio River. (The Indians disagreed with this view.) In 1746, the government began making large grants of Ohio Valley land to speculators. Some 600,000 acres were granted within the present limits of West Virginia.

The most important speculators in West Virginia land were organized into land companies. The **Ohio Company**, organized in 1747, was authorized to claim 200,000 acres of land along the Ohio River and its branches. The **Greenbrier Company**, organized in 1751, got 50,000 acres of Greenbrier Valley land. Some settlers raced ahead of the land speculators. Two hunters, Jacob Marlin and Stephen Sewell, established a hunting camp along the Greenbrier River in Pocahontas County in 1749. During the following year, other settlers moved into the area that is now Greenbrier County. The Tygart and Files families established the first known Monongahela Valley settlements in 1753, in the Tygart Valley of Randolph County.

WV State Archives

LAN 1749 DV REGNE DE LOVIS XV. ROY DE FRANCE, NOVS CELORON COMMANDANT DVN DETACHEMENT ENVOIE PAR MONSIEVR LE Mis DE LA GALISSONIERE COMMANDANT GENERAL DE LA NOVVELLE FRANCE POVR RETABLIR LA TRANQVILLITE DANS QVELQVES VILLAGES SAUVAGES DE CES CANTONS AVONS ENTERRE CETTE PLAQVE A LENTREE DE LA RIVIERE CHINODAHICHETHA LE 18 AOUST PRES DE LA RIVIERE OYO AUTREMENT BELLE RIVIERE POVR MONVMENT DV RENOVVELLEMENT DE POSSESSION QVE NOVS AVONS PRIS DE LA DITTE RIVIERE OYO ET DE TOVTES CELLES QVI Y TOMBENT ET DE TOVES LES TERRES DES DEVX COTES JVSQVE AVX SOVRCES DES DITTES RIVIES VINSI QVEN ONT JOVY OV DV JOVIR LES PRECEDENTS ROYS DE FRANCE ET QVILS SISONT MAINTENVS PAR LES ARMES ET PAR LES TRAITTES SPECIALEMENT PAR CEVX DE RISVVICK DVTRCHT ET DAIX LA CHPELLE

Lead plate buried by the French at the mouth of the Great Kanawha River.

Unlike the settlements in the Shenandoah and Potomac valleys, Virginia's continuing move west of the Alleghenies was not to be peaceful. By the mid-eighteenth century, France was prepared to fight for its claim to this region. This time, the French could back up their claim with more than just words. They were able to send soldiers and Indian allies to meet the Virginia settlers and land speculators. Their ability to reach the Ohio Valley from the north was helped by an unusual Frenchman named Louis Chabert de Joncaire.

Joncaire did for France what Governor Spotswood did for Virginia. He got the French moving again toward the Ohio Valley. As a French soldier, sometime around the end of the seventeenth century, Joncaire had been captured and adopted by the Seneca. Gradually, he came to have some influence among his adopted people. In 1721, they allowed him to set up a trading post near the Niagara Carrying Place. In 1726, Joncaire persuaded the Seneca to allow his post to be rebuilt as a stone fort. The French called the fort the "House of Peace," even though it was secretly intended as a military base.

During the next twenty-five years, Joncaire's post at Niagara grew into a great fortress. The presence of this fortress at the Iroquois "western door" helped to convert the Seneca - the largest Iroquois nation - from enemies to friends of France. The fortress also protected the supply routes from Canada. These routes were needed by anyone who moved into the Ohio Valley from the north. As long as Fort Niagara remained in unfriendly hands, no settler in the Ohio Valley could be sure of peace and safety.

By the middle of the eighteenth century, France and England were moving toward a showdown in the Ohio Valley. The prize for each nation became the Forks of the Ohio, the present site of Pittsburgh. Here, the Allegheny River flowed down from the direction of French Canada and the Iroquois country in the north. Here, it met the Monongahela River flowing up from the frontiers of Virginia in the South.

> *In the year 1749, reign of Louis the Fifteenth, King of France, we, Celeron, commander of a detachment sent by Monsieur the Marquis de la Galissoniere, Commandant General of New France, to re-establish tranquility in some Indian villages of these cantons, have buried this plate at the mouth of the river Chinodahichetha, the 18th of August, near the river Ohio, otherwise Beautiful River, as a monument of renewal of possessions, which we have taken of the said river Ohio, and of all those which fall into it, and of all the lands on both sides, as far as to the sources of said rivers; the same as were enjoyed or ought to have been enjoyed, by the preceding Kings of France, and that they have maintained it by their arms and by treaties, especially by those of Ryswick, Utrecht, and Ax-la-Chapelle.*

Translation of lead plate

How quickly the explosion came can be seen by looking at events by year:

1749 The Ohio Company, which was based in Virginia, established a supply camp on the upper Potomac, opposite Fort Cumberland, Maryland. A French expedition traveled down the Allegheny and Ohio rivers. The French buried lead plates to mark the mouths of major branches, including Wheeling Creek and the Great Kanawha River. The plates asserted that all land drained by the Ohio belonged to the King of France.

1751 The Ohio Company sent Christopher Gist across the mountains to explore the Ohio Valley. His mission was to search out good land for the company and to summon Indian leaders to meet with company managers in 1752. The French established a second fort at Niagara, at the Lake Erie end of the Carrying Place.

1752 Gist undertook further exploration for the Ohio Company. This time he concentrated on the northwestern section of West Virginia. At Logstown, near the Forks of the Ohio, Indians of a mixed Shawnee-Seneca settlement agreed to establish trade with the Ohio Company. They recognized the company's claim to land in West Virginia. In return, Gist offered the Indians English protection against the French.

1753 The French built Fort Presqu'Ile on the Pennsylvania shore of Lake Erie. They built Fort Le Boeuf on the portage leading from Lake Erie to the Ohio Valley. George Washington, of Virginia's militia, visited Fort Le Boeuf with a message from the Virginia governor. The governor's message told the French to clear out. The French commander refused.

1754 The Virginia government sent a work party to build a fort at the Forks of the Ohio. Washington followed with troops. Before he reached the Forks, however, the French had driven the workmen away. The French established their own fort at the Forks and called it Fort Duquesne. Washington fought two battles with the French near the Monongahela River. He won the first but lost the second at Fort Necessity. The French captured this little fort on July 3 and took Washington and his men prisoner. They were sent back to Virginia with a message for the English to stay out of the Ohio Valley. Washington's defeat was the signal for most of the Ohio Valley Indians to go over to the French side of the conflict.

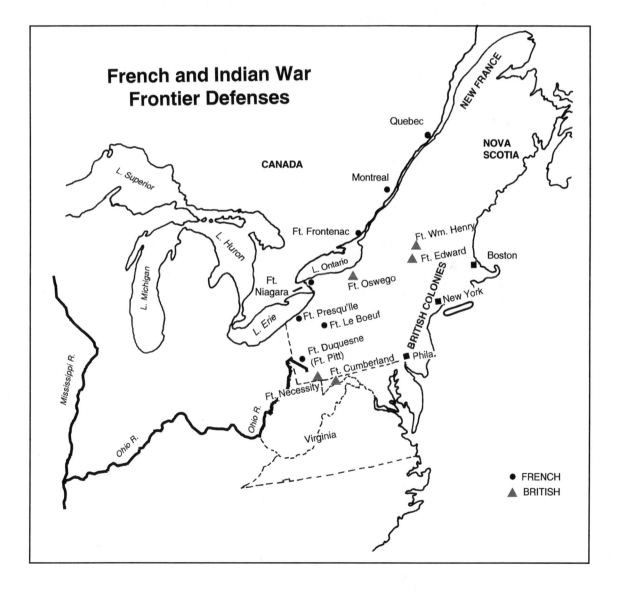

French and Indian War Frontier Defenses

1755 The British government decided to launch full-scale assaults on Forts Niagara and Duquesne. The Niagara campaign bogged down and never really got started, but 1,400 British troops and 450 Virginia militiamen were sent to attack Fort Duquesne. The British were led by General Sir Edward Braddock. About ten miles from the fort, they were ambushed by French and Indian forces and badly defeated. Braddock was killed. His men fled, panic-stricken, back across the mountains.

This battle opened a seven-year-long war between France and Great Britain, with battlefields in many parts of the world and on the oceans. The principal battles, however, were in North America. The eastern half of the continent was the chief prize. In West Virginia and American history, this contest is known as the **French and Indian War**.

Braddock's defeat led to a general Indian assault on the Virginia and Pennsylvania frontiers. All of the settlements in the Monongahela, Greenbrier and New River regions were destroyed. The settlements in the upper Potomac valleys were under frequent attack. Many settlers there abandoned their homes for safer places in The Valley.

Early in 1756, an attempt to counter-attack the Shawnee villages in Ohio produced another disaster. This was called the "Sandy Creek expedition" because it tried to use the Big Sandy Valley of southern West Virginia as an invasion route to the Ohio. This expedition fell victim to bad planning and disorder among the white soldiers. It never even got near the Indian towns.

As long as the French held Fort Niagara and Duquesne, the Virginia frontier remained open to attack. George Washington was in charge of Virginia's frontier defenses. Washington decided to defend the upper Potomac region by constructing a series of forts in the South Branch Valley. He made no attempt to defend the Greenbrier Valley. Despite these efforts, the Indian attacks continued. In 1758 the Indians destroyed two forts in Pendleton County, killing or capturing more than fifty people. This was in addition to attacks on individual settlers and their homes.

The tide began to turn late in 1758. A British army striking through Pennsylvania captured the Forks of the Ohio in November. There, on the ruins of the French Fort Duquesne, the British built Fort Pitt. Another British army captured Fort Niagara in July 1759. In September, Quebec, the greatest French fortress in Canada, was captured. Montreal, the colony's capital, was captured a year later. In February 1763, France and Great Britain signed a peace treaty in Paris. By its terms, Canada and all the French territory east of the Mississippi River was turned over to the British.

By the time of the treaty, an uneasy peace had already settled over the West Virginia frontier. Settlers returned to their homes in the Greenbrier and South Branch valleys. They had returned too soon, however. A new Indian war was already brewing. Conquering the French in Canada brought about two big changes in British government policy toward the frontier region. One change was a new attitude toward the Indians. They were no longer to be treated as equals, or as though they were independent nations. The Indians were to be treated like wards, or children, of the British and colonial governments.

The Indians did not like this at all. They also resented the high prices that British traders charged for the ammunition, tools, and the clothing they needed. A group of Shawnees at Fort Pitt complained in 1762 that the British and colonial authorities had treated the Ohio Valley Indians very well when the outcome of the war was still in doubt. "Butt sence you have conquered ye French in Canada you look on us as nobody." Similar feelings among other tribes led to the new outbreak of fighting in May 1763.

This was called the war of **Pontiac's Rebellion**. Pontiac was an Ottawa leader who organized assaults against Detroit and other British outposts in the region. This time, the Seneca joined in the fighting. They surrounded Niagara while Shawnees and Delawares surrounded Fort Pitt. Every British post in the west was destroyed except Forts Pitt, Niagara and Detroit. Even these three strongholds, however, spent most of the summer of 1763 under attack. That same year, a Shawnee war party headed by the Cornstalk wiped out the Greenbrier settlements a second time. In addition to destroying these settlements, the Shawnees and their allies made raids into the upper Potomac region. The raids in West Virginia continued into the early summer of 1764. By then, however, the Indians had been discouraged by their failure to capture all the major forts and by defeats at the hands of British forces along the upper Ohio. The Indians agreed to peace in return for British promises to keep settlers out of their territories.

3.5 Rebellion and Settlement

The second change in British policy after the French-Indian War concerned the process of settlement. As long as the French were still in Canada, the British government had generally encouraged the steady westward advance of white settlers. Now the government decided to call a halt. On October 7, 1763, the British king issued a Royal Proclamation on the matter. The proclamation established the high ridge of the Alleghenies as the dividing line between Indian and white settlements. Whites who had settled west of the mountains were ordered to get out.

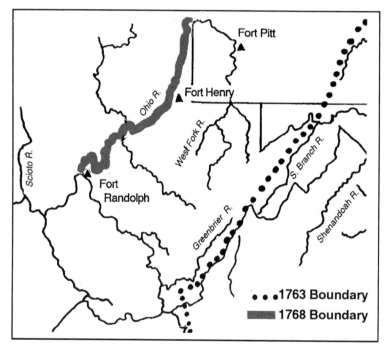

Adjustments of areas open to settlement. Borders of 1763 and 1768 between the British and Indians.

The British government issued this proclamation for two reasons. One was that they had taken over the rich French fur trade in Canada. If this trade was to continue to be profitable, the Indians had to be allowed to hunt and trap furs in peace. Secondly, the war of Pontiac's Rebellion had shown how costly Indian wars were to the government. Since wars always seemed to happen wherever Indians and whites lived too closely together, the British government decided to keep them apart. The proclamation of 1763 kept settlers out of West Virginia's Ohio Valley section for a few years. In 1768, the British government decided to change the policy. It did so in order to provide land for speculators who had been granted western lands before the French and Indian War. Treaties made with the Iroquois and Cherokee that year pushed the new boundary between Indian and white territory to the Ohio River.

Immediately, settlers and speculators rushed into the Ohio Valley, trying to stake out the best land. Several West Virginia communities acquired their first permanent settlers during these years. These included Lewisburg, in the Greenbrier region; Peterstown, near the New River; Morgantown, on the Monongahela; and Wheeling, on the Ohio.

About ten thousand families rushed into the upper Ohio Valley alone between 1769 and 1771. Many of these families settled in the region between the Ohio and Monongahela rivers. This territory became a subject of dispute between Virginia and Pennsylvania. A powerful company of Pennsylvania land speculators tried to organize the region, including a portion of West Virginia, as a separate colony. The company's name for the colony was **Vandalia**. Other land companies opposed the scheme. Eventually, the British government failed to approve it.

Meanwhile, individual speculators pushed their search for land far down the Ohio River. They went two or three hundred miles beyond the frontier settlements to get land that the big land companies or individual settlers could not claim. This took them well into the heart of the Ohio Valley. Of course, this alarmed the Shawnees. During the early 1770s, Indians and whites engaged each other in a growing number of small conflicts. After the Logan Massacre in April 1774 (described in Section 2.2), the Virginia frontier was once again threatened by war.

3.6 Indian Warfare 1774-1795

This war was called **Lord Dunmore's War**, after Lord Dunmore, then the royal governor of Virginia. It pitted the militia of frontier Virginia against the Shawnees and their allies. This time, the British decided to take the offensive instead of waiting to defend their settlements against Indian raids. Lord Dunmore ordered the frontier militia to form two armies. One was made up of men from the Shenandoah Valley and upper Potomac settlements. It was led by Dunmore himself.

This army traveled from Winchester, Virginia, across the mountains and down the Monongahela River to Fort Pitt. From the fort, Dunmore planned to travel down the Ohio to the mouth of the Great Kanawha River. There, at the point of land called Point Pleasant, his army would meet the other British army. The two forces would then march west to Ohio, and destroy the Shawnee villages along the Scioto River.

The second army was made up of men from the settlements in the Greenbrier, New River and upper James River valleys. It was led by Andrew Lewis, a veteran Indian fighter and land speculator. Lewis's army gathered at Lewisburg and marched west to the Kanawha Valley. It reached Point Pleasant on October 8, 1774. At the time, Dunmore's army was still up the Ohio River - near the place where Parkersburg is now. Thus, the Cornstalk was given a chance which he was quick to seize. Instead of waiting for the two armies to get together, the Cornstalk attacked Lewis's army at Point Pleasant early on the morning of October 10.

The Cornstalk had between eight hundred and one thou-

An artist's conception of the Battle of Point Pleasant

sand warriors, including Delawares, Wyandots, Mingos and Ottawas as well as Shawnees. Lewis had about 1,100 militia men. From dawn until late afternoon, the two armies fought each other. Then the Indians withdrew across the Ohio River, falling back to defend their villages. They had not destroyed the white army, as the Cornstalk apparently planned. However, they did cause heavy losses among the frontiersmen.

Still, when Lord Dunmore arrived with his army, the Shawnees were ready to talk. They agreed to give up their hunting grounds in West Virginia and Kentucky. They promised to welcome traders from Virginia and to return all their captives. The Indians also promised to allow white people to travel along the Ohio River in peace.

The Battle of Point Pleasant was one of the most important battles ever fought on West Virginia soil. For one thing, it was the beginning of the end for the Shawnees' control of West Virginia. The war also gave Virginia two important forts located right on the Ohio River: one at Point Pleasant, the other at Wheeling. After 1774, settlements along the Greenbrier and Monongahela rivers grew rapidly behind the protection of these forts. So did the settlements along the upper Ohio, in what we know today as the Northern Panhandle. The Kanawha Valley also attracted settlers, although the Kanawha settlements were not as numerous or as

Prickett's Fort, Prickett's Fort State Park
Marion County

Photo by Steve Shaluta, Jr, West Virginia Division of Tourism

permanent as those along the Monongahela, Greenbrier and Ohio. Further down the Ohio, the Kentucky country also began attracting thousands of settlers. This meant that, for the first time, West Virginia settlements were not the most distant of frontier communities.

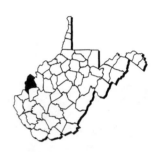

The peace that followed Point Pleasant gave West Virginia's settlements a period of two-and-a-half years to grow and gather strength. Then, in 1777, war broke out again. This time the causes were far more complicated than the usual pressures of whites against Indians. As in 1755, the warfare between Indians and whites was mixed up with conflicts among different groups of white settlers. In 1755, the Shawnees and their allies had sided with French against the British and their colonists. Twenty years later, they sided with the British against the colonists, who now called themselves Americans and were working to create a new nation. This time, from 1777 to 1782, the Indian warfare affecting West Virginia was a part of the American Revolution.

In some ways the Indian war of the Revolution was like a replay of the earlier French and Indian War. This time around, the British acted out the role that had been played by the French. British troops, for example, occupied the bases along the Great Lakes. The most important of the British forts were Detroit and Niagara. Beginning in 1775, authorities at these forts urged the Indians to attack frontier settlements. The British gave the Indians weapons, ammunition and other goods that had been brought from Canada. The Indians used these supplies to launch their raids on Ohio Valley frontier settlements. These attacks were also supported by a number of American settlers who remained loyal to the British. (Thus, these settlers were called "loyalists.")

The Indians did not really attack the frontier in force, however, until the "bloody year of the three sevens," as the first year of fighting was later known. On August 31, 1777, a party of 350 Wyandots, Shawnees and Mingos attacked Fort Henry, at present-day Wheeling. The fort held out through three days of desperate fighting, but lost nearly half of its men. Smaller Indian raiding parties struck during this time at the Greenbrier and Monongahela settlements and at smaller forts along the Ohio. In 1778, new

WV Division of Tourism & Parks

This monument commemorates the Battle of Point Pleasant, in Mason County. The battle was the beginning of the end of Shawnee control in West Virginia.

WV State Archives

Fort Henry, at present - day Wheeling, survived an attack by 350 Indians in August 1777.

attacks were made on the Greenbrier settlements. In 1779, the fortification at Point Pleasant - Fort Randolph - had to be abandoned. Similarly, most of the Kanawha Valley's settlers left their homes until after the war was over.

Apart from the Kanawha Valley, however, most West Virginia frontiersmen did not abandon their settlements, as they had done in 1755. For one thing, there were too many whites in the 1770s for the Indians to drive back across the mountains. Also, the frontiersmen did not wait for armies of professional uniformed soldiers to defend them. Instead, they went on the attack themselves.

The most successful campaign launched from West Virginia into the Indian country during this time was the famous expedition of George Rogers Clark in 1778. With 175 men, gathered mostly in West Virginia and Kentucky, Clark captured Kaskaskia, Cahokia and Vincennes. These were three former French settlements in the Illinois country, now controlled by the British. When the British commander at Detroit came down to oppose him, Clark captured him also. This feat so impressed the Indians of the Ohio Valley that some of them began coming over to the American side.

Another expedition involving the West Virginia frontier was the Sandusky campaign, in the spring of 1782. This campaign ended in defeat, which led to a second Indian attack on Fort Henry in September of that year. Again, the fort held out through three days of fighting between its defenders and 350 Indians and whites. The Fort Henry attackers included loyalists and British soldiers as well as Indians. They flew a British flag and used British ammunition and guns.

The second battle of Fort Henry was fought nearly eleven months after the surrender of the British General Cornwallis to George Washington. Peace talks between Great Britain and the new United States of America were already under way in Paris. Thus, the 1782 battle of Fort Henry is sometimes called the "last battle of the American Revolution." Whether or not we think of it this way, it was certainly the last major conflict of West Virginia's Indian wars. Without support from a European government, the Indians could not fight very long on their own. The Indian raids soon came to an end.

It was in the Ohio Valley that West Virginians performed their greatest service to the cause of American independence. They had helped defend and extend the frontier deep into the Indian country. As a result, the United States was able to claim a large share of territory that the British had conquered from France during the French and Indian War. The British kept Canada, but the United States got the entire eastern half of the Mississippi Valley. Thus, the western border of the new nation became the Mississippi River, instead of the Allegheny Mountains or the Ohio. Without the courage and sacrifices of the frontier settlers and soldiers of West Virginia, Pennsylvania and Kentucky, it might not have turned out this way.

The frontier wars also provided West Virginians with their greatest revolutionary legends. These wars gave them stories of bloodshed, hardship and courage which were told over and over again around the firesides of pioneer West Virginia homes. Many of these stories centered upon famous Indian fighters such as Lewis Wetzel and his brothers Martin, Jacob and John. The Wetzels, motivated by the death of their father at the hands of Indians, claimed to have killed at least thirty-two of them. The Wetzels and people like them left many stories of trickery, stealth, narrow escapes and brutal killings on the frontier.

One frontier hero was Anne Bailey, a small and vigorous woman who spoke English with a Cockney, or urban London, accent. Bailey served as a scout and messenger during the Indian fighting in the Kanawha Valley. Another hero was Dick Pointer, a black slave owned by one of the pioneer settlers of Greenbrier County. Pointer helped hold off attackers in the defense of a Greenbrier Valley fort in 1778. Years later, local whites asked the

3.7 Frontier Heros and Legends

Topper Sherwood

Dick
Pointer

Hero During
Indian Attack
On Fort Donnally
1778
Died 1827
Dedicated July 3, 1982

*Dick Pointer's grave
is in Lewisburg,
Greenbrier County*

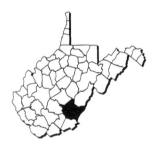

Virginia Legislature to buy Pointer from his owner and, as a reward for his courage, to grant him the "freedom he has long sighed for." Their request was turned down.

In addition to their struggle to defend the frontier, West Virginians contributed in other ways to the American Revolution. For example, two companies of riflemen traveled from the lower Shenandoah Valley counties to Boston in record time during the summer of 1775. They were the first southern soldiers to join the American Army, which was surrounding the British in that city at the time.

Other West Virginia soldiers fought the British in important battles in Eastern Virginia and North Carolina. General Horatio Gates, who led the victorious American Army at the Battle of Saratoga, was a resident of Berkeley County. Andrew Lewis, hero at the Battle of Point Pleasant, led the troops who drove Lord Dunmore and the royal government out of Eastern Virginia in the summer of 1775.

Indian raiding did not end in West Virginia until 1795. But after 1782, Indian raiders came only occasionally and did relatively little damage. The Shawnees left their villages in southern Ohio and moved west to what is now Indiana. They turned over larger and larger chunks of their territory to the new United States government. In 1795, the British finally gave up their forts at Detroit and Niagara. Without these supply bases, Indian resistance to white occupation of the upper Ohio Valley came to an end. Virginia - east and west - was entirely surrounded by Euro-American territory. The Indian presence became nothing more than a memory, as did the claims of territory by France and Great Britain.

The borders of Western Virginia began to assume the shape that some of the West Virginia's boundaries have today. In 1784, Virginia and Pennsylvania settled their border dispute in the upper Ohio region. The boundary they agreed upon is the same as today's West Virginia-Pennsylvania state line. Pennsylvania kept the Forks of the Ohio, the site of Fort Pitt and the growing city of Pittsburgh. Virginia kept the sliver of land along the Ohio River that we know as the Northern Panhandle.

That same year, Virginia gave the United States its claim to the land northwest of the Ohio River. This land began to fill rapidly with settlers during the 1790s. The eastern part of it was admitted to the Union as the state of Ohio in 1803. To the southwest, Kentucky also filled up with settlers and detached itself from Virginia. It became a separate state in 1792.

The Kentucky-Virginia boundary was drawn along the Big Sandy River and its main eastern branch, the Tug Fork. This boundary is the Kentucky-West Virginia border today. In the northeast, the Virginia-Maryland boundary remained the same. It followed the Potomac River from Chesapeake Bay to the Fairfax Stone, at the source of the Potomac River.

Thus, all of the borders of West Virginia's territory appeared on the map by 1792 - except one. This was the boundary between West Virginia and Virginia. It would not be drawn until eighty years after the end of the American Revolution.

Why and how West Virginia detached itself from Virginia is one of the subjects in Part II.

Study Questions - Chapter 3

1. Based on the reading you have done in Chapters 2 and 3, list as many examples as you can that illustrate the strong points of the Indian societies that lived near West Virginia.

2. What are some reasons that Euro-Americans had for giving the title of "king" to minor native American spokesmen?

3. In what ways did Euro-American settlers encourage practices that were harmful to the native peoples' way of life?

4. What were the most positive benefits of cultural exchange from the perspective of the natives? Of the white settlers? Of African-Americans on the frontier?

PART II:
Becoming
a State

Chapter 4:
Land and Law

Who owns West Virginia? This question was central to the wars of the Frontier Period. It remains an important issue today. Yet, the question is not as simple as it might seem. Land ownership involves distinguishing between two other concepts. These are the concepts of **territory** and **property**.

Land ownership also involves some problems which every society has to work out. How does the ownership of land relate to the use of its resources? Should the *owners* of land and resources be treated differently from its *users*? Should a society value some uses of land more than others? How should these values be determined and enforced?

This chapter offers you definitions of the following concepts: **territory, property, land ownership, land use** and **land specu-lation**. It also tells what a **legal system** is. When you finish, you should be able to use these terms and concepts to interpret the events of West Virginia's Statehood Period. You should also be able to explain how West Virginians of that time worked out the issues of land ownership and land use.

4.1 Territory and Property

What is the difference between territory and property? Both of these concepts refer to the ownership of resources, especially land. The difference between them lies in the owners. Territory is the land and its resources that can be possessed and con-trolled by societies or communities. No society, for example, has ever turned the ocean into its territory - except those parts of it that can be controlled from land.

Property, on the other hand, belongs to individuals within a society or community. It can also belong to groups within that society, such as a family, a partnership, or a company. Property refers to many things other than land. Under the American legal system, land has always been dealt with as a special kind of property. For legal purposes, land - and the resources attached to it - is called **real property**. Real property also includes human-made structures such as houses and buildings. Other kinds of property are called **personal property**. This consists of things like clothing, furniture and electronic equipment - the kinds of things you can carry around with you. Real property, on the other hand, remains in some way fixed or attached to the earth.

This distinction is important in West Virginia history because of the way early governments collected taxes. Personal property could be moved around; it could be hidden. Real property was attached to the earth and could not be hidden. Real property was, therefore, easier for authorities to tax.

During the eighteenth and nineteenth centuries, most of the taxes raised by state and local governments in this country were based on real property. Problems with property taxation have been hot political issues during every period of West Virginia history. The subject will be discussed often in this book.

The territory that belongs to an entire society is the property of that society. This is an idea of land ownership that some Europeans brought to North America. In kingdoms, the territory of the society was the property of its king. Thus, the British claimed the lands that they discovered as the property of the king of Great Britain. The French said their American lands were owned by the king of France. In each case, the king's property and the nation's territory were one in the same.

Property owned by governments is called **public property**. Property owned by individuals (or companies or families) is called **private property**. In the European kingdoms, private ownership of land could exist when the king granted a share of his territory (the public property) to an individual or group. European kings granted North American land to private owners in return for public services. Lord Fairfax's

WV Division of Tourism & Parks

Lord Fairfax's huge grant of land from King Charles II was bordered by the Potomac River. Today, the river is the northern border of West Virginia's Eastern Panhandle.

huge grant along the Potomac River came about in this way. One of his ancestors had supported King Charles II against the king's political enemies. In return, Charles gave the ancestor a huge chunk of North American land. Charles also gave William Penn the land that later became Pennsylvania. The king did this to cancel a debt he owed to Penn's father.

The governments that Europeans created in North America continued to carry European ideas of public and private land ownership. The Virginia government granted land in the Shenandoah and Ohio River valleys. In return, the new owners promised to settle a certain number of families on the property within a certain number of years. Virginia also used land grants to pay soldiers - first in the French and Indian War and, later, in the American Revolution.

After the Revolution, the new United States government continued to keep the European ideas of public and private land ownership. The U.S. Constitution, for example, refers to "the territory and other property of the United States." Also, through most of the nineteenth century, the federal government made grants of public land to individuals, to states and to communities. In return, the people and groups who received these grants pledged to use them for public service. Such services included building railroads and setting up schools and universities.

During most of American history, the mere act of settling on the frontier was considered a public service. In eighteenth-century Virginia, a person could get up to 400 acres of land simply by settling on it. A settler had to locate vacant land, build a cabin on it, clear some fields and live there for five years. The only other cost was a small yearly fee. This method of acquiring land was called **tomahawk rights**, because settlers used toma-hawk slashes on trees to mark the boundaries of their land. This practice stayed in effect in Virginia until 1779.

The transfer of public property to private ownership some-times carried conditions which the new owners had to meet. More often, however, the government simply sold the land for cash and made no conditions. This was particularly true in Virginia during the later part of the Frontier Period. Still, private ownership of land also carried duties - some of them permanent. All land owners, for example, had to pay taxes. In the case of frontier land, the government often excused or "forgave" taxes for the first few years. But, sooner or later, the taxes would have to be paid.

Land owners could also lose their property if they failed to meet the proper conditions or duties. When this happened, they were said to have "forfeited" their land back to the government. In other words, their private property became public property once again. If the taxes owed were then paid, the property could be "redeemed" by the land owner. Or, the owner could sell the land to someone else and use the proceeds to pay off the taxes owed.

As long as private owners met all the conditions and duties that came with their land, they could use it as their exclusive property. This means that they could use it in any way they liked. They could also sell it, or pass it on to their children or other heirs.

If you think this sounds complicated, you're right. It *is* complicated. In fact, it's probably fair to say that land issues have taken up more time and energy - and have caused more confusion and frustration - than any other social problem of West Virginia's history. Arguments involving land ownership, land use, and property taxes have been important during every period. It is certainly worth taking some time to learn the basic concepts involved with these issues.

Some of the specific land problems that arose during the Frontier Period will be discussed later on in this chapter. First, however, it's worth taking a look at how Indian theories of land ownership differed from those of the white settlers.

4.2 Land in Indian Societies

Before we discuss land ownership and land use in Indian societies, we need to define the concept of a **legal system**. A legal system is an organized method for enforcing a society's rules and decisions. Today's American legal system is made up of laws, law codes, courts, judges and lawyers. The laws are the rules formally adopted by our society. Law codes bring all the laws together into organized sets of books. If there is disagreement about how to apply the laws, courts are where people resolve it. The court is also a place for trials, for anyone accused of breaking laws. Judges preside over the courts. And, finally, the lawyers make the arguments that are heard by judges and juries in the courtroom.

The Indians did not have such a legal system. They had no law codes, lawyers or courts. They also had no technical equipment for surveying land, so they didn't have the same precise descriptions of individual parcels, or pieces of land, that whites did.

The Indians had no concept of "private property," as applied to the land. Only among the Delawares was it customary for families, during certain times of the year, to be assigned specific hunting territories. Apparently this was an unusual practice, not found among other Indians. Certainly, the idea of an individual having exclusive use of a particular piece of land was completely strange to Native Americans.

The Indians practiced communal land ownership. That is, the entire community owned the land upon which it lived. Frequently, Indian men asked whites to postpone discussions about the land until they could consult with the Indian women. The whites assumed that this was simply a delaying tactic. White men during the Frontier Period weren't used to consulting women on important matters. In Indian cultures, the women had a special relationship with land. The women, for example, were in charge of the farming. It was they who planted and nurtured the land. Before any land could be given up, the Indian women were consulted about its value and worth.

This was only one of many conditions and duties that members of Indian communities felt they had to meet in regard to the land. Other duties extended to their dead ancestors, as well as to other living things with which they shared the land. In this way, the Indians were very religious. They believed that the trees, the flowing creeks and every creature in the forest had its own special spirit. They believed that these spirits should be treated with respect.

This religious attitude was strengthened by a personal love the Indians had for the land. They lived very close to the land. Children played at the edge of the forest. Young boys spent days - or even weeks - in the woods, practicing their hunting skills and playing war games. In the clearings, women and girls planted and cared for crops. They searched for fruits, nuts, berries and herbs. Everyone acquired a close understanding of - and dependence upon - the land around their homes.

These attitudes also were shared by the Indian men. They traveled along well-worn woodland trails to hunt and fight. They "managed" the forest by burning off the undergrowth. (This increased the number of small, tender plants which fed the deer and other game animals.) Some nineteenth-century land agreements contain the statements of Indian men, in which they expressed the pain of being separated from the land they had known so well.

Although the Indians had no sense of "personal property," they had a very well-defined sense of territory. Community members knew precisely which land was the community property. Indian territories included the nearby farming lands and distant hunting grounds as well. The boundaries followed major rivers, mountain ridges and other well-known landmarks.

Indian territories could be lost and won in war. The Iroquois' claim to the Ohio Valley, for example, was based on conquest. No matter how a territory was acquired, however, the

WV Division of Tourism & Parks

Twin Falls State Park, Wyoming County. At least four Indian groups were said to have used this area for hunting. There is no record of Indians in the county after 1799.

land always carried the duty to protect it. One of the Shawnee complaints against their "uncles" in the Iroquois Confederacy, for example, was that the Iroquois had failed to protect Shawnee lands from the whites.

The idea of land as a commodity was strange to the Indians. A commodity is something that can be bartered, bought and sold. "Money, to us, is of no value, and to most of us [it is] unknown," one Shawnee spokesman explained to American officials in 1793. He politely suggested that the government take the money it was offering for Indian land and hand it out among the white settlers. Then, the settlers might go buy land elsewhere and leave the Indians alone.

This did not happen, of course. The Indians had become "addicted" to European trade goods, weapons and ammunition. The chance to sell land in exchange for these goods was very tempting for Indians. Often they had to sell land in order to buy the goods they needed. The Indians rarely sold land because they wanted to, only because they had to.

Why did the whites bother to buy Indian land? After all, they were capturing it steadily through warfare anyway. The answer has to do with the competition for North American territory among the various European governments. The British, French and Dutch based their claims to territory on two things. One was the right of the first "discovery." Thus, Britain's claim to the Ohio Valley was based, first of all, on Batts and Fallam's discovery of the New River in 1671. The French claim was based on the voyages of LaSalle, described in section 3.2.

By 1751, white settlers in the South Branch Valley were cultivating wheat and rye. They had also introduced red clover, causing local Indians to suggest that the settlers had dyed the land in blood.

Another recognized method of claiming territory was through agreements with the Indians. The Iroquois Confederacy placed all of its land under the protection of the British King in 1686. The Iroquois did this in order to get the British to protect their territory from the French. Thereafter, the British claim to the land in the Ohio Valley and south of the Great Lakes was based on the Iroquois' claim to the same land. The British, then, had to respect the Indians' claim in their own laws and courts, because they wanted to use that claim to compete with the French. Later, the United States government, which claimed to have acquired all the Iroquois territory from the British, was placed in the same position.

In effect, European legal theory turned Indian territory into a special kind of private property. The Indians' ownership of this property had to be dealt with, somehow, before the land could be divided up and granted or sold to white property owners. Since West Virginia was not inhabited by Indians in the Frontier Period, the process of getting rid of Indian ownership was a relatively simple one. The British colony of Virginia purchased the Iroquois claims to the land between the Blue Ridge and the Ohio River in 1722 and 1744. Lord Dunmore got the Shawnees to recognize Virginia's claim to this territory in a treaty signed shortly after the Battle of Point Pleasant in 1774. This established a clear **title** to the land, as far as American courts were concerned. (A land title is the record of ownership.) In this way, Virginia followed the Iroquois as the legal "owner" of most of the territory that later became West Virginia.

4.3 the Problem of Land Titles

Before 1776, the Virginia government could not grant or sell land in its territory without the British government's approval. After the American Revolution, however, Virginia rapidly turned its vacant territory into private property. By 1800, nearly all its public land was sold or granted to private owners. After the Revolution, there weren't many legal problems growing directly out of previous Indian ownership of West Virginia land. But the Indian wars, which lasted into the early 1780s, still prevented many new owners from moving in and using their property.

There were plenty of other problems, too. One basic problem was that the Ohio Valley portion of West Virginia had been fought over so much during the first half of the Frontier Period. The land was fought over first by whites and Indians; then by France and Britain; and, finally, by Britain and the United States. Even after the Revolution, important sections of the Ohio Valley were claimed by Virginia and Pennsylvania as well. The problem was this: Under the new American law, the owners of property had to obtain their title from the government. As long as it was unclear as to *which* government would control the territory, no one could be sure whose property was whose. As long as territorial control of the region remained in doubt, the rights of property owners were also in doubt.

One good example of how territorial disputes created confusion for land owners was the **Vandalia** project. Vandalia was a scheme organized in 1769 by land speculators, most of whom were from Pennsylvania. The idea was to set up a separate colony, covering most of West Virginia, southwestern Pennsylvania and the eastern third of Kentucky. Neither the Virginia nor the Pennsylvania colonial governments approved of the Vandalia scheme. The British government, however, could have created the colony on its own, since the king was the "owner" of this entire territory until 1776. In fact, the Vandalia speculators nearly succeeded in getting their plan approved in London. But the first fighting of the American Revolution stopped Vandalia from getting any further there.

After the Revolution began, the Vandalia speculators faced a new claimant to the territory: the new government of the United States. Accordingly, in 1776, they sponsored a proposal to create a fourteenth state. This was to be called **Westsylvania**. The proposed state had more or less the same borders as Vandalia would have had. Again, both Virginia and Pennsylvania opposed the scheme, and nothing came of it.

The speculators revived this scheme after the Revolution in somewhat different form and with a different name: the **Indiana Company**. This time, they did not seek to set up a separate government. Instead they sought to force Virginia to grant them two million acres in northwestern West Virginia. They wanted all the land between the Ohio and Monongahela Rivers, south from the Pennsylvania border all the way to the Little Kanawha. Again, the Virginia government - led by legislators from West Virginia counties - vigorously fought the scheme and won. The Vandalia speculators brought a lawsuit against the government of Virginia. But the U.S. Supreme Court dismissed the suit in 1798.

Between 1802 and 1805, the promoters revived the project yet another time. Again, it was thrown out of court. Meanwhile, the claims of the Ohio Company set off another long series of lawsuits. These speculators also appealed to the United States courts. They lost, but the outcome of their suits was not completely settled until the 1820s.

The Greenbrier Company was able to hold onto its claim of 50,000 acres in southern West Virginia. But here, too, lawsuits and other legal complications dragged out the settlement of land titles until the early nineteenth century. The same thing happened with much of Lord Fairfax's land in the Eastern Panhandle. Virginia seized and sold part of his land during the Revolution. It did so because Lord Fairfax and his heirs were

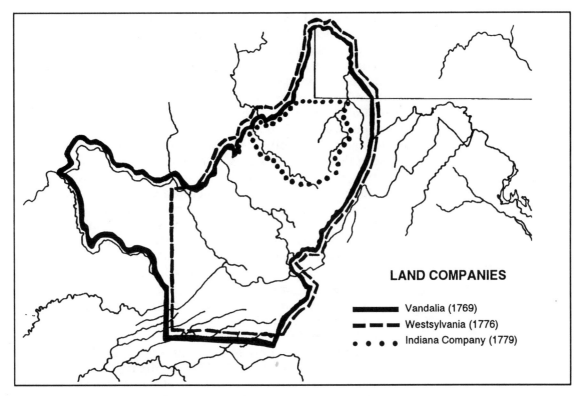

LAND COMPANIES

— Vandalia (1769)
– – Westsylvania (1776)
• • • Indiana Company (1779)

Map of Vandalia, Indiana and Westsylvania

British subjects and loyal supporters of the king. A long and famous legal battle followed. On one side was Denny Martin, the heir of Lord Fairfax and the man for whom Martinsburg was named. The Commonwealth of Virginia was on the other. A ruling by the U.S. Supreme Court in 1816 gave Martin the land. In its ruling, the Supreme Court said that legal authority (or jurisdiction) of the United States was superior to that of Virginia. When it signed its peace treaty with Great Britain in 1783, the United States government had promised to protect the property rights of British subjects, even the loyalists. Thus, the U.S. government had a duty to protect Martin. This case became famous in legal history as **Martin vs. Hunters Lessee**.

Thus, territorial disputes affected land in every part of West Virginia. In the end, things turned out better for some land speculators than for others. Those who held clear titles to the land - generally, titles obtained either from the British government or its colony of Virginia - were more likely to have their claims upheld by the new United States and Virginia governments. These speculators included the Greenbrier Company and the heirs of Lord Fairfax. Those land speculators who had not secured clear titles from the previous governments were more likely to lose their West Virginia land. This included the Ohio Company and the Vandalia promoters. In both cases, the final decision often dragged on and on - long after the Frontier Period. Thousands of families who settled in West Virginia did so under a cloud of uncertainty. They could buy land from the Virginia government after 1776. But there was always the chance they would lose it, if the courts ruled against Virginia's claims in favor of one of the land companies. Unfortunately, this was just the beginning of their problems.

The legal complications mentioned so far came about because of claims by land speculators or companies before the American Revolution. There were also problems after the U.S. government was in place, however. After the Revolution, the state of Virginia adopted a new set of land laws. The Virginia land legislation of 1779 was passed with good intentions, but with bad results. The laws were intended to benefit settlers and other small land owners. Instead, the changes drew the attention of a whole new group of land speculators.

The new laws confirmed the previous "tomahawk rights" for settlers who made claims to small parcels of land, but it also made these rights *transferable*. That is, the rights could be sold to somebody other than the original settler. Many settlers had been driven from their homes by Indian warfare, so they could now claim the tomahawk rights (technically called "pre-emption rights") to their original land. This, after all, was only fair. They could also claim these rights and sell them to speculators - even if they did not return to their original land.

The same thing happened with the land that Virginia promised to its soldiers of the French and Indian and Revolutionary wars. The state did not actually give land to these soldiers. It gave them warrants, paper certificates to be exchanged for land - up to 5,000 acres for officers and 100 to 400 acres for ordinary soldiers. These warrants were also made transferable.

Both of these provisions encouraged land speculation. The new law made it possible for land speculators to go around buying up soldiers' land warrants and settlers' pre-emption rights. The speculators would pay the soldiers or settlers a small sum for their claims. Then they would gather up these claims until they had warrants for thousands and thousands of acres. Then they could exchange the warrants at the state land office in Richmond.

The land office gave the speculators "patents" or deeds for

the actual land they wanted. Most of the land that speculators acquired from Virginia in this way was located in West Virginia or Kentucky. Merchants from Richmond, Philadelphia, Baltimore and other eastern cities acquired up to 500,000 acres apiece in such dealings. Leading politicians did even better. By cashing in land warrants, two politicians acquired more than one million acres each of West Virginia land. Fifty other politicians, including twenty-two legislators from West Virginia, acquired smaller amounts of land.

In part, the territorial conflicts over West Virginia's land were conflicts over different forms of land use. The same was true about the conflict between settlers and speculators.

4.4 Conflicts Over Land Use

The Indians used the land primarily for hunting the wildlife on it. The French held essentially the same position because of their interest in the fur trade. When the British took over the French empire in North America in 1763, they also shared this view of wilderness land. But the defeat of the Indians and their European allies ended the time when hunting and trapping would be the primary use of West Virginia's land. The white settlers of West Virginia intended to use the land mainly for agriculture. Hunting was an important sideline with them, just as agriculture had been for the Indians. The primary plan of most settlers, however, was to clear the land of its trees in order to grow food crops. They also used much more timber for fuel and building purposes than the Indians did. And the settlers were much more numerous than the Indians. All of this meant that the arrival of settlers in West Virginia increased the agricultural use of the land. It also made wildlife and furs scarcer. This was one reason why the Indians fought the change.

The differences regarding land use were more subtle between settlers and speculators, however. Both groups valued the land for its agricultural purposes. Both tried to get the best agricultural land they could. But there were two differences between settlers and speculators and they were far-reaching ones. First, speculators sought to acquire large tracts of land, extending to many thousands of acres. Settlers could make do with much smaller amounts - say, a few hundred acres of land. Secondly, speculators did not obtain land mainly for their own use. They hoped to resell it to others after its value had increased. Most settlers, on the other hand, expected to live on their property. They planned to build homes on it and grow food for their families. Many settlers were also willing to sell their land.

Sometimes, they were offered a better price for the improvements they had made - cleared fields and new buildings, for example. The settlers who sold their land often moved farther west to start the same process all over again.

The dictionary defines "speculator" as someone who expects to make a large profit quickly on something he buys and sells. The land speculators of early West Virginia history fit this definition in theory - but not in practice. West Virginia's speculators expected to make large profits quickly. But they rarely did. Some speculators, such as Lord Fairfax and the Greenbrier Company, made their profits steadily and slowly. Others didn't make much profit at all, which was the case with the Ohio Company. One way or the other, the effect that speculators had on early West Virginia history was the same. The effect was bad.

The idea behind land speculation was to get to the best land before the settlers did. Speculators wanted to acquire land cheaply - even for free - and then sell it at a nice profit when the settlers came in. This worked very well in the Shenandoah Valley during the 1730s and 1740s. In The Valley, there were no Indians or foreign soldiers to interfere with the process.

But the Indian wars interfered with this process when it spread to the Ohio Valley section of West Virginia. Settlement in the Ohio Valley didn't grow steadily, as it had in the Shenandoah. In the Ohio Valley it started and stopped, over and over again. Speculators and settlers arrived there at about the same time. They joined with each other in fighting the Indians. A good example was Andrew Lewis. Lewis, one of Virginia's greatest land speculators, led an army in the Battle of Point Pleasant - an army made up mostly of settlers. But in peacetime, the settlers and speculators competed with each other for the best land.

The competition for land was greatly affected by the hilly or mountainous nature of most West Virginia territory. The best type of property for agriculture is flat or gently rolling land, where crops are more easily planted and cultivated. Such land is relatively scarce in West Virginia. It is found in large amounts only along the major rivers. But even there, the flat land - called "bottom land" - is strung out in narrow ribbons, between the river and the nearby hills. Along the lower Ohio and Kanawha rivers, where bottom land is most plentiful, it is never more than a mile or two wide.

Speculators and settlers agreed that flat or rolling land was best for agriculture. But there was a difference in the amount of land that each group needed. Speculators wanted as much land as they could acquire cheaply. They knew that they could never make a profit trying to sell small tracts of expensive land. There was too great a supply of land then for it to sell at a very high price. Thus, the speculators hoped to make a profit by selling large amounts of land at low prices.

To acquire a large amount of good land in West Virginia, a speculator would have had to choose it very carefully. Take George Washington, for example. He was West Virginia's best-known land speculator. In 1770, Washington came out to the Ohio Valley to choose for himself the lands that he wanted. He held land

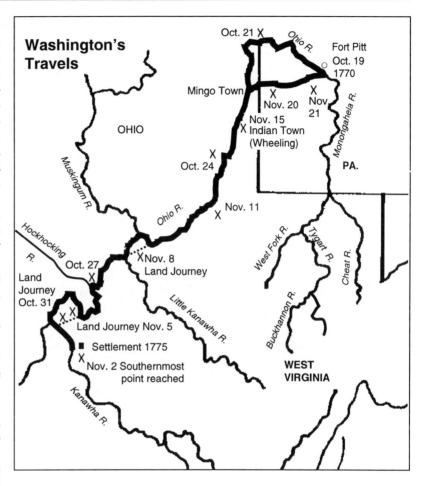

Washington's Ohio River journey, 1770, and settlement, 1775.

warrants worth over 30,000 acres. He had acquired most of these warrants from other soldiers in the French and Indian War. Washington surveyed his property so as to get only bottom lands along the Ohio and Kanawha rivers. The nearby hills he regarded as worthless for agricultural purposes, so he left them out of his tracts.

Other speculators with French and Indian War land warrants also chose bottom lands. Another example is the Savage Grant, acquired in Cabell County by several military officers. This grant included the site of the present-day city of Huntington.

By the time of the American Revolution, Washington and other early speculators had snapped up the biggest tracts of West Virginia's best agricultural land. This included the bottom lands

along the Ohio and Kanawha and along the lower stretches of these rivers' larger branches. It also included other wide, level stretches along the Monongahela and New rivers and the broad highland valleys drained by the Greenbrier and Potomac. There was plenty of good land left in West Virginia after 1779. But this land was scattered along the smaller streams in fairly small parcels.

Speculators who came later than Washington did not choose as carefully as he did. They could have made hundreds of small, individual surveys to get valuable flat land. Instead of doing this, they continued to use their land warrants to block out huge tracts. The boundaries of these later tracts ignored the land's natural features. They included many thousands of acres of unwanted hillsides, as well as the more desirable parcels of level land. The

Early speculators snapped up the biggest tracts of West Virginia's best farm land, including wide stretches along the New River.

speculators took the hillsides in order to acquire good land in large amounts. When they resold the land, they often did the same thing. They made settlers who bought their land take the bad along with the good.

Most of the speculators who acquired large amounts of West Virginia land did not live in West Virginia. Many of them did not even live in Virginia. They hired local surveyors to mark off the boundaries of their land. They got local politicians and lawyers to help them obtain deeds from the Virginia Land Office in Richmond.

But the professionals hired by the speculators were not always well-trained. Sometimes the surveyors worked hastily and sloppily. They defined the boundaries of many tracts in terms of landmarks such as trees or rocks, which later disappeared. And Richmond was a long way from the hill country where these surveys were being made. Travel to the land office was difficult and slow.

For these reasons, it was relatively easy for different speculators to acquire titles to overlapping pieces of land. The overlap could have been due to bad surveying. But it could also happen if one speculator bought a large piece of land with military warrants, and then later found that someone else owned pre-emption rights to some part of it. Most of all, it could happen when the same land was bought and sold over and over again because of non-payment of taxes. Almost all speculators tried to avoid paying taxes on their wilderness land. Originally, they acquired the land, hoping for a quick sale and profit. When the land failed to sell quickly, they naturally did not want to add to its cost by paying taxes on it year after year. Sometimes the

speculators who lived outside Virginia did not know exactly where their land was - or how much in taxes they owed. Sometimes these questions could not even be answered because of errors in the surveys and descriptions of the land.

The Virginia government had the right to seize and resell all land on which the taxes were unpaid (or delinquent). But the government did not enforce this rule consistently. Some land was for-feited and resold. Other delinquent land stayed on the books without forfeiture.

A non-resident speculator whose land was forfeited and resold could later bring suit in the courts. He could claim he had been treated unfairly. Often the courts would agree, even after the state had resold the land to someone else. The

WV Division of Tourism & Parks

courts would tell the state to give the land back to the original speculator. The settler who had bought the land from the state would find that he was being forced to buy his land a second time from the original owner. Some settlers had to repeatedly repurchase their land. In some cases, they even had to buy the buildings, fields and other improvements that they themselves had made.

Most settlers would have been happy to resell their land at a profit. In this sense, there was a little bit of speculator in most settlers. But the settler's main purpose was to build a home and grow food for a family, which did not require huge amounts of land. Settlers, then, could be more flexible than speculators in locating their land. They could take advantage of small stretches of bottom land. They could also find room for con-toured fields on the rounded hilltops. They could graze their

The Cranberry Glades, in Pocahontas County, are meadows in a highland valley 3,100 feet above sea level. The glades are cut by many winding streams, the largest of which is the Cranberry River.

cattle in the natural highland meadows, called "glades" or "balds."

In other words, there were lots of places in West Virginia where small farmers could build their homes. But there were few places where small land owners were safe from the confusion caused by land speculators. Many enterprising settlers decided that owning West Virginia land was too much of a gamble. Land titles were more secure in Ohio and Kentucky. The land was generally better there also. That is why many people who had defended their homes with great courage against the Indians and the British moved on to other states after the Revolution. It was easier to move west than to quarrel in the courts with speculators and land companies.

Other people stayed in West Virginia, but their children or grandchildren moved west. Thousand upon thousands of people traveled west along the Ohio River without ever stopping to take a gamble on West Virginia. No doubt the challenge of creating a farm in this rugged hill country scared some people off. Certainly some others were scared away by the bad reputation acquired by Virginia's land system.

For all of these reasons, West Virginia received only a small share from the stream of westward migrants who poured across the mountains after the Revolution. In 1790, for example, only 20,000 people lived in the Ohio Valley section of West Virginia, while Kentucky was home to 70,000. We can never be sure exactly how many people - or what kinds of people - West Virginia lost as a result of its land problems. We can be sure, however, that land problems had a bad effect on the growth and development of our state.

4.5 Lawyers and Squatters

West Virginia's land problems did turn out to be beneficial to two groups in the state. One group consisted of lawyers who learned to specialize in all the legal problems involving land. In the nineteenth century, West Virginia became known as a great place for land lawyers. Nearly every land owner needed legal advice about titles and boundaries. The owner might have lots of land or just a farm. He might win his lawsuit or lose it. In any case, the lawyer always got to charge a fee.

Another group of people who may have benefitted from the situation were "squatters." Squatters used land that belonged to someone else. It was a fairly common thing for someone to "squat down" on a small patch of land in this way. He would throw up a cabin, plant some grain and vegetables, and stay there until the land owner came along to ask for payment or collect rent. If he wanted to make trouble for the land owner, a squatter could keep from getting kicked off the land for years, using legal tricks or simple evasion. Or, the squatter might simply move further up the creek, where he could squat down on someone else's land. In most states, squatters were attracted to the frontier. In West Virginia, they seem to have stayed long after the frontier passed.

Who were these people? Who would prefer squatting to owning land or moving away to the west? Like the people who bypassed West Virginia, we will probably never know just who the squatters were or why they acted as they did. But we can make some good guesses. Squatters probably included a large number of people who were less ambitious than the average settler. These were people who were not so concerned with acquiring property and improving their lot. Squatters may have included people who did not understand the land laws. They may have included people who wanted to stay close to relatives, but who were unable for some reason to buy suitable nearby land. Or, it may be that many squatters felt that they had a right to use vacant land that was owned by someone who lived far away.

This view would not have been supported by the courts, which usually upheld the rights of property owners. But it would have been a popular view among the squat-ters' neighbors. During the Statehood Period - and for many years afterward - West Virginians came to resent the fact that so much of their best land was owned by non-resident land speculators. They disliked paying property taxes when non-resident owners often got out of paying them. The typical West Virginia settler worked hard to secure and defend a good title to his own land. Squatters took a different approach to the land prob-lem, but it is likely that they still enjoyed some degree of social ap-proval.

The land issues of the State-hood Period created many prob-lems for later citizens of West Vir-ginia. First, there was the practical matter of figuring out exactly who owned what parcels of land. It took judges, lawyers and surveyors most of the nineteenth century to clear up all the overlapping land claims. It also took a long time to get all the land properly recorded on the tax rolls. Until this was done, any investment in West Virginia land had the reputation of being very risky. It was something that few smart or ambitious investors would have wanted to do.

Aside from legal problems, there were also ethical problems concerning the matters of land ownership and use. Ethical problems involve questions of right and wrong. Should the land be divided up into small parcels or large blocks? Was it better for land to be used to *produce* things than to be bought and sold as a *commodity* itself? Should it be used primarily for the benefit of local residents? Or did non-resident owners have equal rights? These questions had to be answered by the leaders who decided Virginia's land laws and property-tax policies during the nineteenth century. Thus, these matters all became political issues. To understand how these issues worked out, it is important to understand West Virginia's political system as it evolved during the Statehood Period. This is what Chapter 5 is all about.

Study Questions - Chapter 4

1. What do the concepts of *territory* and *property* have to do with the matter of paying taxes on land?

2. From the standpoint of women, what were some of the advantages of the Indian theory of land ownership?

3. How did land speculators, settlers and squatters differ in their ideas about land use?

4. How did settlers and soldiers earn the right to free land during the Frontier Period? What problems did these rights cause in the Statehood Period?

Chapter 5:
Why West Virginia Became a State

From the time of its first settlement until 1776, West Virginia was part of the British royal colony of Virginia. Then Virginia joined with the twelve other "original states" to form the United States of America. From 1776 to 1863, West Virginia was part of the Commonwealth of Virginia, as the Virginia state government was called. Then, during the Civil War, West Virginia achieved independence from Virginia. It became a separate state within the United States. This is what we mean by "West Virginia statehood."

How did West Virginia statehood come about? Like many historical questions, there is both a short answer and a long one. The short answer describes certain specific events between 1861 and 1863, when West Virginia's leaders created a new division of Virginia's territory and government. These events are briefly described, beginning on page 94. The long answer covers a much longer period of time. It involves other events and attitudes that convinced many West Virginians that separate statehood was a good idea. The long answer involves the reasons that led people to support the division of Virginia when the opportunity arrived. This answer also requires an examination of those West Virginians who did not think the division was a good idea. It is important to know how these dissenters influenced the statehood process and the new state, once it was born. This chapter explores the long answer.

There were three basic factors that prepared the way for West Virginia statehood. One was **democracy**, the political philosophy that developed in the United States during and after the American Revolution. The second was **sectionalism** within Virginia. The third was the **Civil War**. Without any one of these factors, an attempt to divide Virginia would never have succeeded.

"All men are created equal." These words are from the Declaration of Independence, adopted by the Congress of the United States on July 4, 1776. The notion that all men are equal was the central value in the political philosophy of democracy. This philosophy attracted a lot of support during the Revolution. This support widened gradually until, by around 1830, democracy had become the dominant political philosophy in the United

5.1 Tools of Democracy

States. Still, it did not attract support from everyone. Some influential Americans opposed the spread of democracy throughout this period. And, even among democracy's supporters, there was disagreement about the best way to put democratic values into practice.

What precisely did democracy mean, as it developed in American society during this period? For one thing, it did not mean social or economic equality. The people who wrote the Declaration of Independence and the Constitution of the United States were all males. Many of them owned slaves. They did not wish to make all people equal in wealth and social status. Nor did they wish to make women equal to men, or blacks equal to whites.

The Founders' belief in equality did provide a *basis* for extending political rights to women and to blacks. It also provided a basis for programs that reduce differences in social status and wealth. But the Founders did not initiate these developments themselves. Their notion of equality was very restricted, compared with ours today. Considering the standards of their own time, however, their attitudes were truly revolutionary.

Thus, "All men are created equal" really only applied to white men and, during the Statehood Period, it only applied to political matters. In other words, democracy meant that all white men should have an equal voice in the organization and workings of government. Just how this was to happen in practice was pretty much left up to the individual states. The Constitution of the United States specified that all voters would be allowed to choose the members of the national House of Representatives. Indirectly, voters also participated in electing the president and the United States senators. But the individual states were left to decide exactly who would be allowed to vote. The states also specified how state and local governments were to be organized and run. This meant that there was a great deal of diversity among the various state governments after the Revolution.

During the early nineteenth century, the states gradually adopted similar democratic practices. Three such practices were especially important: **white manhood suffrage, popular election** and **equal representation**.

White manhood suffrage meant that every white male adult was allowed to vote and hold office. ("Suffrage" is the technical term for the privilege of voting.) Traditionally, the right to vote was granted only to white males who owned a substantial quantity of land. A few states also extended suffrage to free black men, but Virginia was not one of these.

Popular election meant, simply, that most state and local government officials had to be chosen by the voters. This would include the governor, members of state legislatures and, in most states, judges and top executives, such as the state treasurer. Popular elections also included county officials - such as sheriffs, clerks and judges - and the mayors and councils of towns. Traditionally, government officials had been chosen by other government officials.

Equal representation, or *equal apportionment*, meant that all election districts should include roughly the same number of people. How authorities defined the election districts was a very important issue; it affected the extent to which elected officials were truly representative of the people who voted. The United States Constitution specified equal apportionment for the districts that elected congressmen - members of the U.S. House of Representatives. It even specified that seats in the House had to be reapportioned every ten years to allow for population changes in congressional election districts. But the national Constitution said nothing about state legislatures. Moreover, it included a controversial provision that allowed Southern states to count three-fifths of their slave population for purposes of congressional apportionment. This three-fifths proportion was called the *federal number*.

Many Southern states used the federal number - or counted slaves in some other way - to apportion state legislative election districts. Supporters of democracy in the South criticized this practice. They said that slaves should not be counted for purposes of apportioning election districts because slaves could not vote. Instead, supporters of democracy proposed the "white basis" of apportionment. This meant that election districts should be designed to contain roughly equal numbers of white people. This way, the apportionment of legislative seats would not be equal in terms of total population, but it would be equal in terms of actual voters.

Between 1789 and 1850, all but two American states adopted the practice of white manhood suffrage and popular election. All but two of the Southern states, where slavery was legal, had adopted the "white basis" of equal apportionment. The two exceptions were Virginia and South Carolina. Thus, Virginia was an exception to the general trend toward greater political democracy in the United States. Virginia's failure to go along with the democratic trend was one of the reasons for sectionalism in

5.2 Sectionalism in Virginia

the state.

Sectionalism is a term which describes a certain pattern of political conflict. This pattern occurs when conflict develops between geographic sections of the same political system. The most familiar example of sectionalism in American history is the conflict between the Northern and Southern states, leading up to the Civil War. There can also be sectional conflict within smaller political systems such as counties, cities and towns. It can be found in medium-sized systems, such as states. In fact, sectionalism has been more persistent at the state level than at any other level in American history. In some form or another, nineteenth-century sectional conflict took place in nearly every U.S. state.

Sectional conflict usually is rooted in disagreements about government policy affecting resources. Natural resources such as minerals, waterways and different types of land are usually distributed unevenly across the map. Thus, when a disagreement arises about how to use or develop resources, it is natural for this disagreement to be expressed in geographic or "sectional" terms.

This is what happened in Virginia. The state's sectional conflicts were rooted within the variations of its different types of agricultural land. Eastern Virginia, lying east of the Blue Ridge Mountains, consisted mostly of rolling or level land. Much of this land lay within reach of deep tidal rivers, good navigation routes for ships carrying plantation products to distant markets. It was well-suited to farming in relatively large units called plantations.

During the seventeenth century, Virginia plantation owners learned to specialize in a single crop, tobacco, which sold well in Europe. Raising tobacco required heavy labor, however, and plantation owners came to depend on slaves to undertake the work. Gradually, an aristocracy of large land owners and slaveowners emerged in Eastern Virginia. Even people who were not part of this aristocracy - small farmers and merchants in towns like Norfolk and Richmond, for example - tended to depend upon the aristocracy in some way or another. Thus, during the eighteenth century, the Virginia aristocracy provided the undisputed political, economic and social leadership of the state.

During the last half of the eighteenth century, the aristocracy of Eastern Virginia produced a very impressive group of political leaders. In fact, the leaders of Virginia were the leaders of the United States. They included four of the first five U.S. presidents: George Washington, Thomas Jefferson, James Madison and James Monroe. Virginia also produced John Marshall, the greatest chief justice of the United States Supreme Court, and other important leaders such as Patrick Henry, George Mason, George Wythe and Richard Henry Lee.

After 1820, however, the Virginia aristocracy began to decline. It declined in wealth and in its influence outside of Virginia. It also declined in self-confidence and, thus, in its openness to compromise. After James Monroe, Virginia produced only one other president who lived there at the time of his presidency, John Tyler. The only nineteenth-century Virginian who came close to matching the abilities and achievements of the state's eighteenth-century leaders was Robert E. Lee. Lee was not a politician, but a military general.

The land in Western Virginia did not lend itself to the development of a plantation system. Much of it was too poor or too hilly to justify extensive cultivation by large gangs of slaves. Much of Western Virginia's best agricultural land was located in highland valleys, where the growing season is too short for crops like tobacco. A few tobacco plantations did spring up in the Kanawha and Ohio river bottom lands. But these rivers carried crops westward, to different markets than those of Eastern Virginia.

As a result, Western Virginia developed a more diversified agriculture than Eastern Virginia. It produced a complete range of farm sizes and types. These types ranged from a few plantations to tiny clearings along mountain streams, where "backwoods" farmers grew food for their families - much as the frontiersmen had done. The region also produced a variety of farming specialties. Most farmers grew corn and other grains such as wheat, rye, barley, oats and buckwheat. Most also raised a few cattle, hogs or sheep. During the early Statehood Period, farmers in different districts of Western Virginia began to specialize in different products. The Valley became a wheat-producing region. The Greenbrier and

WV State Archives

Much of Western Virginia was too poor or too hilly to justify cultivation by large numbers of slaves. This drawing shows slaves being transported from Virginia to Kentucky in 1847.

South Branch valleys specialized in raising cattle and horses. The Monongahela and Ohio river counties developed a reputation for sheep-raising. Farmers in the Ohio and Kanawha bottom lands grew corn and wheat, as well as tobacco.

5.3 Sectionalism and Trade

Western Virginia also developed a more diversified mix of industries. Iron manufacturing first appeared in the Northern Panhandle and The Valley between 1810 and 1830. Then, it spread to the Monongahela Valley. Salt manufacturing developed in the Kanawha Valley, above Charleston. Martinsburg became a place for flour mills and woolen factories. Manufacturers in Wheeling built wagons and boats, wove textiles and made nails, along with a variety of other iron products. Harpers Ferry was a center for weapons production.

Section 7.2 contains a more detailed discussion of West Virginia's economic development during this period. The point

WV State Archives

here is that Western Virginia's resources and their development led to significant political differences with Eastern Virginia. One of the most important differences concerned transportation development. The early leaders of Virginia proposed an extensive network of roads and canals. The idea

The salt works in Malden, Kanawha County, used coal and natural gas to boil salt water, or "brine," to make salt. Salt-making was one of West Virginia's earliest industries.

was to link Eastern and Western Virginia so that each region's growth would benefit the other. George Washington was a particularly avid booster of this idea. In 1786, the Virginia General Assembly formally supported a transportation program that Washington helped design.

The roads and canals of such a system, however, would run mostly in an east-west direction - across the mountains, which run largely north-to-south. Everyone could see that the cost of such a network would have been very high. And the burden of these costs would have fallen mostly on the state government of Virginia.

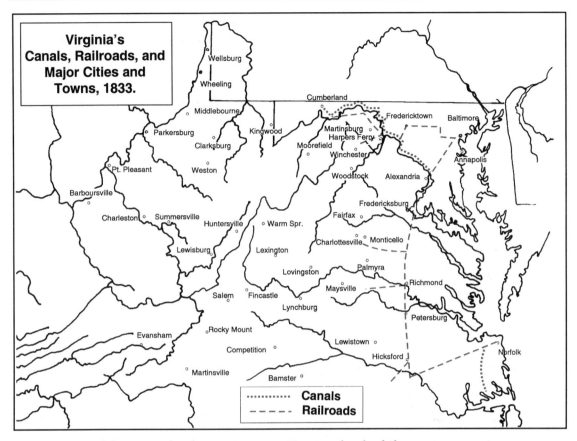

Virginia's Canals, Railroads, and Major Cities and Towns, 1833.

Wellsburg
Wheeling
Cumberland
Middlebourne
Fredericktown   Baltimore
Parkersburg   Kingwood   Martinsburg
                                      Harpers Ferry
Clarksburg   Moorefield   Annapolis
                                    Winchester
Pt. Pleasant   Weston   Woodstock   Alexandria
Barboursville
                                          Fredericksburg
Charleston   Summersville   Fairfax
              Huntersville   Warm Spr.
                                    Charlottesville   Monticello
Lewisburg   Lexington
                        Lovingston   Palmyra
                              Maysville   Richmond
          Salem   Fincastle
                        Lynchburg   Petersburg
                Rocky Mount
Evansham   Lewistown
          Competition
                              Hicksford   Norfolk
      Martinsville
                  Bamster

············· **Canals**
- - - - - **Railroads**

In spite of the costs, leaders in Western Virginia backed the transportation program. Certainly, they had much to gain from it. New roads and canals would have added to the value and productivity of mountain land. The new system would have made it easier for farmers and manufacturers in the Ohio Valley and other areas to send their products to lucrative markets in the east.

Eastern Virginia planters had much less to gain from a new transportation program. Their system was already in place. They could count on the tidal rivers of the Chesapeake Bay and the roads that extended to river towns like Alexandria and Richmond. Eastern Virginia residents were also afraid that they would have to pay higher taxes if the government built new roads and canals in Western Virginia. They were particularly afraid that the proposed program might cause a shift in the tax burden from real property (land) to personal property. To eastern plantation

Eastern Virginia's transportation systems developed at a faster rate than those in the west.

owners, this meant a shift in taxes from land to slaves. There were slaves in Western Virginia, but not nearly to the extent that they were found in Eastern Virginia. For this reason, eastern leaders and land owners began to see the issue of transportation development as a threat to the institution of slavery. After 1820, the aristocracy opposed the transportation network that Western Virginia wanted - or, at least, the support they gave it was lukewarm.

5.4 Sectionalism and Democracy

Eventually, Western Virginia developed an aristocracy of its own. Like Eastern Virginia's, the western aristocracy consisted of the richest land owners. Most of these land owners, however, didn't own tobacco plantations. They had acquired much of Western Virginia's wilderness land. Western Virginia land owners knew that a transportation-development program would have made their land much more valuable. They also knew that, if they were going to get what they wanted, they would need more power in the Virginia state government.

White manhood suffrage, popular election and equal apportionment would have increased the political power of voters in Western Virginia. All these things would have contributed to the spread of democracy in Virginia. This is one reason why western aristocrats wanted more democracy in Virginia, unlike their counterparts in the east. Western Virginians saw democracy as an opportunity to win the network of roads and canals they desired.

Western leaders had other reasons for supporting democracy. Generally, the ideal of equality was more popular in Western Virginia than it was in the east. This ideal had grown out of the frontier, during the wars with the Indians and British. In frontier warfare, each man had counted; each had to pull his own weight. This kind of patriotism, which West Virginians had developed during these years, made them very eager to join in the national trend toward democracy. They resented the fact that Virginia always seemed to lag behind.

Even if Western Virginia's aristocratic leaders had opposed democracy, they would have faced a much more diverse group of followers at home than Eastern Virginia's leaders ever did. For example, Charles S. Morgan, an aristocratic leader of Morgantown, voted against the popular election of governors at the state Constitutional Convention of 1829-30. This made his followers at home very unhappy. Morgan never held an elective office in

Western Virginia again. Instead, he moved to Richmond and was appointed to a job with the Virginia government.

The growing sectional conflict between Eastern and Western Virginia reached its first crisis in 1829-1830, when leaders from around the state gathered for a convention in Richmond. The convention was held to consider changes in the state's constitution.

Eastern Virginia leaders dominated the Constitutional Convention of 1829-30. Western leaders - along with the easterners who believed in the principles of democracy - made appeals for white manhood suffrage, popular elections and equal apportionment. All were rejected. In fact, the constitutional convention rejected most of the changes that westerners favored.

Again, *popular election* meant that most state and local government officials would be chosen directly by the voters. As it was, Virginia's state and local authorities remained appointed - selected by other government officials. The governor himself was selected by the legislature. So were the principal judges and just about everyone else, down to the lowliest county official. Only the members of the legislature, called the General Assembly, were actually elected by the voters.

White manhood suffrage - the right to vote for all white men, not just land owners - would have given counties west of the Blue Ridge a majority of voters in the state.

Similarly, equal apportionment on the "white basis" would have given the western counties, where there were more whites, a majority of seats in the General Assembly. Convention delegates from Eastern Virginia refused to permit this. Instead, they forced the adoption of a formula which divided the state into four districts. The districts were the Tidewater, the Piedmont, the Valley and the Trans-Allegheny. The map on the next page shows each of these districts on a map of Virginia. It also shows the number of state delegates and senators that was given to each district by the constitutional convention. Opposition from the western counties caused the convention to agree to consider reapportionment of the legislative districts, but not until 1841.

The constitutional changes of 1829-30 were submitted to the voters for approval. Voters in the Trans-Allegheny section overwhelmingly rejected them. But in other parts of the state, the voters approved the convention's work. For the first time, Wheeling newspapers issued calls to divide or "dismember" the state.

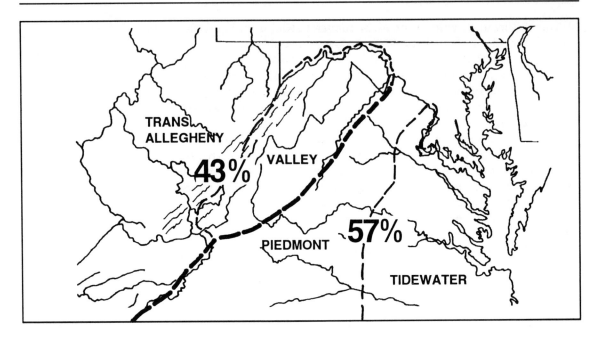

TRANS
ALLEGHENY

43%   VALLEY

57%

PIEDMONT

TIDEWATER

Four voting districts defined by the 1829-30 Virginia convention. The percentages refer to combined senators and delegates in the General Assembly. It is worth noting that the white population of the Western sections was growing more rapidly than the East.

In 1832, a new sectional quarrel broke out in the General Assembly. Western legislators put forward a proposal to abolish slavery and a plan showing how Virginia's slave population should gradually be set free. Eastern Virginia legislators were horrified by this idea. They used their control of the General Assembly to defeat it.

Sectional conflict intensified again in 1841. Under terms of the constitution of 1830, the General Assembly failed to provide for a new apportionment of legislative districts. Western leaders called a convention, which met in Lewisburg in 1842. This convention repeated western demands for manhood suffrage, popular election and equal apportionment. It also emphasized transportation issues that were important to Western Virginia. Westerners continued to agitate these questions until 1850. Then the General Assembly called another convention to make constitutional changes.

The convention of 1850-51 started out again with deep disagreements between leaders from the east and west. In fact, the convention nearly broke up without completing its task. In contrast to 1829-30, however, the delegates of this convention found a way to compromise on most issues. They agreed to the principles of white manhood suffrage and popular election. In

1851, Virginia held its first statewide election for all public officials, extending from the governor and top judges all the way down to county officials. All white males - those who owned land and those who did not - were granted the right to vote that year. Under the new system, the first two candidates for governor were both from West Virginia - the loser from Charleston, the winner from Bridgeport.

Another compromise was worked out on the matter of apportionment. Eastern Virginia leaders again refused to give up their control of the General Assembly. But they agreed to an increase in western representation. They also agreed to commit themselves to an eventual reapportionment on the white basis by 1865 at the latest.

During the 1850s, sectional conflict in Virginia declined. Western leaders won a greater share of control in the state government at Richmond. Thus, they came closer to realizing their goal of improved transportation. The Baltimore and Ohio Railroad was completed between Harpers Ferry and Wheeling, which answered the transportation needs of northern West Virginia. Significant progress was also being made on another rail line linking Charleston and Richmond. In the mountainous parts of the state, roads such as the Weston and Gauley Bridge turnpikes were built or improved.

Moreover, leaders in both sections of the state showed greater willingness to compromise. Western officials abandoned their criticisms of slavery. Instead, many of the most influential western leaders pledged to defend slavery if Northern abolitionists attacked it. Eastern Virginia pulled out of its long economic depression. The former tobacco-growing region began to diversify its agriculture. Richmond emerged as the largest manufacturing center in the South.

If these trends had been allowed to develop under peacetime conditions, it is highly unlikely that Virginia would have ever been divided. Sectional conflicts probably would have declined to manageable levels, as they did in other states. In 1860, however, Virginia was again plunged into a sectional crisis. This time the conflict originated outside the state.

In November 1860, Abraham Lincoln was elected President of the United States. Leaders in Southern states claimed that the new president and his followers would use the federal government's power to abolish the institution of slavery. One month after Lincoln's election, the Southern states began to withdraw, or secede, from the United States.

In February 1861, seven Southern states joined together to form a new government, the **Confederate States of America**. On April 12, fighting broke out between the Confederate government and the United States at Fort Sumter, near Charleston, South Carolina. This was the beginning of the bloody conflict known as the Civil War.

If Virginians had been left to themselves, they probably would have remained neutral during the Civil War. Only a handful of Virginia voters had supported Lincoln's election. Most of these lived in the Wheeling area. There was a much larger group of pro-Confederate Virginians, but they were still a minority. Although pro-Southern people were found all over the state, they were concentrated in Eastern Virginia. Most Virginians did not wish to take sides. In 1860, they had voted for presidential candidates who promised them peace.

5.5 The Civil War

During the six months between Lincoln's election and the outbreak of the war, Virginia leaders tried desperately to work out a compromise. George W. Summers of Kanawha County was the most prominent leader of this peace movement. Eventually, however, the movement failed. Virginians were forced to choose sides. In February 1861, a special convention met in Richmond to discuss the problem. Members of the convention talked and argued for two months. Then, on April 17, 1861 - five days after the battle at Fort Sumter - the Richmond Convention voted 88 to 55 for Virginia to secede from the Union. On May 23, the voters of the state approved the convention's decision and Virginia formally joined the Confederacy. According to the theory of secession, Virginia was now no longer a part of the United States.

President Lincoln did not believe in this theory of secession. He said the states had no right to secede and that the United States had the duty to oppose secession by military force. A majority of people in the Northern states approved of his position. So did a majority in northern West Virginia. A majority of northern West Virginia delegates voted against secession at the Richmond Convention. A majority of voters in northern West Virginia did likewise in the election of May 23. But delegates and voters in other parts of West Virginia were more favorable to secession. The Eastern Panhandle counties were almost evenly divided on the issue. Southern West Virginia voters and delegates favored secession.

So, once Virginia seceded, fighting between West Virginia's

northern and southern troops developed quickly. On May 25, Ohio and Indiana soldiers crossed the Ohio River at Wheeling and Parkersburg. They were joined by pro-Union troops from the Northern Panhandle region of West Virginia. This army moved quickly eastward to push Confederate Virginia troops away from the Baltimore and Ohio Railroad. The first battle between the two sides took place on June 2, 1861, at a covered bridge at Philippi. The Union troops were victorious. The Battle of Philippi was the first full-scale fight of the Civil War after the opening battle at Fort Sumter.

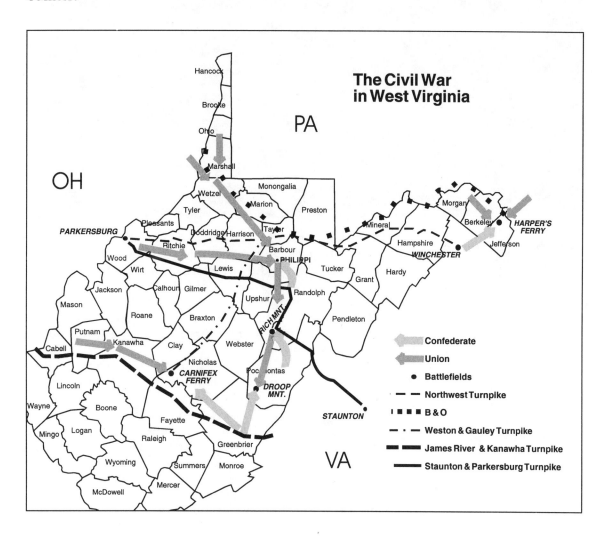

WV State Archives

The covered bridge at Philippi, Barbour County, was the first full-scale fight of the Civil War after the opening battle at Fort Sumter.

The Union forces in northern West Virginia won another important victory on July 11, at Rich Mountain in Randolph County. Meanwhile, on July 9, another Union army from Ohio invaded the Kanawha Valley. Confederate forces were soon driven from this region. Union forces also managed to win control of the Baltimore and Ohio Railroad in the Eastern Panhandle counties. A Confederate counterattack in August 1861 failed to undo these victories.

The Union forces remained in control of northern West Virginia from the summer of 1861 until the end of the war. The Kanawha Valley was also under Union control, except for a brief period in 1862. Otherwise, there were occasional Confederate raids and guerilla warfare behind Union lines. The Confederates remained in control of the Greenbrier Valley, however, until November 6, 1863, when the Battle of Droop Mountain was fought. This battle, in Pocahontas County, was another decisive Union victory. It extended Union control of West Virginia territory almost to the present borders of the state.

It is hard to exaggerate the importance of the Civil War to

West Virginia statehood. The outbreak of fighting shattered the sectional peace between Eastern and Western Virginia. Virginia's secession from the Union led to a revival of proposals to divide the state. The war led national officials, such as President Lincoln, to support the statehood project. The swift Union military conquest of northern West Virginia and the Kanawha Valley gave statehood advocates a safe place to work. This conquest, plus Union control of the B&O Railroad, determined West Virginia's boundary with Virginia as it was drawn in 1863.

To appreciate the importance of military events, it is useful to compare what happened in West Virginia with what happened in Tennessee. There were as many opponents of Confederate secession in East Tennessee as there were in West Virginia. Tennessee Unionists lived deep inside Confederate territory, however. Despite repeated attempts, Union military forces did not win complete military control of East Tennessee until the last year of the war. The battle lines kept surging back and forth across Tennessee. This meant that there was no definite territory under Union control that could become the basis for a new state, even though East Tennessee Unionists wanted one. Thus, East Tennessee remained purely a geographical expression, while West Virginia became the name of a new state.

> On the 5th of August Lieutenant Wagner of the Engineers arrived at Gauley Bridge with instructions from General (William) Rosecrans to superintend the construction of such fortifications as might be proper for a post of three regiments ... We fortified the post by an epaulment or two for cannon, high up on the hillside covering the ferry and the road up New River. An infantry trench, with a parapet of barrels filled with earth, was run along the margin of Gauley River till it reached a creek coming down from the hills on the left... On the side of Gauley Mont facing our post, we slashed timber from the edge of the precipice nearly to the top of the mountain, making an entaglement through which it was impossible that any body of troops should move. Down the Kanawha, below the falls, we strengthened the saw-mill with logs, till it became a blockhouse loopholed for musketry, commanding the road to Charleston, the ferry, and the opening of the road to Fayette Court House..."
>
> *Jacob D. Cox, Brigadier-General, Union Army*
> *Military Reminiscences*

5.6 Making the New State

The Civil War made West Virginia statehood possible, but it did not make it easy. The statehood leaders worked under conditions that were uncertain and dangerous. All of West

Virginia, except the Northern Panhandle, was threatened by Confederate guerrillas and raiders. One such Confederate raid almost resulted in the capture of Francis H. Pierpont, one of the most prominent leaders for West Virginia statehood. The Confederate Virginia government considered participation in the statehood movement to be a crime. If Pierpont had been captured, he would certainly have been imprisoned in Richmond and possibly hanged.

The legal process for creating a new state from the territory of an old one was very complicated. A few statehood leaders wished to bypass this process completely. They simply wished to create "New Virginia" by staging a revolution. But this was essentially what Old Virginia had done when it seceded from the United States. The Confederate states were staging a revolution, trying to win their independence by military force. President Lincoln and Union supporters considered such a process to be unlawful and wrong. This discouraged West Virginians from trying to win their independence from Virginia in the same fashion, even though it would have been simpler to do it

WV State Archives

Union troops posted at Gauley Bridge, Fayette County.

this way.

Instead, West Virginia achieved separation from Virginia by the following procedure:

1. A convention of West Virginia Union supporters met in Wheeling on May 11, 1861. This was called the First Wheeling Convention. Its purpose was to organize opposition to secession. It also provided for a second convention to be held if Virginia voters approved of secession - which they did on May 23.

2. The Second Wheeling Convention met on June 13, 1861. It created a new Virginia government with headquarters in Wheeling. This was called the "Restored" or "Loyal Virginia" government. In theory, it took over the role that the Virginia government had given up when it joined the Confederacy.

3. The U.S. Constitution required Virginia's permission for a new state to form in its territory. The Loyal Virginia government at Wheeling gave this permission. The Second Wheeling Convention gathered again in August and adopted a "dismemberment ordinance." This ordinance provided for the creation of a new state called "Kanawha," and included 39 counties. An election was held in these counties in October 1861. Because it took place during a war, only 19,000 out of 48,000 eligible voters in these counties voted in this election. The voters approved the dismemberment ordinance by a vote of 18,408 to 781.

4. Another convention met in Wheeling in November 1861 to write a constitution for the new state. This Constitutional Convention named the new state West Virginia. It added nine more counties to the new state, including several that were still under Confederate control. The convention adopted government institutions based on Ohio and New England examples. However, it still failed to abolish slavery.

5. In February 1862, the constitution was finished. In May, the new state applied to Congress for admission to the Union. Congress debated the matter until December 1862. Congressional leaders approved of statehood on one condition. They

Independence Hall, in Wheeling was the meeting place of the second Wheeling Convention in June 1861. At that time, the building was called the "Custom House."

WV Division of Tourism & Parks

Topper Sherwood

On April 20, 1863, Abraham Lincoln issued a proclamation stating that West Virginia had met all the conditions needed for statehood. This statue of Lincoln stands outside the state Capitol in Charleston.

required West Virginia to abolish slavery in its territory before it could officially become a state. This was done by means of an amendment to West Virginia's constitution, adopted in March 1863.

6. Meanwhile, President Lincoln was debating the legality and wisdom of West Virginia statehood with members of his Cabinet. The six Cabinet members were evenly divided, three in favor of statehood, three against. Finally, Lincoln gave his approval. He signed the West Virginia statehood bill on December 31, 1862. On April 20, 1863, he issued a proclamation stating that West Virginia had fulfilled all the conditions required for statehood. He said it would become a separate state in sixty days.

7. On June 20, 1863, West Virginia began its official existence as a state. Arthur H. Boreman of Parkersburg became its first governor. Waitman T. Willey of Morgantown and Peter G. Van Winkle of Parkersburg became its first United States Senators. James H. Brown of Charleston became the first chief justice of the West Virginia Supreme Court. (Francis H. Pierpont of Fairmont was still recognized in West Virginia and the Union as governor of "Loyal Virginia." He moved his headquarters from Wheeling to Alexandria, where his government could be on Virginia soil.)

In some ways, the years immediately following statehood were as frustrating for West Virginia leaders as the previous years had been. Each step that brought West Virginia closer to statehood also created enemies for the new state and its leaders. These enemies included Virginia Confederates whose home counties were now part of the new state. There were also West Virginians who supported the Union, but who were opposed to the creation of a new state. There were early statehood supporters who then changed their minds rather than agree to the abolition of slavery. Other people turned against the statehood leaders because they did not like President Lincoln or the congressional leaders who had backed statehood. By 1865, it became clear that the supporters of West Virginia statehood were outnumbered by enemies within their own new state.

When the Civil War ended, some statehood leaders worried that their opponents would try to reunite West Virginia with

Virginia. They took desperate measures to prevent this. They adopted laws which made it illegal for ex-Confederates to vote or hold office. They also adopted state loyalty oaths, which suspected rebels had to take before they could practice their professions or take part in political life.

These measures probably lost as many pro-statehood supporters as they gained, but they did keep West Virginia's original leadership in office for five years after the war. Then, in 1870, the opposition won a slight majority in the state elections. This election gave West Virginia new leadership - one that included many former Confederates. The statehood leaders were thrown out of office. Their 1863 constitution was replaced by one that was modeled on the Virginia Constitution that had been in effect before the Civil War.

The Statehood Era produced some remarkable West Virginia leaders. The most famous West Virginian of this era was **Thomas Jonathan Jackson** - or **"Stonewall" Jackson**, as he is commonly known.

5.7 Heros of the Statehood Period

WV State Archives

He was born in Clarksburg in 1824. Although his family included wealthy land speculators and political leaders, Jackson himself had a difficult childhood because of the death of his parents. He grew up in Lewis County, in the home of an uncle, on a beautiful bottom-land farm called Jackson's Mill.

Jackson's family managed to get him appointed to the United States Military Academy at West Point. But his military genius was not readily apparent there, and he followed an obscure career before the Civil War. During the sectional crisis of 1861, Jackson opposed the statehood movement in West Virginia and supported the secession of Virginia.

He became a West Virginia hero nevertheless. His brilliance as a Confederate general earned Jackson the love of his fellow rebels and the admi-

Stonewall Jackson

ration of military experts all over the world. Jackson showed a genius for quickly moving his troops and catching the enemy off-guard. When he was killed on May 10, 1863, at Chancellorsville, Virginia, the hopes of the Confederacy suffered a serious blow.

John Brown was not a West Virginian. He was not born in the state. But he died here, and the cause and manner of his death were factors that helped bring on the Civil War.

Brown was an abolitionist. He believed in the elimination of slavery, and was unwilling to wait for peaceful and legal means to accomplish the task. Instead, he planned a violent attack on the U.S. arsenal, or weapons storehouse, at Harpers Ferry. He planned to distribute the weapons to Jefferson County slaves, whom he planned to lead in a slave rebellion. He hoped the slaves would rise up against their masters in a revolution that would spread across the South. Brown and a little band of men - including free African-Americans as well as whites - attacked Harpers Ferry on October 16, 1859.

But Brown's military skills were not equal to his ideals. He and his men were quickly captured by a U.S. Army unit. Several were killed, while Brown himself was wounded. Accused of treason against the Commonwealth of Virginia, Brown was tried and executed at Charles Town in December 1859. In death, he became a martyr to the cause of freedom and equality in the Northern states. Two years later, when Union soldiers marched into the South, they sang the words of "John Brown's Body," with the chorus: "...But his truth is marching on."

WV State Archives

John Brown

Francis H. Pierpont of Fairmont was the governor of the Loyal Virginia government and a principal leader of the statehood movement. He was one of the few West Virginia leaders who was openly critical of slavery during the 1850s. Pierpont guided West Virginia and its statehood movement through the most dangerous years of the Civil War.

James H. Brown was a rich lawyer and land owner from Charleston. He supported statehood, but he defended slavery and other Virginia institutions. He did not own slaves himself, however. He also defended the Union and the statehood movement vigorously at a time when most members of his class remained neutral or supported the Confederacy.

George W. Summers, of Charleston, was one of those who remained neutral. He was West Virginia's best-known political leader before the Civil War. He worked tirelessly to promote peace between the North and the South in 1861. When the peace movement failed, Summers withdrew from public life, refusing to take sides. He also refused to support the statehood movement. Though he favored a new state, he disapproved of the way that it was created.

Samuel Price of Lewisburg was West Virginia's leading expert on land law. He was also a successful land speculator. Although he opposed Virginia's secession, he went along with it.

In 1863, Price was elected Lieutenant-Governor of Virginia's Confederate government in Richmond. After the war ended in 1865, the voters of Greenbrier County elected him to the West Virginia state Senate. The West Virginia Legislature refused to let him serve, however, because Price was a former Confederate.

After political rights were restored to ex-Confederates, Price played a leading role in the Constitutional Convention of 1872. He was elected to be a U.S. senator from West Virginia in 1875.

Perhaps the most mysterious West Virginia leader of this period was **John S. Carlile** of Clarksburg. Carlile was a determined enemy of Virginia's secession from the Union and an early supporter of the new state. He was elected in 1861 to the U.S. Senate from the Loyal Virginia government.

Then, in 1862, Carlile turned against the statehood movement and tried to wreck its chances with Congress. Historians have never been sure just why he did this. Presumably, it was the slavery issue that led him to change his mind. Carlile did not believe that Congress had the right to force Virginia to free its slaves. In any case, he managed to offend nearly every political group in West Virginia before he was finished. Shortly after his term in the Senate ended, he moved away from the state.

Laura Jackson Arnold was the most prominent heroine of the Statehood Era. She was the sister of Stonewall Jackson and, like him, suffered many personal tragedies. Her brother was a leading Confederate general. Her husband, a rich and elderly land speculator, was also a Confederate sympathizer. But Mrs. Arnold's sympathy was with the Union. She was particularly sympathetic toward the young Union soldiers who were stationed near her home in Beverly, Randolph County. She nursed wounded soldiers from both armies and generally did what she could to lessen the boring and lonely aspects of military life. Her husband used her wartime activities as the basis of a divorce suit he brought against her after the war.

Study Questions - Chapter 5

1. Applying information you gained from reading this chapter, explain why:

a. Western Virginians didn't like the Virginia government to use the "federal number" in counting the population for voting purposes?

b. Leaders in Virginia during the first half of the nineteenth century resisted the changes accompanying new ideas?

c. Western Virginians wanted a good transportation system across the mountains into Eastern Virginia, but eastern leaders opposed the plan?

d. Western Virginians did not like the Virginia government's property-ownership requirement for voting?

e. West Virginia today has three congressmen in the U.S. House of Representatives and California has fifty-two?

2. What experiences did Western Virginians share that caused them to feel a "frontier spirit?"

3. In 1832, western delegates to the Virginia Assembly proposed ending slavery. Suggest several reasons you think the Western Virginians did not support slavery. Look for at least three "clues" in your text, including pictures.

Chapter 6:
State Government

Under the U.S. Constitution, West Virginia's new state government was equal to Virginia's government in every way. As far as formal political institutions were concerned, the separation of the two states was complete, total and permanent.

But it was not quite that simple. West Virginia remained tied to Virginia in certain ways. When the new state was being created, its leaders specifically rejected the idea of giving it an entirely new name, such as "Kanawha." Instead, they kept "Virginia" as part of the state's name. In 1872, a new set of leaders rewrote the West Virginia Constitution to make it more like Virginia's. There were also other continuing links between Virginia and West Virginia. In fact, West Virginia's political life did not grow away from its Virginia origins until the 1880s.

Thus, we find a two-fold problem in interpreting the history of West Virginia's Statehood Period. We want to understand the state's differences with Virginia. But we also need to understand the similarities. To put it a little differently, we need to identify what was "western" about the part of Virginia that became West Virginia; and we also need to learn what was "Virginian" about the west.

One way to study this problem is to look at the history of the Statehood Period as the history of an emerging **political system** in West Virginia. When you finish reading this chapter, you should have a better idea of what is meant by the term "political system." You should be able to recognize and distinguish between the two components of a political system - **political institutions** and **political culture**. You should also be able to distinguish between **formal** and **informal political institutions**. Finally, you should be able to apply all of these concepts to the interpretation of events that happened during West Virginia's Statehood Period.

Idea and Issues:
The Emerging
Political System

What is a political system? It is a system for handling the disagreements and conflicts that occur among people living within a society. A political system also includes mechanisms for defining and enforcing the laws and customs of the society. And it includes ways of managing the relations that the society extends to other societies.

6.1 The Branches
of Government

Before 1776, Virginia was part of the political system of the British Empire. Today, West Virginia and Virginia, like all other American states, are parts of the larger political system of the United States. Thus, U.S. states - as political systems that are parts of a larger system - do not perform all the functions of *independent* political systems. They cannot make treaties with foreign countries, for example. They cannot establish state religions, or award titles of nobility, or pass laws on topics that the U.S. Constitution reserves for the federal government. But, otherwise, states have *most* of the qualities found in the political systems of other societies.

A political system consists, first of all, of **formal political institutions**. These are the parts of a system that are organized and established by law. For example, the United States and every one of the fifty states has a written **constitution**. Each constitution describes a method of creating laws, enforcing them, and a method for amending the constitution. Every constitution establishes the state's legislative, executive and judicial institutions.

Amending a constitution means changing specific parts. Constitutions can also be completely rewritten. The United States Constitution has never been rewritten. But it has been amended twenty-six times. The states amend and rewrite their constitutions more frequently. West Virginia is not typical in this respect, however. Its constitution has been rewritten only once, in 1872, and there have been only seventeen amendments since that time.

The **executive branch** enforces the laws of the state. The governor is the head, or "chief executive," of this branch. In 1822, Virginia created another executive agency called the Board of Public Works. It consisted of the state auditor, treasurer, the attorney general and the heads of other administrative departments. (West Virginia copied the Board of Public Works into its political system and, in fact, gave it more power than it had in Virginia.)

The **legislative branch** of government creates the laws of the state. In Virginia, the legislative branch is called the General Assembly. West Virginia abandoned this term. Its legislature is called simply the Legislature. In every state but Nebraska, the state legislature consists of two "houses," or "chambers." In West Virginia, the "upper" house is called a state Senate. The "lower" house is a House of Delegates. The state Senate is smaller and its members serve for longer terms.

The **judicial branch** of state government provides trials for people accused of breaking state laws. It also settles disputes that arise between individuals or groups in the state. These disputes are brought before the courts in the form of lawsuits.

Today - just as it was in pre-Civil War Virginia - **state courts** operate at an intermediate level between local and federal courts. **Local courts** operate at the county level and generally rule on minor crimes or disputes involving small amounts of money. **United States district courts** operate in every state and provide federal trials for people accused of breaking U.S. laws. They also hear lawsuits involving disputes between people or groups living in different states.

Before statehood, the U.S. Congress created a federal court for the district of Western Virginia. In 1863, this became the district of West Virginia. In 1905, West Virginia was divided into two judicial districts - one in the northern part of the state and one in the southern. Since then, the number of federal judges in our state has continued to grow, but the number of federal-court districts remains the same.

In 1809, Virginia established a two-tiered system of state courts and this was continued by West Virginia. The lower courts were called **circuit courts**. They were so named because the presiding judge traveled from county to county within a specified district or "circuit." The circuit judge held court in each county at least three times a year. In each county, the judge was assisted by a circuit-court clerk and a "commonwealth's attorney," or prosecutor. (In Virginia, before 1851, these offices were all appointive. The compromises made at the constitutional convention of that year made them elective.)

The highest state court in Virginia was called the **Court of Appeals**. This court heard appeals of decisions made by local and circuit courts. Until 1837, this was also the court that dealt with most lawsuits involving land titles. Then, pressure from Western Virginia leaders caused the law to be changed. From West Virginians' standpoint, land cases were better heard by circuit courts - right in the counties where land disputes occurred.

West Virginia's first state leaders adopted Virginia's court system with only minor changes. But the writers of both of West Virginia's constitutions - the original one of 1863 and its replacement of 1872 - quarreled fiercely over another institution, that of the county government.

As an institution, the "county" originated in England. In the seventeenth century, the British colony of Virginia created the first counties in America. Under Virginia law, counties were governed by **county courts** composed of **magistrates** or **justices of the peace**. (Both terms were used.) Individually, the justices acted as judges in cases involving minor crimes and disputes in their neighborhoods. Three or four times a year, the justices of a county gathered and acted together as the "county court."

In contrast to later state and federal political systems, the county courts mixed the judicial, executive and legislative powers together. The justices made the laws for a county; they ruled in legal disputes; and they nominated one among themselves to be the county's chief executive officer, the **sheriff**. The governor appointed the sheriff, but he usually appointed whomever the county justices nominated. Whenever a justice died or retired, the others on the court simply chose a new one. Usually, they picked the new justice from among their own relatives and friends.

County courts were the key to the political power of Virginia's aristocracy. Justices tended to be chosen from among the richest and most prominent families in each county. This was the way these families shared control of the county governments. But their power extended to other offices as well. County sheriffs were chosen from among the members of the county court. Sheriffs had the power to decide when and how to hold elections for members of Virginia's General Assembly. And the General Assembly chose the governor, the judges and other important officials of the state.

The institution of the county court helps to explain why West Virginia developed its own version of the Virginia political aristocracy. In each county, east and west, the courts tended to concentrate political power in the hands of a few families. But, during the Statehood Period, the county court became unpopular with most West Virginians. It was, after all, the least democratic of Virginia's institutions. In 1851, county offices - along with state offices - did become elective positions. But, otherwise, the system was unchanged before the Civil War.

Then, in 1862, the first West Virginia Constitutional Convention decided to get rid of the Virginia county court system entirely. It its place, convention delegates substituted a New England form of local government, called the "township system." The township system, however, was too big a change for most West Virginians. As it was rewritten in 1872, the West Virginia constitution brought back the county court. This time, however, the justices were elected, as they had been under the Virginia constitution with the democratic reforms of 1851. Unfortunately, this didn't work out either. Finally, in 1880, West Virginia adopted a constitutional amendment that created West Virginia county government in its modern form.

The term **county court** was retained in the new county political system adopted in 1880. But the court's membership and functions changed drastically. Each county elected three commissioners who, together, made up the county court. This three-member court retained its role as the county's combined executive and legislative body. It also kept its power to appoint officials such as coroners and county health officers. But, after 1880, West Virginia county courts lost their judicial functions. They no longer decided lawsuits or held trials.

Magistrate courts retained their original Virginia form in West Virginia until 1974. Each county was divided into magisterial districts. Each district elected one or two justices of the peace, or "J.P.s," who heard cases involving small sums and minor offenses. A constitutional amendment replaced the old J.P. courts with magistrate courts in 1974.

Election machinery was another political institution controlled by state constitutions. Under the old Virginia system, sheriffs had control of election procedures. They decided when the vote would be held and they appointed the people who supervised the voting.

6.2 Election Machinery

Voting was done orally. This meant that the election officials - and anyone else standing nearby - heard the voter express his choice out loud. Some Virginia leaders thought oral voting was a manly expression of a citizen's opinion. But the practice had its undemocratic side. It must have made some people afraid to vote against rich and powerful candidates. It probably discouraged some people from voting altogether. Oral voting was one of the first Virginia practices that West Virginia got rid of. The state's first constitution in 1863 established the secret paper ballot as the method of voting in West Virginia. During the 1872 Constitutional Convention, some delegates made an attempt to restore oral voting. But this proposal was rejected and secret balloting has remained the rule.

Before 1890, political candidates or parties gave out the **ballots** which voters used to vote. A voter accepted the ballot, or "ticket," offered by the candidate or party that he favored. Then he stuffed that ballot into a special box.

In 1890, West Virginia adopted the **Australian ballot**. This ballot was prepared by state election officials and handed to each voter. It listed *all* the candidates and political parties in a uniform fashion, without giving an edge to any party or candidate. The voter simply marked his or her choices.

During the 1950s, voting machines began to be used in West Virginia elections. These machines used a modified form of Australian ballot, and that form survives today with computer-voting systems. However, many informal political terms still survive from the earlier forms of voting. Words such as "ticket," "poll" and "ballot stuffing" go back to the days when different methods of voting were used.

6.3 Political Parties and Patronage

In addition to its formal institutions, every political system has **informal institutions**. These informal institutions are not established by constitutions or other laws. They come into use as customs or habits. Political parties, for example, started out as informal institutions.

A **political party** is an organized group of individuals who have joined together to influence the selection of political candidates and officeholders. Parties also attempt to influence government policies and to influence overall government operations. And they convey information about government operations and political candidates to the general public.

Political parties started out in the United States as temporary alliances between groups (or "factions") of politicians. But by 1800, parties had assumed permanent form in most states. During the nineteenth century, almost all voters came to think of themselves as members of some national political party.

Between 1830 and 1852, the two major national political parties were the **Democrats** and **Whigs**. These parties became institutions that helped bridge the differences between Eastern and Western Virginia. Both parties were well-represented in both sections of the state. Thus, it was in each party's interest to promote sectional compromise.

During the 1850s, however, the national Whig party broke into pro- and anti-slavery factions. In 1860, the Democratic Party broke up the same way. When faced with an issue as bitterly divisive as slavery, neither party was able to develop a compromise position that appealed to all its members. The weakening of the political parties meant that there was one less thing holding the nation - and Virginia - together.

In 1856, a new national political party emerged, called the

Republican Party. From the start, the Republicans took a definite position against the growth of slavery. This anti-slavery position had great appeal in the North, but very little in border states such as Virginia. Abraham Lincoln was the Republican presidential candidate in 1860. He won the presidency, but nearly all his votes came from the Northern states. In Virginia, Lincoln got less than two thousand votes. Most of these came from the Wheeling area, with some also from Preston County and from Parkersburg.

Archibald Campbell was a bold and vigorous spokesman for the Republican Party in Western Virginia in 1860. So was his newspaper, the *Wheeling Intelligencer*. The Republicans had little popular support in the state, but the statehood movement depended on the party's success. More specifically, the movement depended on the support of President Lincoln and the powerful Republicans in Congress. Thus, most statehood leaders followed Lincoln and Archibald Campbell into the Republican Party.

After the Civil War, the Republicans were joined by the majority of veterans who fought on the Union side. African-American voters also were overwhelmingly Republican because of the party's position against slavery. The party recruited enough new voters in northern West Virginia, in fact, to give it control of certain counties there - namely, Grant, Preston, Upshur, Taylor, Morgan, Hancock, Ritchie, Tyler, Marshall and Monongalia.

But, as popular as it had become in the north, the Republican Party did not have enough votes to gain control of the entire state. West Virginia Republicans were outnumbered by several kinds of voters in 1865. Non-Republican voters included pro-Confederate Democrats, pro-Union Democrats, former Whigs and young men who had no previous party membership.

Gradually, these factions grouped together into a reorga-

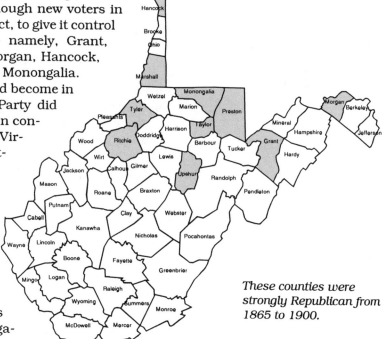

These counties were strongly Republican from 1865 to 1900.

nized version of the Democratic Party, which enjoyed great appeal among Confederate veterans. The Democratic Party was initially successful in counties around the southern, eastern and central parts of the state. Democratic voters were numerous enough to win control of West Virginia in 1870. The party held onto its control of state government from then until 1896.

Patronage is another informal political institution. This is the practice of awarding government jobs, contracts, or other benefits to people on the basis of their political support of a candidate or party. In nineteenth-century Virginia and West Virginia, there were not many state or local government jobs to award. But there were numerous U.S. government jobs, especially after the Civil War. President Lincoln, for example, appointed Archibald Campbell in 1861 to be the U.S. postmaster at Wheeling. Lincoln was the Republican president, Campbell was the leading Republican in Wheeling, and the postmastership was the most desirable federal job there.

It was well understood that service to a political party was the chief qualification for obtaining a patronage job. This was not a matter of formal law. It was a matter of custom. As the number of government jobs grew in West Virginia, political patronage became increasingly important as an institution in state politics.

6.4 Political Culture

Political systems also include some features that are not organized or defined well enough to be called "institutions." But these features are still very important in political life. Such features are part of the **political culture**. We can define political culture as the sum of a society's practices, values, and beliefs that make its political institutions work.

We can get a good understanding of political culture by examining the ways that political leaders and their followers exchange information. Political leaders in any system need to know what concerns the people. They need this information in order to develop government policies that will attract public support. They also need to pass information back to the people. They have to explain their policy positions, criticize the policies of their rivals, and strengthen their own political support.

During the Statehood Period, the principal means of exchanging information was through oral communication. That is, citizens and their leaders talked to each other. By and large, the printed word was far less effective as a means of reaching people, certainly less so than it is now. Other mass media, such as movies, radio and television, didn't exist.

Thus, an oral political culture was well-suited to the way people lived in West Virginia before 1880. Except for a few towns and one city (Wheeling), most people lived in isolated places. The nature of the land meant that farms and homes were scattered along the valleys of small streams. There were no daily newspapers outside of Wheeling before 1880. Weekly newspapers were found only in the larger towns. Postal service was slow and irregular. Telegraph service was found only along the railroads before the Civil War. In these circumstances, face-to-face communication was the most effective way to convey political information and win followers.

Because of this, a legal institution called **court day** became the most important expression of oral political culture. Court day was the day when the circuit-court judge came to a particular county. This happened in each county three or four times a year. Court days were times when the county's important lawsuits and criminal trials were held. But they were also social and political occasions. People from all over the county came to the county seat on court day.

Many people watched the trials as a form of entertainment, but others came to visit, gossip, or shop. The county militia or volunteer-soldier unit usually held its drills on court day; young men competed in foot races and other athletics. There were shooting matches; and sometimes, two or more fellows who'd had too much to drink entertained each other with a fight. It was an occasion for people to visit their friends and relatives from other parts of the county.

But the highlight of court days were the political speeches. The courthouse was often populated with lawyers on court days. Some of the lawyers had cases before the court - but not all of them. Court days gave these men the chance to compete against each other, showing off their skills at making speeches. They used speech-

Joseph Diss Debar, a French immigrant, drew these lawyers traveling to court day in the 1840s.

WV State Archives

WV State Archives

Joseph Diss Debar's sketch of the men he called "gentlemen justices."

making to display their courtroom style and, thus, to drum up business for themselves.

People who listened to the speeches at the courthouse were sometimes informed - and often entertained - by the lawyers. Some listened quietly. Others heckled and asked questions. Afterward, the speaker might be "cornered" for a private conversation or two.

Of course, many court-day speakers were candidates for political office. These men found that court day was an especially good time to advertise their political views and promote their party positions. Following the circuit court always gave a politician the chance to widen his circle of friends and acquaintances. He could then appeal to these new acquaintances for support in his campaign.

Supporters, in turn, recruited others from among their relatives, friends and neighbors at home. If he won office, the politician became able to reward government jobs or contracts to his particularly effective backers. This cemented his alliance with his local supporters.

The West Virginia politicians who traveled from county to county on court days were usually richer and better educated than the people they spoke to. They were often land speculators or agents of other out-of-state speculators, who owned West Virginia land. They took full advantage of Virginia's undemocratic political institutions to build up their own power. Yet many of them worked to change those institutions. [See section 5.4, page 86.] And they had a more democratic relationship with the people than the formal institutions of Virginia provided. Specifically, the oral political culture of Virginia added an informal democratic element to the state's undemocratic political system. A government whose leaders spoke face-to-face with citizens was democratic in a psychological sense. Citizens who could talk directly to their leaders had power that was just as important as the power to vote and hold office.

The oral tradition of political culture was Virginian. But it persisted in West Virginia long after the new state was established. Especially in central, southern and eastern West Virginia, politicians continued to campaign in the traditional manner. They traveled from place to place, making speeches at court days, reunions, picnics, religious gatherings and other festive occasions. They continued to develop supporters on a face-to-face, friends-and-neighbors basis. They kept their followers through personal friendship and personal favors.

West Virginia's statehood movement attracted some leaders who appealed to voters through this traditional political culture. But, for the most part, pro-statehood leaders represented northern and western communities, where a new political culture was taking shape. This new culture was based on newspapers and other printed forms of communication. It was also based on well-organized rallies and campaigns involving thousands of campaign workers.

Politicians of the new culture were generally not skilled in using the personal, face-to-face techniques of the traditional political culture. They tried to appeal to supporters on the basis of issues. They were not successful. After the Civil War, they were not able to win much support outside the northern and western parts of the state.

West Virginia's statehood leaders preached "democracy" to the state's new citizens. Their constitution of 1863 defined some of the most democratic formal institutions that West Virginia has ever had. But these leaders could not keep control of the state government by peaceful, democratic means. As peacetime conditions returned, political leaders who were skilled in the oral political culture of rural Virginia surged forward again. Their reorganization of West Virginia's formal political institutions in 1872 was based on Virginia's traditional political culture. That culture dominated politics in most of West Virginia's southern half for more than a generation after the Civil War.

After 1880, the industrial economy began to bring different conditions of life through central and southern West Virginia. Only then did the traditional political culture begin to change.

Study Questions - Chapter 6

1. Under West Virginia's first constitution, state senators served terms of *two* years, delegates served *one* year, and governors served *two* years. The second constitution increased the length of terms to *four* years for state senators, *two* years for delegates, and *four* years for governors. What might be some reasons in favor of and against increasing the terms of these officials and making elections less frequent?

2. Virginians chose the candidate they wanted by oral or voice-voting. The first West Virginia constitution made the secret ballot the voting form used in our state. Which kinds of people would prefer a voice vote? Which would prefer the secret ballot?

3. Why is political patronage an important power for government officials?

4. Nineteeth-century political candidates mostly used public speaking to get the support of the voters. Political candidates today have very different ways of trying to get votes. Name as many different ways as you can in which candidates try and get votes today. Are these ways of getting votes a part of our political institution or part of our political culture?

PART III: Becoming an Industrial Society

Chapter 7:
The Industrial Period

West Virginia became an industrial society during the nineteenth century. Industrialism brought changes to the state that were every bit as great as the political changes that created it - maybe even greater. Unlike statehood, however, industrialization was a more gradual and uneven process. It affected different places at different times, and in different ways.

The most intense changes brought by industrialization took place in the years between 1850 and 1930. This is the period we identify as the **Industrial Period** in this book. In some parts of West Virginia, however, industrialization began long before 1850. It continues to take place in our own century. Industrialization, then, is an ongoing process. We can trace its beginnings and say something about its initial impact upon our society. But no one is certain when (or whether) the process of indutrialization will end.

Ideas and Issues:
Industrialization

Industrialization has widespread effects on the cultural, social and political life of a society. Basically, however, it is an economic change. It begins with changes in people's economic lives - in the ways that they use their available resources to produce goods and services. In order to appreciate how vast these changes were, it is first necessary to describe the economic life of West Virginia as it existed before the process of industrialization began.

In economic terms, the Frontier Period might just as well be called the "Forest Period" of West Virginia history. The pioneer settlers of that time depended heavily on the resources of the forest. Like the Indian and prehistoric inhabitants before them, West Virginia settlers relied on hunting and on gathering forest products. The most obvious example is game animals. Deer, turkey, bear and smaller animals provided settlers with meat and skins for clothing and trade. It is no accident that one prominent symbol of West Virginia, the mountaineer, is a forest character carrying a hunting rifle and wearing clothes made from animal skins.

The forest provided many things for West Virginia settlers. Besides game animals, there were cool, clear streams with an

7.1 Before
Industrialization

abundance of fish. There were nuts, berries, fruits, maple syrup and wild honey to be harvested. There was also a large variety of edible and medicinal herbs.

Ginseng and ramps are two of the most famous plants in West Virginia's forests. Ginseng is a root which became important in American trade with China during the 1780s. West Virginia settlers traded ginseng with area merchants. The merchants, in turn, passed it along until ginseng eventually reached the New England seaports. From there, the root entered the China trade.

Ramps were not traded. They were consumed locally. They provided the first fresh greens available in the spring. In fact, ramps could often be found when there was still snow on the ground. To people who had plenty of meat in the winter but had gone for months without fresh vegetables, ramps were a great delicacy. Their freshness and abundance more than made up for their unpleasant smell.

Forests also provided wood for every kind of construction. The characteristic house of the Frontier Period was the log cabin. The forts which played such an important role in the wars of the period were protected by palisades, or walls, of logs. For that matter, so were the Indian villages of the late Prehistoric Period. The Mound Builders even buried their dead in log tombs.

The forest provided the basic resources of food, clothing, fuel and shelter during the Frontier Period. It also provided products, such as animal skins and ginseng, which could be traded for goods that the forest did not offer.

In 1880, West Virginia was still heavily forested. Forest products were a vital part of its economy. But the economic base of the Statehood Period was agriculture, which involved a variety of economic activities. Technically, farming refers mainly to horticulture, the raising of plants. But West Virginia farmers were also herdsmen or graziers, who raised pigs, cattle, horses and sheep. Some farmers learned to specialize in one or more of these activities. That is, they concentrated on producing crops or herds for sale. This made them **commercial farmers**. But the majority of West Virginia farmers during the Statehood Period remained **subsistence farmers**, whose families consumed most of what they produced.

The difference between commercial and subsistence farming was, to some extent, a difference in location. By 1820, commercial farming was well-established wherever there was good land and access to transportation. Subsistence farming was especially common in the central and southern counties.

But it was found in the poorest and remotest districts in every county in the state.

For many, however, there was no clear separation between commercial and subsistence farming. Most commercial farmers produced food for their families as well as specialized products. Many subsistence farmers would have produced for the market if West Virginia's transportation system had been better. Since distant markets were hard to reach, farmers generally did not try to reach them - unless they lived close to a good road or a major river. But nearly every farmer produced something - or gathered something from the nearby forest - which could be traded for cash or for needed products that the settlers could not produce for themselves.

One of the first processing operations to become established in West Virginia was distilling. This is the process of turning corn or grain into whiskey or fruit juice into brandy. The method of distilling was well-known to all immigrants from the British Isles, though it seems to have been a specialty of people from Scotland or Ireland.

7.2 Industries of the Frontier Period

The distilling industry in West Virginia was born out of necessity - from the difficulty of transportation. When roads were bad and markets were distant, liquor was much easier and cheaper to sell than grain or fruit. Fruit cannot be stored for long periods unless it is dried. Grain is bulky and had a low economic value for its weight. Distilling it concentrated the volume and increased the value per unit of weight by as much as tenfold. Thus, whiskey was often the first thing a farmer sold, once he started producing more grain than his family and animals could eat. During the late eighteenth century, the corn whiskey of the Monongahela Valley acquired a reputation as being among the best available in the United States.

National Park Service Photo

Making illegal "moonshine" whiskey dates back to the 1790s. These federal and local officers in eastern West Virginia were photographed after uncovering a hidden still in 1950.

But liquor was also tempting as an object of taxation. In 1791, the United States government imposed a federal tax, called an excise tax, on whiskey. The result was a violent protest called the Whiskey Rebellion, which broke out in western Pennsylvania and nearby sections of Ohio and Monongalia counties.

During the Civil War, the federal government again imposed an excise tax. But it did not make any serious effort to collect the tax until 1879. During the next decade, West Virginia's backwoods whiskey makers became famous for their resistance to the tax. The untaxed whiskey and brandy they made was called **moonshine**. The name was a traditional British word for illegal goods that are produced or handled by night.

William A. MacCorkle, who was state governor in the 1890s, once said that the federal court in West Virginia prosecuted more moonshiners than any other federal court in the country. MacCorkle offered no proof of this assertion. But during those years, the image of the hillbilly - dressed in the backwoods clothes of the 1880s and carrying his whiskey jug and rifle - became a popular symbol of West Virginia and of the mountain sections in nearby states.

A more typical and widespread symbol of agricultural development was the **mill**, which ground grain into flour or meal.

Mills operated through a combination of large stones. One stone revolved around and crushed the grain against the other. The first mills were operated by muscle power, either human or animal. These were called tub mills. But by the end of the eighteenth century, water-powered grist mills appeared in the most-developed agricultural districts. Water-powered lumber or saw mills followed close behind. Saw mills processed timber into planks and beams, which were much more convenient to use than logs. The appearance of gristmills and sawmills in a neighborhood was usually a major step toward economic de-

WV State Archives

An eighteenth-century grist mill on Dropping Lick Creek, Monroe County.

velopment. Mills opened the way to commercial agriculture, which gradually replaced the hunting and subsistence farming of the frontier.

Glade Creek Grist Mill, Babcock State Park
Fayette County

Another step toward agricultural maturity was the capacity for people to make the glass and metal materials required by a comfortable and successful farm life. Pioneer settlers rarely had window glass, and they used wooden pegs in place of iron nails, which also were scarce. But the farmers of the Statehood Period increasingly built houses with clapboard siding and plenty of windows. Beginning in 1742, iron was manufactured in the Eastern Panhandle. In the Northern Panhandle, iron manufacturing began in 1794. Glass and pottery making began in the Morgantown area around 1800.

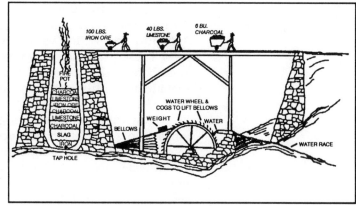

The workings of an iron furnace.

Between 1820 and 1830, Wheeling grew into a diversified manufacturing center. At first it specialized in goods that were needed in commerce, such as wagons and boats, or in agricultural processing. Its products included glass, leather, cotton and woolen textiles, whiskey, beer, lumber and small loosely-rolled cigars which became famous as "Wheeling Stogies."

In one sense, the establishment of iron and glass furnaces constituted the beginning of industrial growth in West Virginia. But industrial growth is not the same thing as industrialization. Iron and glass are manufactured products. So are the products of agriculture and forestry, such as whiskey, lumber, flour and meal. But these products had been made in European and American societies for centuries. The methods for making them had been perfected hundreds of years before. There was nothing in this kind of industrial growth that could cause the sweeping social changes brought by industrialization.

West Virginia Collection, WVU Library

The establishment of iron and glass plants, in a sense, represents the beginning of industrial growth in West Virginia. This iron furnace operated near Morgantown (Monongalia County).

7.3 The Bases of
Industrialization

Industrialization in West Virginia began with the everyday manufacturing and processing operations we've just described. But industrialization went beyond this and created new products. These products were being manufactured in great variety, in substantial quantities, and in radically new ways. More specifically, industrialization involved three interrelated kinds of changes.

First, there was **technological change**, a process with three components: (1) *Mechanization*, which means increasing the power and efficiency of machines to do work formerly done with the muscle power of human beings or animals; (2) *invention*, which means creating new machines or applying them to create new products; and (3) *innovation*, which means using existing machines, processes or products in a new and more efficient way.

Secondly, there was a great increase in the **amount of energy** that was available to do work. This was partly because of improvements in the efficiency of machines that used traditional energy sources, like falling water and burning wood. But of much greater importance for West Virginia was the harnessing of new energy sources, especially the energy found in the "fossil" fuels: petroleum, natural gas and coal. The discovery and exploitation of these new energy sources was the greatest single factor in stimulating West Virginia's economic growth during the Industrial Period.

Finally, there were changes involving **work relations**. The new sources of energy and new technology changed the nature of work itself. Workers were required to perform in entirely different ways - and for different reasons - than they ever had before. These new work requirements involved both social and cultural change. They also involved a great deal of social conflict, since workers resisted the changes which industrialization brought into their lives. The use of new energy sources gave West Virginians the greatest economic opportunities they had ever known. But, at the same time, the accompanying changes in work relations were among the greatest difficulties the state had ever faced.

To a considerable degree, West Virginia's industrialization was dependent upon developments in other places. The beginning of mechanized transportation provides a good example. In 1787, James Rumsey, a Maryland native then living in Shepherdstown, successfully demonstrated the value of steam engines in propelling a boat upstream on a river. Unfortunately, Rumsey was not successful in getting the financial backing he needed to make his mechanical boat a practical success. Thus, the steamboat did not come into general use until inventor Robert Fulton got backing from New York investors in 1809.

The first steamboat on the Ohio River was built to Fulton's plans in Pittsburgh in 1811. In 1816, Henry M. Shreve and two other Wheeling residents built the *Washington*, whose size and speed demonstrated the economic value of steamboats on inland rivers. But Wheeling remained only a minor center of steamboat construction. Most of the steamboats traveling up and down the Ohio were built in cities like Louisville, Cincinnati or Pittsburgh. By 1900, river traffic began to shift from steamboats to more powerful barges and towboats. Charleston became a center for the construction of these vessels and their engines.

A similar thing happened with the railroad, the nineteenth century's second major invention in mechanized transportation. Many West Virginians recognized the advantages of rail transportation for conquering their steep hills and shallow swift-flowing rivers. But, while railroads were more practical than steamboats for reaching most parts of the state, building railroads wasn't that much easier. The Virginia government's reluctance to support railroad projects (for the reasons discussed in Section 5.2) was an important cause of tension between Eastern and Western Virginia before 1861. It was a costly and complicated business to lay railroad lines in such challenging territory.

West Virginians lacked the money and experience to undertake such projects themselves. Once again, they depended on outsiders for help. In 1834, the Maryland-based Baltimore & Ohio Railroad extended from Baltimore to Harpers Ferry. In 1842, the B&O reached Cumberland, Maryland, the commercial outlet for the South Branch Valley. But it didn't reach Wheeling until 1853 or Parkersburg until 1857. Another planned railroad, linking the Kanawha Valley and Eastern Virginia, made even slower progress. This rail line wasn't finished until 1873, when it opened between Richmond and the new city of Huntington. The new system was called the Chesapeake and Ohio Railroad, or C&O.

The invention of the telegraph followed shortly after the steamboat and railroad. It spread rapidly, first as part of the railroad system. Telegraph wires were strung outside of the railroad districts in West Virginia by the Union armies during the Civil War. Telegraph service made possible a great expansion in the speed with which information traveled between places and this, in turn, helped improve the exchange of resources and products. Postal service also became more rapid and widespread with the advent of railroads.

Combined with the mechanization of printing, the communication services of the early Industrial Period made possible the spread of daily newspapers. There had been no daily newspapers in West Virginia before 1850. In fact, Wheeling was the only town with a daily paper until 1880. (The year before, Wheeling became the first West Virginia town to adopt the telephone, which had been invented in Massachusetts.) By 1900, however, daily newspapers had spread to Charleston, Huntington, Clarksburg, Parkersburg, Morgantown, Fairmont, Martinsburg, Bluefield and Beckley. By 1910, every county in the Mountain State had at least one weekly paper.

7.4 Industrialization and Manufacturing

West Virginia had three important centers of industrial development before 1880: Harpers Ferry, the Kanawha Valley and Wheeling.

Factories at Harpers Ferry made weapons for the United States Army. The oldest factory was called the Harpers Ferry Arsenal. This aresenal was owned by the U.S. government. It was established in 1799 at the insistence of ex-President George Washington, whose family owned property in Jefferson County.

The Harpers Ferry Arsenal was organized like a factory. But it made most of its weapons in a traditional handicrafts manner. That is, each Harpers Ferry musket or rifle was essentially the product of craftsmen working with hand tools. Each part of the rifle was unique, and so was the entire weapon. Thus, no single weapon was exactly like any other. This is one reason why Harpers Ferry's weapons are prized so highly by gun collectors today.

However, the traditional method of making guns did not represent the standard of efficiency that military leaders wished to attain. They wanted all parts of a particular type of weapon to be fully interchangeable. That is, parts from one gun could be used to repair another gun. A supply of spare parts would insure that all weapons could be usable all of the time. This would save time and money on gun repairs. Under battlefield conditions, it could also save lives.

This principle could be applied to many other products. In fact, the **principle of interchangeable parts** is used in the manufacture of most industrial products today.

A New England-born inventor named John H. Hall put the principle of interchangeable parts into operation at Harpers

Ferry between 1824 and 1840. Hall had come to the Army's attention by inventing a new kind of rifle. In 1819 the Army decided to adopt Hall's rifle. But it asked him to set up his factory at Harpers Ferry rather than in his home town of Portland, Maine. Apparently military leaders hoped that Hall's new manufacturing methods would rub off on the nearby arsenal. Hall made his own manufacturing operation one of the most fully mechanized in the country.

In order to produce parts so nearly identical that they could be used interchangeably, Hall had to make all of the parts with machines. He designed and built most of the machines he needed himself. He also designed a system of precision gauges which measured each part against a predetermined standard. In this way production was **standardized**. This meant that the manufacturing process no longer had to depend upon the skill and judgment of individual craftsmen. Hall's rifles were produced entirely by machines - lock, stock and barrel. Eventually the method of manufacturing standardized interchangeable parts by a mechanized process became known as "the American system." Harpers Ferry was one of this system's birthplaces.

West Virginia Collection, WVU Library

John Hall's rifle works at Harpers Ferry, Jefferson County, relied on new technology and a traditional source of energy, water power. The rifle works were destroyed during the Civil War, when this photo was taken.

Hall's Rifle Works at Harpers Ferry used a new technology. But it relied upon a traditional source of energy - water power. Water wheels harnessed the rapids of the Shenandoah River to a system of gears and pulleys which made Hall's new machines work. The salt industry of the Kanawha Valley was just the opposite. It was an industry that used new sources of energy to power old forms of technology. To bring heat to the old-fashioned process of boiling salt-water or "brine" to make salt, the Kanawha

A United States Model 1841 percussion rifle, made at the Harpers Ferry Armory using the "American System" of manufacturing.

Huntington Museums

saltmakers turned to coal and natural gas. To drill deep into the earth to find brine that would yield a higher volume of salt, they perfected many of the drilling tools and techniques which were later used to obtain oil and gas from deep in the earth. New technology and new energy sources came together in West Virginia's third center of pioneer industrialization. This was Wheeling, where two Pittsburgh men, Peter Schoenberger and David Agnew, established the Wheeling Iron Works in 1832. Unlike Harpers Ferry, Wheeling had no significant source of water power. And it had no iron ore or other raw materials, as did the iron furnaces located near the Cheat River east of Morgantown. But it had excellent transportation for its day, thanks to the Ohio River and a federally-financed highway - the National Road - which linked Wheeling to Cumberland, Maryland, and the commercial cities east of the Appalachian Mountains. Wheeling had one other resource: abundant supplies of coal.

Schoenberger and Agnew's innovation was to apply Wheeling's energy sources to machinery and processes that were already being used to make a variety of iron products, especially nails. They did this by using steam engines fueled by coal. Water power had been used in the process, but steam drove the machinery in much the same way - and it was more efficient and reliable.

Other Wheeling manufacturers quickly adopted coal-fueled steam engines to other purposes. By 1834, Wheeling had steam-driven flour mills, sawmills and distilleries - as well as iron factories. All together, these operations consumed more than one million bushels of coal. In 1840, Pittsburgh was generating more steam power than any other American city. Wheeling was second. This changed as rail transportation distributed coal more widely and cheaply. But Wheeling's future as an industrial center was secure.

Harpers Ferry and the Kanawha salt-making district didn't survive as industrial centers for very long after the Civil War. Neither did the iron-producing region near Morgantown. But the Wheeling area continued to develop. During the 1850s, the city became the leading American manufacturing center for flint glass, or lead crystal, which was used in making glass bottles and tableware. Wheeling also became known as the Nail City and adopted all the latest inventions and innovations in the manufacture of iron products. In 1859, Wheeling manufacturers began to make raw iron (or pig iron) themselves rather than import it from backwoods iron furnaces. In 1884, they adopted the Bessemer process for turning molten iron into steel. In 1887, a Wheeling manufacturer invented a technique for producing welded steel pipe. Such pipe came to be of great importance in the production and distribution of oil and natural gas.

During the 1890s, Wheeling became a major center for the manufacture of sheet metal. The city's steelmakers adopted the practice of corrugating steel sheets, or wrinkling them to increase their strength. They also galvanized the steel, which means they coated it with zinc to prevent rust. These innovations became the basis for a new array of standardized roofing materials. Sheet steel could also be stamped

WV State Archives

The Belmont Nail Works in Wheeling.

into floral and geometric designs to form pre-fabricated ceilings for buildings. Such products were among the first standardized building products available in the United States. Other sheet-metal specialties included garbage cans, tin cans for food containers and sheet steel for automobile bodies. [See photo on page 142.] Wheeling and other communities along the Ohio River produced all of these products.

In 1900, Wheeling and its suburbs contained about one-third of West Virginia's manufacturing facilities. Another 25 percent was found in other Ohio River communities, such as Newell, Wellsburg, Moundsville, Parkersburg, Point Pleasant and Huntington. Emerging twentieth-century industries also caused new industrial towns, such as Weirton and Follansbee, to be built along the river.

There were reasons why manufacturing clustered along the Ohio River. One reason was the cheap and easy transportation that the river made available. Another was the abundant water. As manufacturing grew more mechanized and complicated, industrial processes generated more heat. Water was needed for cooling. Another reason was the wide, level bottom land along the river.

Like nineteenth-century agriculture, twentieth-century industry flourished on flat land. This was partly due to changes in energy sources. Natural gas and electricity could be carried to individual machines through pipes or wires. Unlike water wheels and wind mills, these new sources of heat and power could easily be transported wherever they were needed. Thus, the designs of factory buildings began to spread outward. They became low and wide, rather than tall and narrow. Such buildings outgrew all but the largest valleys of West Virginia. During the 1920s and '30s, the state acquired a major new manufacturing industry, the chemicals industry, which spread out along the major rivers, especially the Kanawha.

Away from the major rivers, West Virginia manufacturing stayed relatively small-scale and usually was tied to agriculture, forestry, or mining. Much of this manufacturing was simply processing - like saw- and grain-milling. But technological change affected these older, simpler industries too. Sawmills, for example, greatly increased their output using steam power and improved machinery. Between 1870 and 1920, West Virginia's lumber production soared - while its virgin forest practically disappeared.

The abundance of wood led to the manufacture of simple wood products, such as chairs in Charleston, clothespins in Richwood and tool handles in Charleston and Buckhannon. It also led to a small amount of paper manufacturing. These products were cheap and uncomplicated compared with the rifles made in Harpers Ferry or the steel in Wheeling. But they were all made with the same idea in mind: new technology being used to produce standardized products. Thus, even West Virginia's smaller operations were part of the trend toward standardization. The habits and values of industrialization had spread to virtually every corner of the state.

7.5 Industrialization and Agriculture

West Virginia agriculture was also transformed by technological change. The state's hilly terrain was not as well-suited as the Midwestern states for large-scale agricultural production. With the introduction of mechanized farm equipment, however, much larger fields began to be cultivated. Also, improved transportation - especially the railroad and gasoline-powered truck - greatly increased farmers' access to markets. This, in turn, enabled farmers to specialize in cash crops. For example, the construction of a railroad in the South Branch Valley in 1910 transformed that area into a fruit-growing region. The new railroad gave farmers the chance to ship their fruit crops and other products to markets in the big Eastern cities, rather than just turn it into brandy as farmers had done in the past. Later, long-distance trucking helped the Christmas-tree industry in the same area.

Another effect of industrialization upon agriculture was to increase the size of local markets for farm products. Farmers could grow food to sell in nearby industrial communities as well as in distant markets. For example, industrialization in the Kanawha Valley raised the commercial benefits of producing milk, butter, poultry and eggs. Farmers in the Greenbrier Valley could ship these perishable products swiftly westward over the C&O.

But industrialization also had negative effects on agriculture. For one thing, it led to a declining farm population. Industrial cities and mining communities offered ambitious young people easier ways to earn money and more enjoyable ways to spend it. Thus, after 1900, West Virginia's farm population steadily declined. Still, West Virginians did not easily abandon their ties with the land. Part-time farming or gardening remained a common occupation among all kinds of workers, as is still the case today.

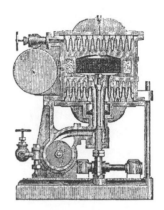

Refrigeration
Machine-1875

Another negative effect of industrialization was the drop in food prices. Food prices in the late nineteenth century declined faster than those of any other product. This decline was good for consumers, but it meant that commercial farmers made less money on what they sold.

Farmers also paid more than their share of taxes. This was because state and local tax policies still reflected the older emphasis on taxing *real* property, that is, land. Factories, machinery and industrial products were considered to be *personal* property. (This also included "intangible" or "unseen" property, such as bank deposits and stock held by industrial companies.) Traditionally, personal property was not taxed as heavily as real property. This made many farmers angry. Beginning in 1882, farmers and their allies joined in political protest movements aimed at tax reform.

The greatest impact of industrialization in West Virginia came about through energy production. Coal mining in West Virginia developed slowly before 1880. The basic reason for this was poor transportation. Until the transportation problem was solved, coal production grew significantly only in those areas that were close to large rivers, such as the Kanawha Valley and the Northern Panhandle. These districts also had local industries that used coal.

The opening of the state's vast coal resources depended

7.6 Industrialization and Energy

upon the building of a two-part rail network. One part of the network consisted of the "trunk lines," the main rail lines connecting the coal areas to big cities (and thus, to big coal markets) in the East and Midwest. The other part consisted of feeder lines, which branched out from the trunk-lines to West Virginia's narrow and rugged valleys, where the most easily-mined coal was found.

The Baltimore & Ohio (1834-57) and the Chesapeake and Ohio (1867-73) were the first two trunk-lines in the state. But neither of these railways did much to encourage feeder lines to be built, so the feeders advanced more slowly - in brief spurts of construction. Meanwhile, new trunk lines were laid across southern West Virginia, tapping the state's richest deposits of coal.

Primary among these was the Norfolk and Western (N&W) Railway, built between 1884 and 1890. The N&W ran through Bluefield, Welch, Williamson and Huntington, linking them with several states in the Midwest. Running east, the N&W went as far as Norfolk, Virginia. Another railroad, the Kanawha and Michigan Railroad (K&M), connected the Kanawha Valley with Detroit in 1886. The Virginian Railway, completed in 1910, went south to Princeton from the K&M terminus on the Kanawha. Then it ran east to the seaports of the Chesapeake Bay.

Gradually, the feeder network expanded across the state from the trunk-lines. As it did so, each feeder line created a fairly well-defined coal-mining "field." Thus, the Elk Garden or Elkins field developed along a feeder road which gradually extended southward from Piedmont on the B&O (1881) to the new town of Elkins (1889) to a C&O feeder in the upper Greenbrier Valley (1901). The Fairmont coal field expanded along the Monongahela River Railroad south to Clarksburg and north to Morgantown. In southern West Virginia the Kanawha and New River fields spread out along the C&O and its feeders. So did the Tug Fork and Mingo coal fields along the N&W and the Winding Gulf field on the Virginian Railway.

The completion of the Ohio River Railroad from Wheeling to Point Pleasant (1884) and to Huntington (1888) gave West Virginia its first north-south railroad. The Coal & Coke Railroad, completed in 1906, crossed the center of the state from Elkins to Charleston. A C&O feeder in the Guyandot Valley was the last major coal-carrying railroad developed in the state. It ran from Huntington to Logan and was completed in 1914. The mining operations along this route were known as the Logan coal field.

The map on page 129 illustrates the railroad network as

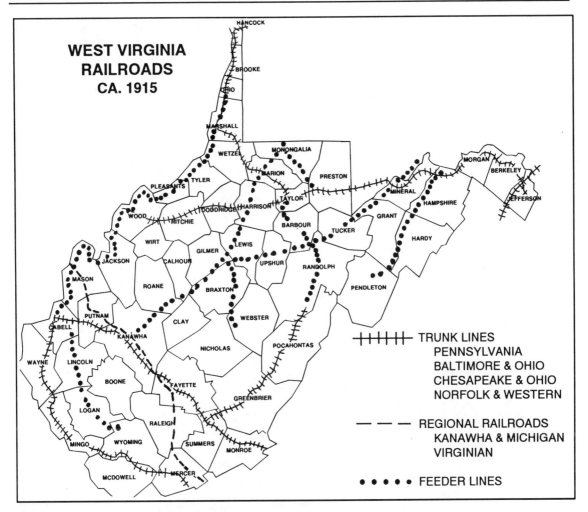

WEST VIRGINIA
RAILROADS
CA. 1915

┼┼┼┼┼ TRUNK LINES
PENNSYLVANIA
BALTIMORE & OHIO
CHESAPEAKE & OHIO
NORFOLK & WESTERN

— — — REGIONAL RAILROADS
KANAWHA & MICHIGAN
VIRGINIAN

• • • • • FEEDER LINES

it existed in West Virginia around 1915.

Oil production in West Virginia began in 1860 at Burning Springs, in Wirt County. Although it was disrupted by the Civil War, oil production expanded immediately after the war was over. It leveled off at about 300,000 barrels a year during the 1870s and '80s.

The big leap in oil production came with the opening of the Mannington (1889) and Sistersville (1892) oil fields, in the northern part of the state. During the next decade, oil discoveries occurred in a wide arc of locations, stretching between Morgantown and Charleston and west to the Ohio River. Production increased to more than 16 million barrels by 1900. Then, it leveled off again and declined.

Natural gas was usually found in or near the oil fields. Gas production, beginning in 1890, expanded from a small amount to more than 300 million cubic feet in 1917, the peak year.

During the first half of the twentieth century, West Virginia was one of the leading energy-producing states in the nation. It was the country's number-one natural gas producer between 1906 and 1924, and it became the leading coal producer in 1927. Oil production declined somewhat after 1917, but the state still remained one of the largest producers of oil for some time.

There was also the promise of renewed use of water power in the Mountain State. The invention of the dynamo generator made it possible to generate electricity by the force of falling water. This **hydroelectric** energy could be transmitted by wires, just like other forms of electricity. The invention of steam turbines also made it possible to generate electricity from coal-fired steam boilers. With an abundance of so many different energy sources, West Virginia's industrial future seemed assured.

Much of West Virginia's coal was marketed outside the state. These men hauled coal around 1900.

Industrialism and the accompanying rise in energy production didn't benefit everyone in West Virginia, however. For many state residents, the years after 1900 were full of economic disappointment. One reason for this was the failure of the state's wealth of new energy sources to attract more manufacturing industries. Manufacturing was always an economic boon to a region. It usually generated higher wages, profits and taxes than other types of industry. But relatively few factories were drawn by West Virginia's wealth of industrial fuels. Instead, producers sold the bulk of the state's coal, oil and gas to industries elsewhere. During the early twentieth century, as much as 90 percent of the coal and natural gas produced in West Virginia, for example, was marketed outside of the state. More often than not, the Mountain State's fuels were shipped by pipeline, railroad, by wire and barge to factories in Ohio, Pennsylvania and other states. This export of energy meant that West Virginia lost many of the social benefits associated with manufacturing.

Another result of the state's energy-resource drain was that some business and political leaders joined with farmers in demanding the reform of West Virginia's tax structure. They wished to shift a larger share of tax burdens from farmers and small property owners to railroads, pipelines and energy producers. The Legislature of 1901 created a special tax commission to deal with this problem.

In 1903, the Tax Commission recommended a system of **severance** taxes on coal, oil and natural gas. These taxes would have been applied to the fuels when they were extracted or "severed" from the earth. The idea was that this would keep more of the value of these resources in West Virginia, even though the bulk of the energy products would still be shipped to other states.

Of course, the energy industries did not like the idea of severance taxes. They managed to persuade enough legislators to defeat them in 1903, and again in 1905. The same thing happened when reformers proposed severance taxes in 1909, 1915, 1931, 1933 and 1953. In fact, the state didn't enact any severance taxes on its energy resources until 1971.

This wasn't the only tax on energy producers, however. In 1922, the state Legislature enacted a special tax on the sales of business and industrial products. This was called a **business and occupation** tax. This tax was higher for coal and natural gas producers than it was for manufacturing industries. Thus, to some extent, the business and occupation tax made up for the export of energy resources from West Virginia to other states.

Another goal of reformers was to limit property taxes for small land owners. This was accomplished by a constitutional amendment, adopted in 1932. The **Tax Limitation Amendment** set ceilings on the amount of money that local governments could raise by property taxes. The Tax Limitation Amendment also transferred certain services and duties that once had been carried out by local governments to the state government. An earlier reform had ended the state's role in collecting property taxes altogether. Thus, with all its new burdens, the state had to find new sources of public revenue. One source was a sales tax on all purchases made in West Virginia. The state's first sales tax was adopted in 1933.

Perhaps the greatest disappointments caused by industrialization in West Virginia were in the area of labor relations. Work-relations problems usually involved two related types of

7.7 Industrialization and Labor

conflict. One type grew out of workers' attempts to win higher wages - or to prevent their employers from lowering wages. The other type of conflict grew out of workers' resistance to the kinds of discipline and the hazards that industrial work involved. Like many other changes associated with industrialization, these conflicts began far back in the Statehood Period. They continue to be problems in our society today.

Agricultural labor was as physically demanding as almost any industrial job. Spring planting and the fall harvest made for long days full of hard work. But the work was more varied than industrial labor. Agricultural tasks changed with the seasons, and there were slack periods. There was time to go fishing in the hot days of mid-summer while the crops matured. After the harvest, crisp autumn days were perfect for hunting and butchering meat. Mid-winter was a time to work indoors, mending and fixing equipment and tools. This was also the time when some farmers became part-time lumbermen. They felled trees and used teams of horses to drag the logs to large streams. With the early spring floods, the logs could be floated downstream and sold in river towns.

Timbering

Rural life was no picnic. It had its own kind of routine and drudgery. The isolation of farm life in the mountains often led to boredom, and cash didn't come easily to families on subsistence farms. Industrialization, meanwhile, had created a growing number of consumer goods - everything from bicycles and cameras to pianos and fishing reels. Many poorer people of backwoods West Virginia were cut off from this new wealth of goods. Most of them could get by on what they grew or made for themselves - but that didn't mean they wanted to.

Thus, there were plenty of people who were ready for change. They were eager for new kinds of work and the cash incomes that factory jobs offered. This was especially true as the nineteenth century drew to a close, and it was especially true of young people. There were many workers for whom any change was likely to be an improvement. African-Americans - many of them former slaves - still worked hard on Southern farms they didn't own, even after the Civil War. Other workers immigrated to West Virginia from Ireland and other countries in Europe. These immigrants often came from rural areas where landless peasants lived near starvation. For all of these people, industrial labor in the United States offered the promise of a better life.

No matter what a person's reason for taking an industrial job, it still posed problems of adjustment. Like farming, industrial work had its seasonal patterns. But these were different from agricultural seasons. Times were "good" whenever there was "plenty of work." During these times, employers wanted workers on the job all day long, every day, month after month. A working day's length could run as high as sixteen hours. For steel workers who drew the "swing shift" every other week, it might be twenty-four. On the other hand, industrial workers might face long months when there was little or no work at all.

Industrialization also increased the speed and regularity of work. The new American system of manufacturing required that employees work as steadily and reliably as their machines. Standardized parts, in other words, meant standardized production; and standardized production required standardized behavior. Very often, the worker who operated a factory machine had to perform the same task over and over again, hour by hour, day by day. This is such common behavior today that it may be difficult to understand how new it was to someone living in the nineteenth century. But people are not born knowing how to obey red and green lights, to pull start- and stop-levers, or even how to work by the clock. They have to be taught. They have to be persuaded or forced to do tasks in a regular, predictable manner without being told what to do each time. This kind of behavior is called **industrial discipline**.

People who had been brought up on farms had trouble getting used to the demands of industrial workplaces. They frequently violated their employers' rules, if they could do so without losing their jobs. In cities like Wheeling, they often could not get away with it. In these industrial centers, there were usually plenty of other people around who could take a worker's job. In more isolated locations - such as Harpers Ferry, or the coal-mining "camps" of southern West Virginia - employers had more trouble finding workers to fill the vacant posts.

Before 1865, the owners of the Kanawha salt works solved the labor-shortage problem by using slaves. Some of the enslaved salt workers were the property of the salt makers. But many of them were hired or leased from owners in Eastern Virginia. In any case, slaves did much of the dreary and dangerous work of making salt. This solution was no longer possible after the Civil War, of course, when slavery was abolished.

Free workers in out-of-the-way locations could usually get

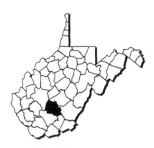

National Park Service Photo

For young men from rural areas, a job in the mines may have held the promise of a better way of life; but people who had been brought up on farms often had trouble getting used to the demands of industrial workplaces. This Fayette County miner was photographed in 1907.

away with bending their employers' work schedules - at least when business was good and workers were in high demand. Factory managers at Harpers Ferry, for example, had to deal continuously with workers who slipped away during planting or harvest time to work on their own family farms. Similarly, factory officials had to deal with absenteeism in July and August, when workers left to avoid the heat and diseases of mid-summer.

Coal mine operators had to deal with similar problems. Native miners frequently disappeared for short periods to work on their family farms, or to go hunting and fishing. European immigrants also insisted on observing their traditional holidays. Carousers of all races and ethnic groups frequently took Monday off to recover from their weekend activities.

In order to attract and hold workers in isolated locations, employers had to tolerate such behavior. They also had to build houses for the workers to live in and stores where they could buy their supplies. These facilities appeared first at Harpers Ferry and the Kanawha salt district. Later, they spread to most of the coal camps in West Virginia and to some of the lumber camps as well.

Originally, the purpose of such facilities was to attract a reliable labor force. But when "times were bad," things were different. These were the times when there wasn't enough work to go around and, during these periods, pools of extra workers were created. Then, the company houses and stores became weapons which employers could use to enforce industrial discipline.

7.8 Industrialization and Wage Strikes

In most industries during the Industrial Period, there were routine swings between good and bad times. In the coal industry, for example, the spring brought "slack time." This was the season when demand for heating coal was low. Coal buyers didn't begin to store coal for the winter until late summer and fall. If a coal operator often had trouble finding workers, he might just keep his workers employed through the slack periods. But generally, operators preferred to fire their extra workers when business was poor and then rehire them later, when it improved. Here, then, was a situation that was entirely different from the seasonal slack times associated with agricultural labor. This was the modern problem of **unemployment**.

Most West Virginia industrial workers, especially coal miners, routinely faced a few weeks' unemployment during the

Industrial Period. But these weeks could lengthen into months and, during an economic depression, even years. Entire mines could close down. All the jobs in a community could disappear. This happened in the Kanawha salt industry during the 1870s. The industry had declined in the 1850s, and then was hit hard by the Civil War. An economic depression from 1873 to 1879 finished it off. Former African-American slaves, who provided the largest part of the industry's labor, were forced to move to other jobs in other places. Many of these workers moved east, to the newly-opened mines of Fayette and Raleigh counties.

Library of Congress

Some workers were able to hold onto their jobs during depressions. Employers sometimes hesitated to fire skilled workers, who would be hard to replace when business got better. To trim their payrolls, employers cut wages instead. This frequently led to strikes. The workers banded together and refused to work, hoping to force employers to restore their old level of wages. During the 1870s, for example, wage strikes took place at the salt works and coal mines of the Kanawha Valley. Another strike began in the summer of 1877, after a series of wage cuts by the B&O Railroad. Forty employees in Baltimore walked off their jobs and immediately were joined by 1,200 train workers down the line in Martinsburg. The strike quickly spread to Wheeling, Pittsburgh and Chicago. Within a month, it had spread to nearly every other railroad center in the nation. The B&O strike became one of the most famous strikes in American history.

To attract workers to West Virginia, coal companies often built housing and public facilities -- at times constructing entire "company towns." Pictured here is company housing at Hemphill, McDowell County.

A similar wave of strikes took place in 1894 - another time of economic depression. This wave began in the southern West Virginia coal fields and swept northward. Besides coal miners in several parts of West Virginia, the strike involved iron, glass and pottery workers in the Northern Panhandle, and streetcar conductors in Wheeling. This strike was not successful. Few strikes that were caused by depression-time wage cuts were.

7.9 Other Strikes:
Men Against
Machines

But there were other kinds of strikes. Industrial craftsmen frequently struck when their jobs or working conditions were threatened by the introduction of new machines. An example was the "clock strike" at the Harpers Ferry Arsenal in 1842. Until this date, the operation of the government-owned factory there contrasted sharply with the mechanized production of Hall's Rifle Works. Hall was proud of the fact that his machines did not require skilled labor. He relied heavily on teen-aged boys to operate the machines "with a few men to supervise and keep the tools in good order." Little training or experience was needed for these jobs. However, regularity, punctuality and reliability were essential. To work properly, mechanized production had to be run by the clock.

Despite repeated efforts by military authorities to change things, the government armory continued to be dominated by skilled craftsmen. The workers controlled the pace and length of working days. Older skilled craftsmen worked shorter hours than young inexperienced hands. The pace of work was irregular. Workers took time off for personal errands, card games, fights and drinking. Absences and tardiness were common. Workers resisted attempts to change this. In 1830, a superintendent who tried to impose stricter rules was murdered by one of the workers he fired. Because he challenged this leisurely and traditional approach to work in his own factory, John Hall was disliked and shunned by both the leaders and the people of the town.

In 1841, however, the Army took over direct management of the armory. The officer in charge promptly banned drinking on the job and other irregular practices. He also installed a clock and required each worker to put in a ten-hour day. This led to the strike of 1842, when the craftsmen tried to regain control of their working procedures. They were unsuccessful. During the next fifteen years, the armory was fully mechanized. Skilled craftsmen steadily lost ground to unskilled machine "operatives."

Then, in October 1859, John Brown and his small band of abolitionists invaded Harpers Ferry and seized control of the arsenal for thirty-six hours. This action attracted nationwide attention and was one of the incidents that brought on the Civil War. The furious hatred which Brown's action aroused among Harpers Ferry's citizens was partly due to worker resentment against the innovations and inventions of other "Yankees" such as John Hall. **John Brown's Raid severely damaged the arsenal.**

It was finished off by military destruction during the Civil War. Floods on the Shenandoah River swept away Hall's Rifle Works soon afterward.

A similar strike came about as a result of technological changes in the iron industry. The adoption of the Bessemer process of steel making brought an end to the role of iron "puddlers," who had previously been very important to iron making. Puddlers were skilled workers. So were the "nailers," who had been important in making iron nails. The new availability of cheap mass-produced steel threatened both the puddlers' and the nailers' jobs.

On June 1, 1885, the puddlers, nailers and other skilled iron workers of Wheeling went on strike. The strike lasted for nearly a year. Like the Harpers Ferry strike, the Wheeling strike was unsuccessful. Some of the nailers got back their old jobs. The rest of the strikers lost their jobs permanently to machines. A similar strike lasting from 1892 to 1896 nearly wrecked Wheeling's glass industry.

Flint glass blowers were skilled workmen whose skills gave them control of the glass-making process. Glass factory owners wished to end this control and to raise the output of glass workers. A four-year struggle between 1892 and 1896 ended in a victory for employers. But the victory was a hollow one, for this strike spelled the end of Wheeling's leadership in the glass tableware and container industries.

Ironically, one of the glass workers who was forced to leave Wheeling during these years turned out to be the industry's greatest inventor. This was Michael T. Owens. He was unable to find work in Wheeling because of his labor union-organizing activities. So he moved to Toledo, Ohio. There he found financial backing for a series of inventions which made it possible to make bottle and building glass by machine. The corporations that Owens founded later opened branch plants in West Virginia; but the headquarters of his company (along with most of the profits) remained in Ohio.

Perhaps the greatest confrontation between workers and machines in West Virginia history, however, was not a strike but a contest. This was the legendary contest in 1870 or 1871 between John Henry and the steam drill at the Big Bend Tunnel on the C&O Railway. It is hard to be sure of the exact basis of truth for this legend. But there probably was a strong tunnel- construction worker named John Henry. And he probably did

Iron Works

National Park Service Photo

The Big Bend Tunnel, in Summers County, where the legend of steel-driver John Henry was born.

engage in a contest with a steam-powered drill. The idea was to see which could drill holes in hard rock most effectively, the man or the machine. According to the legend, John Henry won the contest but died soon afterward, supposedly from his exertions during the race.

John Henry was an African-American, but his story has come to stand for the pride that all workers feel in doing work with their own hands. The story also stands for the mixed emotions that most workers felt about machines during the Industrial Period. Through folk music, John Henry's story spread across West Virginia, to the nation and even the world.

It has to be pointed out, however, that a railroad worker like John Henry wasn't likely to die from the effects of a race with the new technology. Workers in the Big Bend Tunnel were more likely

West Virginia State Archives

The streets of Monongah following a mine explosion near there in 1907. The hearse is taking caskets to the mine, where 361 miners were killed.

to have been killed by falling rocks. Industrialization brought with it a great increase in safety hazards for workers. "Roof falls" were a common cause of death and injury among tunnel-construction workers and among coal miners. So were various lung diseases, caused by breathing rock dust or coal dust. As many as 700 workers may have been killed, for example, by breathing silica dust while digging the Hawks Nest Tunnel in Fayette County during the 1930s. The tunnel disaster is considered the worst industrial accident in American history. Coal mine explosions were another serious hazard. The greatest coal mine disaster in American history took place at Monongah, in Marion County, on December 6, 1907. Some 361 miners lost their lives in this explosion.

West Virginia State Archives

Spectacular industrial accidents killed dozens or even hundreds of workers and made the newspaper headlines. But, actually, the greatest cause of death and injury were the more ordinary events, involving only one or two victims. Disabled workers were a common sight in the Kanawha salt region during the 1870s. In any railroad town, one never had to go far to find someone who'd lost an arm or leg in a train accident. Particularly dreadful accidents took place in the iron and steel mills, with their huge machines, furnaces and giant vats filled with molten metal. Crippled or diseased workers gathered around most of the mines and factories in the state. They sold food or newspapers, offered to perform simple tasks, or simply begged - anything to earn a living when they were no longer able to work.

Industrial work was often dangerous work. The Hawks Nest Tunnel in Fayette County was dug as a 40-foot-wide "water pipe" for an electric-power station. Hundreds of workers died from silica dust they breathed during the tunnel's construction.

Thus, industrialization had two sides: a good and a bad one. It carried new opportunities and new problems. It brought new ways to earn money and new products to spend it on. But it also changed people's lives and threatened their livelihood - specifically, with unemployment and industrial accidents.

All the changes brought by industrialization were often beyond the control of individuals, families, or communities. Industrial societies, then, required new forms of social organization. These new forms are called **bureaucracies** and they are the subject of Part IV of this book.

Study Questions - Chapter 7

1. Practice applying what you have learned in this chapter by naming some products with interchangeable parts that we use quite often. What are the interchangeable parts found:

        a) in a flashlight.
        b) in your ball-point pen.
        c) in your TV set.
        d) in a power mower.
        e) in your shoes.
        f) in a razor.
        g) in your car or truck.
        h) in a camera.

2. Some resources in our state were becoming scarce in certain areas more than 150 years ago. Find evidence in the text to prove this.

3. Often, changes brought about by technology in one industry lead to even more discoveries and new industries. Describe the changes resulting from the following:
        a) development of salt-drilling machinery.
        b) scarcity of wood supplies for salt furnaces.
        c) a search for new sources of power for nail-making machines.
        d) development of the Bessemer process.
        e) a need for a non-rusting (or rust-resistant) metal.

4. What advantages did river transportation have over railroad transportation? What advantages did the railroad have over river transportation?

5. Processing farm and forest products required energy. How many energy sources can you name that were available to Frontier and Statehood Period industrial workers in West Virginia?

Chapter 8:
The Economic System

Industrialization is basically a change in a society's **economic system**. Thus, in order to understand industrialization, it is important to understand exactly what an economic system is. This chapter will examine the basic concepts of an economic system. When you have finished it, you should be able to apply your understanding of these concepts to West Virginia's economic system as it evolved during the Industrial Period.

An economic system is a system for producing and distributing goods and services. *Which* goods and *which* services vary from society to society - and from time to time. So do the methods of production and distribution. But every society has some kind of economic system.

As we have seen, industrialization raised the importance of manufactured goods and lowered the importance of agricultural products. It also raised the importance of energy resources (such as coal and natural gas) and raw materials (such as timber and metallic ore) from which the manufactured goods were made.

Industrialization also increased the number and variety of services that people used. In pre-industrial times, an agricultural society required relatively few services. But the new industrial society needed all kinds of new, expanded services - transportation, communications, banking, education, legal work, management, engineering, law enforcement, medicine, insurance and, above all, government services. The expansion of these services - and of the institutions that provided them - will be discussed in detail in these pages.

Ideas & Issues:
Industialization and The Economic System

Changes in production included mechanization. It also included the new "American system." This meant dividing manufacturing into specific steps and assembling products out of standardized, interchangeable parts. In the twentieth century, this system became known as **mass production**.

Similar changes occurred in the area of distribution. Mass production lowered the cost of products, which meant that more and more people could afford them. It also lowered the cost of shipping products. Mechanized transportation - steamboats,

8.1 Production, Distribution and the Business Cycle

railroads, river barges and trucks - allowed West Virginia manufacturers to ship their merchandise farther from the point of production. It also became easier for merchants to bring products in from other states, other regions, even other countries.

Product distribution was also improved by better communications. Telegraph, telephone and postal service made it easier to exchange information about a product's quality and availability. Also, the growth of newspapers encouraged the growth of advertising. So did the spread of national magazines, which appeared around 1900, and of radio networks, established during the 1920s.

Advertising as we know it today - with brand names, slogans and symbols - began during the 1890s. For the most part, early advertising induced West Virginians to buy products that were made elsewhere. A Maryland distillery, for example, coined the slogan "Mountain water makes the difference." Its "Old Export" brand of whiskey was so widely advertised in West Virginia that some people thought the slogan was the state's motto. By the same token, two Wheeling companies coined slogans and symbols that became famous far beyond the borders of the Mountain State. One was the Wheeling Corrugating Company, which made "Wheeling"-brand buckets, tubs, garbage cans, roofing and fencing materials. The other was the Bloch Tobacco Company, manufacturer of "Mail Pouch" tobacco.

Topper Sherwood

Steel products like these were manufactured in Wheeling and distributed around the country, beginning in the early part of the twentieth century. The object on the far right is a small space heater.

The developing nationwide communications networks became known as **mass communications**. Newspapers, magazines, radio and television networks, all involved with mass communications, are called the *mass media*. In industrial societies, the mass media have become as important to the distribution of goods and services as mass production has in producing them.

Aside from production and distribution, another feature of industrialized economic systems is their capacity for **economic growth**. Economic growth takes place when an economic system produces an increasing volume of goods and services. There can be several causes of such growth. The agricultural economy of the United States grew rapidly in the nineteenth century, for example. Economic growth occurred partly because more and more new land was being brought into production. The economy grew, in other words, by adding more resources. The economy also grew as a result of population growth. Population growth produces economic growth - as long as there are enough new resources to meet the demands of the new people.

Another important stimulus to economic growth is increasing **productivity**. Productivity increases whenever a system (or a firm or an individual) turns out more products (output) without increasing the amount of resources (input) used to make them. The same thing happens when the amount of input declines while the output remains the same. In both cases, the productivity increase represents a saving of resources. Economic growth can result if this saving is then invested into production or distribution.

Economic change in a capitalist economy, such as the U.S. economy, is a very complex phenomenon. This is because the basic economic decisions are made by a large number of people. Such economic questions include: What should we produce? How do we produce it? How do we distribute it? How much do we produce? What do we do with the savings from any increased productivity?

All these decisions are made by private individuals, firms and organizations with little or no interference from government. Because industrial growth was the result of thousands and thousands of private decisions, it took place unevenly in long swings called **business cycles**. When economic growth was rapid, the economy was said to have "expanded." There was an increased volume of production, and plenty of jobs. The most rapid periods of expansion were called economic "booms." Since people were generally better-off during these upswings, they liked to think of booms as normal, instead of seeing them as part of an economic cycle that also included a downswing.

When growth slowed down, the economy "contracted," resulting in unemployment. The worst contractions or "busts" were known as **depressions**, though ordinary people referred to them simply as "hard" or "bad" times. Depressions occurred regularly during the nineteenth century. The one beginning in 1857 struck particularly hard blows at the Kanawha salt industry and the iron manufacturers of the Monongahela Valley.

The 1873-1879 depression was the longest of the nine-

Boom

ECONOMIC EXPANSION

ECONOMIC CONTRACTION

Thousands of Business Decisions

Hard Times

Business cycles during the Industrial Period have been marked by "booms" and "busts." These miners are applying for unemployment benefits in Beckley in 1978.

teenth century. But the depression of 1893-1897 was the "deepest," causing the worst unemployment. Other depressions took place in 1884-1885, 1907, 1913-1914 and 1920-1921. The worst depression of all began in 1929 with the "Great Crash" of the stock market. The **Great Depression** extended until 1941, when the United States began to prepare for World War II. The Depression led to more government regulation of the national economy. Thus, it marks the end of the first, largely unregulated phase of American industrialization.

8.2 Economic Development

What you have read so far was true of the United States economic system in general and of West Virginia's economic system in particular. West Virginia's nineteenth-century leaders were especially eager to play a big role in the national economic scene. They felt that their state's economic development had been held back by the pre-statehood policies of Virginia. Freedom from Virginia would eventually stimulate economic growth, they said. The favorite term for this anticipated growth was **development**. West Virginia's political leaders of the late nineteenth century equated "development" with "progress." They opposed any policy that they thought might hamper the state's development. Still, the problems caused by West Virginia's industrialization would not go away.

Economic development in the Mountain State has never been exactly the same as national development. The Northern Panhandle is an exception. Its growth paralleled that of the nation more closely than any other part of West Virginia. Elsewhere, the state's development differed from overall national development in three important ways:

> **1.)** Commercial agriculture did not contribute to economic growth in West Virginia in the same way that it did in the South and Midwest. This spared West

Virginia from many of the evil effects of slavery and of one-crop agriculture, both of which troubled the South. But the state also failed to reap the accumulated wealth that agriculture produced for the Midwest. The relative weakness of West Virginia's commercial agriculture had long-term effects on its economic growth. Early U.S. farming communities became manufacturing centers for many of the twentieth century's most valuable consumer goods - appliances, automobiles and the like. Thus, the relative weakness of West Virginia's commercial agriculture had long-term effects on its growth.

2.) At the same time, West Virginia's manufacturing industries were not as numerous, as strong, or as diverse as those of the Northeast or Midwest. The exception was the Northern Panhandle's iron, steel and glass industries. So were the chemical industries that began locating in the Kanawha Valley in 1914. There were also a few small glass- and metal-fabricating plants established in the Morgantown-Fairmont-Clarksburg area around 1900. But, otherwise, the state failed to attract its share of the nation's manufacturing growth. In fact, with the exception of chemicals, West Virginia failed to attract any of the industries that grew most rapidly between 1900 and 1990. These included automobiles and other transportation industries; military equipment; consumer goods; entertainment (motion pictures, television and recording); electrical machinery; and electronics.

3.) West Virginia became more dependent than any other Eastern state on **extractive** industries. Extractive industries include agriculture and fisheries; but here, the term refers mainly to coal mining, timbering, and the production of petroleum and natural gas. In other words, an extractive industry is one whose main activity is extracting or harvesting natural resources directly from the earth. The extractive industries were vital to the growth of the American economy. But they did not bring the wealth that West Virginia's leaders had expected. The state's growth kept pace with national growth, but it remained one of the poorer states in the Union. This chart shows how the per capita (or

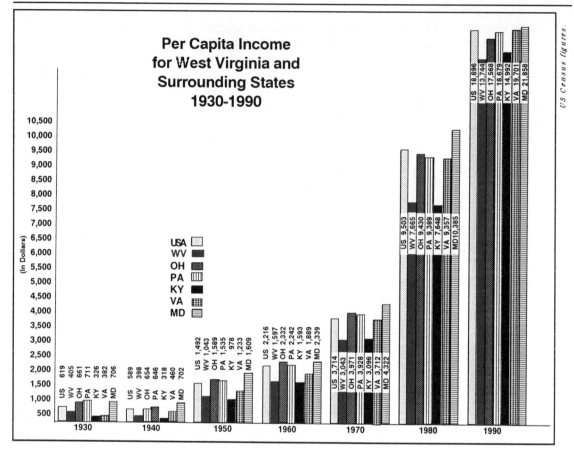

Per Capita Income for West Virginia and Surrounding States 1930-1990

(In Dollars)

10,500
10,000
9,500
9,000
8,500
8,000
7,500
7,000
6,500
6,000
5,500
5,000
4,500
4,000
3,500
3,000
2,500
2,000
1,500
1,000
500

USA
WV
OH
PA
KY
VA
MD

1930
US 619
WV 405
OH 661
PA 711
KY 326
VA 382
MD 706

1940
US 589
WV 398
OH 654
PA 646
KY 318
VA 460
MD 702

1950
US 1,492
WV 1,043
OH 1,589
PA 1,535
KY 978
VA 1,233
MD 1,609

1960
US 2,216
WV 1,597
OH 2,332
PA 2,242
KY 1,593
VA 1,889
MD 2,339

1970
US 3,714
WV 3,043
OH 3,971
PA 3,928
KY 3,096
VA 3,712
MD 4,322

1980
US 9,503
WV 7,665
OH 9,430
PA 9,389
KY 7,648
VA 9,357
MD 10,385

1990
US 18,696
WV 13,744
OH 17,568
PA 18,679
KY 14,992
VA 19,701
MD 21,858

US Census figures.

per person) income of West Virginia from 1930 to 1990 compared with that of neighboring states and the United States as a whole.

The disappointments of West Virginia's economic development - particularly its failure to match the nation's economic growth - have always been puzzling. The state's mineral and timber resources seem to be an obvious guarantee of wealth. The scenery and climate make it a pleasant place to live. It is centrally located in the eastern half of the country. Boosters had recited these facts over and over since the 1860s, and yet the state's economy failed to grow as rapidly or as diversely as they predicted. Why? The answer is important. It's important because the state's disappointment with economic development is linked to so many other problems (labor violence and inadequate government services, for example) that have been associated with industrialization.

The answers to questions about West Virginia's economy require some discussion of the state's industrialization. The issue involves the resources that sustain an economic system. Of course, these resources include fuels and raw materials. But they also include cultural values, and the social, political and economic institutions that determine how a society uses the materials at its command. In this wider sense, there are four types of *economic* resources: **natural resources, human resources, capital** (money) **and management.**

Capital, as a social resource, actually means more than just money. It is a society's investment in the machinery and tools for producing goods. Capital represents the means of production. Any society that wants to develop its resources needs capital. This was West Virginia's problem through much of the Statehood and Industrial periods.

Investment capital can come from several sources. It can come from government. It can come from banks, which gather the accumulated savings of a community. Or, it can be the accumulated profits of older forms of economic activity, such as agriculture or trade. West Virginia failed to gather much capital from any of these sources. Its commercial agriculture was not profitable enough - nor were its commercial cities large enough - to accumulate large pools of investment capital for economic development.

Before 1838, Virginia's economic policies discouraged the establishment of banks in our state. The United States government took over supervision of the nation's banks in 1863. But here, too, federal economic policy did little to encourage development in West Virginia. For most of the Industrial Period, U.S. banking policy encouraged the accumulation of capital in the larger cities of the Northeast, the Midwest and West Coast. These policies made it harder to accumulate capital or borrow money in developing states such as West Virginia.

The state's best chance for accumulating capital, then, was from government. But here, again, there were disappointing results. During the nineteenth century, the federal government owned millions of acres of land in the Midwest, West and in parts of the South. The government was able to grant or sell much of this land for purposes of economic development. But Virginia's public lands had been owned by the *state* government. During the Statehood Period - a time when economic development had scarcely begun - Virginia's land policies had allowed much of West Virginia's land to be absorbed by land speculators.

8.3 Economic Resources: Capital

Virginia did invest some tax money in building turnpikes and other public-transportation improvements. Even this effort produced disappointing results. First, Virginia's investment in West Virginia transportation was never enough to overcome the economic problems posed by the mountainous terrain. And, secondly, these efforts caused the Virginia government to go deeply into debt. After statehood, West Virginia's leaders took this early example as a warning. The writers of both state constitutions included a clause prohibiting the state government from financing economic development in this way.

So, with only limited sources of local capital at their disposal, West Virginia promoters had to look outside their state for the investment capital they needed for economic growth. They often found it. But outside capital usually came with strings attached. People who invest money in distant places, quite naturally, do it with the primary thought of making a profit on their investment. They do not necessarily have a personal stake in communities where they themselves don't live. They do not invest their personal talents in promoting the community's welfare; and they generally do not allow considerations of that welfare to interfere with the profits they seek.

This was largely the case with West Virginia's outside investors. Moreover, the profits from their investments generally flowed out of the state. They added to the capital resources of such places as Baltimore, Philadelphia, New York, Boston, Chicago and Cleveland. That is, the largest share of the profits earned in West Virginia were spent and reinvested elsewhere. Thus, the state's capital shortage continued to be a problem, even after industrialization was well under way.

8.4 Natural Resources

The **natural resources** of a society represent its environmental heritage - its land and the sources of wealth found on it or under it. West Virginia's land, as we have seen in Chapter 4, was badly entangled in a legal mess created by generations of land speculation.

In some parts of the country, notably cities, land speculation led to the rapid accumulation of profits. These profits then were invested in other forms of local economic activity. But the legal problem of land titles prevented this from happening in West Virginia. The land-title problem even caused troubles for West Virginians who owned their land. It was part of the reason why many of them lost control of the timber and mineral wealth of their land.

Complications caused by faulty surveys and conflicting land claims during the Frontier and Statehood periods meant that almost anyone could get a claim to West Virginia land. This was especially true of southern West Virginia, where pioneer land speculators had made the largest claims. Most small property owners had secure titles to their land by 1890. But proving such a title was another story. It was sometimes a costly and lengthy process.

Rather than face such ordeals, many small land owners entered into deals with unscrupulous land lawyers and land dealers. The lawyers or dealers agreed to drop their claim to the surface of the land. But, in return, the land owner had to give away the mineral or timber rights. These rights meant that ownership of the minerals and timber passed from local owners to the land dealers, who usually sold them to non-resident investors. In this way, large land companies came to acquire much of West Virginia's timber and mineral wealth.

There were also a great many West Virginians who sold their mineral and timber rights cheerfully and knowingly for a very small price. One reason was that, at the time when these deals were made, local owners did not know the potential wealth of these rights. The coal, oil, or natural gas lying underground was not worth much to a land owner who lacked the capital to develop these resources. Even trees standing on a hillside meant little to someone who lacked what it took to cut them down and get them to market. State land owners were faced with the choice of selling their minerals and timber to developers for small

> "The first coal mines were put in at Pidgeon Creek, over on the Mingo County side of the mountain. The Chafins owned all the land around there - around Turner and Ragland - but they didn't know what it was worth. The coal speculators came in and those Chafins practically gave that land away. The companies had already started putting up houses for their workers and they talked about building schools. One fellow told the Chafins his company would name a school after them if they sold their land to him. That closed the deal. Yessir, that family must have really thought they were getting something when that company named a school after them...."
>
> — Raymond Chafin,
> Logan County

amounts of cash or getting nothing at all. Many of them, naturally, decided to sell.

As we know today, West Virginia's environment was magnificently endowed with rich minerals and timber. But the *relative* value of these resources was not as great in the Industrial Period as it is now. The century between 1870 and 1970, as discussed previously, was an era of cheap energy. West Virginia's fuels and raw materials were vital to industrialization. But they were not rare. Thirty-six other states produced coal. Even more produced timber. West Virginia's extractive industries had plenty of competition.

West Virginia's central location was another mixed blessing, from an economic point of view. It was easy for the state's energy producers to reach the big industrial markets of the Northeast and Midwest. But Maryland, Pennsylvania, Ohio, Kentucky, Indiana and Illinois were energy-producing states too. These states also had much larger cities and more manufacturing industries than West Virginia did, which made them closer to the richest energy markets.

This competition was especially stiff in the coal industry. The price of coal was based on the costs of mining it and of getting it from mine to market. West Virginia's hilly terrain made it cheaper to open a coal mine during the Industrial Period. This was because coal mining, at that time, depended upon a relatively simple technology. A hillside coal mine could be operated by means of a "drift" or tunnel sloping into the hill. The shafts that had to be built for Midwestern mines were much more costly. But hilly terrain also made coal transportation more expensive in West Virginia. Railroad trunk-lines and feeders were both more costly to build here than in less mountainous states. This meant that the railroads generally charged more to carry freight. Considering the greater distance of West Virginia mines from their markets, the coal here generally cost more to ship than coal from competing states.

Apart from this, West Virginia coal operators were more dependent on the railroad companies than their competitors were. The hilly terrain made it difficult for more than one rail line to be constructed over a particular route. Few mining (or timber or oil-producing) communities had more than one railroad. This meant that the producers had to ship on the railroad companies' terms or not at all. The Norfolk & Western, which was run by a group of Philadelphia capitalists, forced coal operators along its West Virginia line to sell their coal through another Philadelphia

Deep Mine, 1890

Cass Scenic Railroad
Pocahontas County

firm. The C&O also had its own marketing agency. The B&O punished uncooperative or unfriendly coal operators by withholding the railroad cars they needed to ship their coal. Thus, West Virginia's coal producers had little ability to control their markets or their transportation costs. This helps to explain why they fought so bitterly to retain control over their workers and the communities where the miners lived.

Thus, in an era of cheap energy, West Virginia energy products competed at a disadvantage with the products of nearby states.

Human resources represent the human energy and skills which a society puts into its economic system. During the Industrial Period, West Virginia's human resources were drawn from roughly the same groups that provided labor to other parts of the country. For the most part, these were the native descendants of Europeans who came here during the Frontier Period, and a number of African-Americans who migrated from Virginia and North Carolina after the Civil War.

8.5 Human Resources

Immigrants from Ireland and Germany settled in the Northern Panhandle and the Monongahela Valley during the Statehood Period. During the Industrial Period, more Irish settled along the railroads. In varying numbers, other ethnic groups found their way to West Virginia's various industrial districts. These included: Italians, Poles, Hungarians, Russians, Jews, Swiss, Greeks, Czechs, Slovaks, Croats, Serbs, Slovenes, Spaniards and French-speaking Canadians. In this way, West Virginia came to be as well-endowed in its labor force as it was in raw materials and fossil fuels.

In the case of human resources, there was a problem of distribution. For the most part, West Virginia's extractive industries originally developed in the least-populated sections of the state. This meant that the new industries required the creation of new communities. Again, the trend was most pronounced in the coal industry. Coal operators who opened mines in central or southern West Virginia - and in the more isolated parts of the Monongahela Valley - could not attract and hold workers in backwoods districts with little housing. They had no choice but to build "company towns." But in doing so, the coal operators created captive communities, which could be exploited unfairly in many ways. Company towns intensified conflict between employers and workers. The bitter "mine wars," which broke out

Housing was one of the ways that some coal companies enforced industrial discipline among their workers. These striking miners and their families are being evicted from company houses, probably some time in the early 1930s.

in the early 1900s, were to some extent struggles for control of these towns.

Developing a society's human resources means more than just putting people to work. It means developing the population's full economic potential. Education is an important tool for developing this potential. As developed in New England during the early nineteenth century, public education was designed to instill industrial discipline in workers while providing them with basic reading, writing and mathematical skills. Public schools taught children to be punctual and to follow instructions. Teaching them to read and write meant that employers could train them more easily for specific jobs. Thus, education was a way of preparing a general population for a variety of industrial jobs. It was an important foundation for a diversified economy.

But West Virginia's educational efforts lagged behind those of the industrial states of the Northeast and Midwest. There were several reasons. One was the influence of Virginia. Despite repeated false starts, Virginia failed to establish an effective statewide system of free public schools before 1861. West Virginia required such a system under both its constitutions. But the system was slow to become established, and it remained poorly financed throughout the Industrial Period.

One problem was the resistance by many state taxpayers against paying higher taxes for schools. Small property owners already paid more than their share of taxes. They rejected the idea of increasing their tax burdens to benefit education. Railroads and owners of extractive industries resisted paying more taxes for any reason. Mine owners, in particular, feared that additional taxation would add to the cost of their product, which would hurt them in their competition with coal producers from other states.

Hilly terrain was also a problem, as was the scattering of the industrial population to hundreds of isolated locations such as coal camps. This increased the cost of making schools - or most other services - available to everyone who needed them. So, the most rapid educational progress came about in cities and towns, especially Wheeling.

In one way or another, the weaknesses of West Virginia's

educational system would haunt the state for decades. By the end of the twentieth century, for example, services - more than manufacturing - had become important as a way to stimulate economic growth. This was not only true in West Virginia, but in the United States and in most other industrialized nations of the world. Service businesses can be simple, everyday enterprises, such as restaurants or barber shops. But the most lucrative service industries involve the management of information by a highly trained work force. Financial services and health care are good examples of such service industries. Schools became very important in attracting service businesses of this type. Until the 1990s, however, West Virginia's educational system compared unfavorably with those of many other states. This limited the state's immediate ability to develop such industries.

A similar problem affected the growth of manufacturing in West Virginia after 1980. Industries involving simple processing or assembly tended to decline in the United States during the '80s. They tended to move to newly developing countries such as Korea, Mexico, or Brazil. The most lucrative manufacturing, like the most lucrative services, became "information-intensive." Information-intensive products are designed and made on the basis of scientific and technical knowledge. Such industries are called high-technology or "high-tech" industries.

The introduction of higher technology meant that manufacturers increasingly depended on a more highly-trained and innovative work force. Human resources, then, became at least as important as the materials, or natural resources, from which high-tech products were made. Thus, these industries tended to grow in regions that invested heavily in their educational systems during the Industrial Period. West Virginia began an effort to catch up, educationally, in 1989. It was financed by higher taxes, bonds, and lottery ticket sales.

Another way to develop and maintain human resources is to provide services for protecting workers from accidents, disease and unemployment. Twentieth-century industrial leaders resisted efforts to establish such services at public expense. They insisted that such problems were private matters, often to be handled by the workers themselves. Pressure from other groups - labor unions, middle-class reformers, small businesses and agricultural spokesmen - caused West Virginia to begin providing services of this sort.

The state Legislature adopted West Virginia's first mine

WV State Archives

During the early part of the Industrial Period, children often went to work in West Virginia's mines and mills. In 1910, some two million children were working in U.S. industries, averaging two or three dollars a week.

safety regulations in 1883. To enforce them, the state established a system for mine inspection. Subsequent changes in the law increased the number of mine inspectors and prohibited employing children under the age of fourteen in the mines. The Legislature of 1901 passed a factory-safety law and created a state employment bureau to help unemployed people find work. Other developments of this type included a "workmen's compensation" law, designed to compensate workers injured on the job (1913), factory inspection (1915), and a state health department (1915). Yet, like the schools, these services remained poorly financed and under-staffed, largely for the same reasons. The state's services did not approach the national standards of human-resource development until the federal government began to finance and supervise them in the 1930s.

8.6 Management and Entrepreneurs

Management represents a society's capacity to organize its economic activity. Managerial skills may not be needed very much in a subsistence economy. That is, a subsistence farmer has relatively few choices to make and these are likely to be the same choices year after year.

Management is of great importance in stimulating economic growth for an industrial society. Managers decide which economic opportunities to exploit. They devise strategies for combining the capital, human and natural resources so as to increase productivity. They decide what to do with the savings created by greater productivity. They decide, for example, whether to turn savings into a profit for capital investors or whether to turn it into higher wages for the workers.

Managers provide a general direction to an economy, making guesses about the future. These guesses, or "projections," are a mixture of gambling and planning. If the projections are correct, they can be followed by successful managerial decision-making. There is no adequate English word for someone who actively undertakes this kind of work, so we use a French word whose root means "to take on." The word is **entrepreneur**. The general array of innovative managerial and organizational skills is called **entrepreneurship**. In a capitalist economy, entrepreneurship is provided by business firms and individual businesspeople.

Judging from its early industrial leadership, West Virginia was well-provided with managerial resources. Some of the state's outstanding pioneer industrialists came from New England or Pennsylvania. Examples include the arms manufacturer John H. Hall of Harpers Ferry and nail makers Peter Schoenberger and David Agnew, both of Wheeling. But there was native managerial talent as well. During the 1850s, for example, some Kanawha salt producers foresaw the decline of their industry and reduced their investment in it. They made new investments in coal and timber production. In 1856, a group of Greenbrier Valley merchants, land speculators and prosperous farmers, led by Allen T. Caperton of Union, organized the White Sulphur Springs Company. Their objective - and they were successful at it - was to modernize and expand West Virginia's leading resort facility. Similarly, much of the initiative for organizing the Burning Springs oil field in Wirt County came from lawyers, businessmen and bankers in Clarksburg, Parkersburg and Weston.

This illustrates the initiative and imagination with which West Virginia business leaders seized new opportunities during the Statehood Period. Unfortunately, we can never know whether they would have succeeded. The Civil War dealt each of these locally-owned and locally-financed ventures a serious blow at a critical time. By the time that peacetime conditions returned to southern and central West Virginia, it was too late. The region was much poorer and much further behind the Northeast and the Midwest, where production and profits had been stimulated - not hurt - by the war.

Probably for this reason a different sort of entrepreneurship became common in southern West Virginia during the Industrial Period. Managers in that part of the state became "middle men." They were the local agents of non-resident investors or companies. At the fringes of this group were slippery "fly-by-night" operators, who called themselves "distinguished land

White Sulphur Springs

Greenbrier County, WEST VIRGINIA

attorneys." These were the people who scurried around the backwoods counties and secured leases on people's timber and mineral rights. Then, they hustled out to the big cities and peddled the leases to developers.

At the other extreme were West Virginia middle men who creatively made use of their limited business opportunities. They led development in many West Virginia cities and towns - establishing banks, streetcar lines, hotels and electric and gas utilities. Some groups of local businessmen even started the construction of feeder railroads, a very expensive undertaking. This was the case in Huntington, Charleston, Clarksburg and Morgantown. Except for Clarksburg, each of these railroad projects had to be completed by outside capitalists. Still, many local entrepreneurs successfully established small coal, oil and timber-producing companies along the railroads near their towns.

Southern West Virginia's coal operators - like the managers in towns - were often limited in capital and, thus, in their freedom to operate. Normally, the coal operator did not own his own land. Instead, he leased his mineral rights from a land company. He got his railroad cars and rail services from one of the trunk-lines, and sold his coal through a marketing firm - also likely controlled by the railroad.

An exception to this rule was Justus Collins, who established his first coal mine in Mercer County in 1897. Later, he added more mines in McDowell, Fayette and Raleigh counties. By establishing mines along different rail lines - the N&W, C&O and the Virginian - Collins managed to prevent the railroads from dominating his business. Instead, he established his own coal-marketing firm with its headquarters first in Cincinnati and later in Charleston.

Independent businessmen were more common in the northern part of the state. The north had a more diversified economy before the Civil War, which helped it to accumulate more local capital. Life there was also less disrupted by the war. The principal Wheeling glass, iron and steel companies were all locally owned and locally managed. So were the two largest coal producing firms - the Fairmont Coal Company and Davis Coal & Coke. Fairmont Coal was established by James B. Watson of Fairmont, his son Clarence W. Watson, and his son-in-law A. Brooks Fleming. Davis Coal & Coke was established by Henry Gassaway Davis, a Maryland native.

Davis's West Virginia operations were based first in Piedmont, Mineral County, then later in Elkins. Elkins was built in

1888 and named for Stephen B. Elkins, Davis's son-in-law. Stephen Elkins was a full partner in the Davis family's West Virginia mining, feeder railroad, commercial and banking operations. But Davis and Elkins were, to some extent, outsiders. Their principal homes were in Baltimore, Washington, or New York. They built vacation homes at Elkins in the early 1890s and visited there regularly.

Johnson N. Camden of Parkersburg, however, was a full-fledged West Virginian, a descendant of pioneer settlers and statehood-era politicians. Camden started out in land speculation in central West Virginia, but soon switched to the oil industry. After the Civil War, he became the state's leading oil refiner. Later, Camden joined into a coal-mining venture with the Watsons of Fairmont and in various other enterprises with Davis and Elkins. Camden built a feeder railroad that extended southward from Clarksburg to Weston, Buckhannon and Richwood. He also built the Ohio River Railroad.

Other West Virginia business leaders emerged during the early twentieth century. Michael L. Benedum, of Bridgeport, was an oil producer; and Earl W. Oglebay and Ernest Weir were steel manufacturers. As the century progressed, however, northern West Virginia's industries came more and more under the control of non-resident corporations. The management of these firms were based in cities such as Baltimore, Pittsburgh, or New York. Benedum and Oglebay retained control of their operations, but moved their headquarters out of the state - Benedum to Pittsburgh and Oglebay to Cleveland. Weir's operations at Clarksburg, Morgantown and Weirton also came to be directed from offices in Pittsburgh. By 1930, northern West Virginia's managers, like those of the south, had become mostly middle men. Only one major industrial corporation kept its headquarters in West Virginia. This was the Wheel-

WV State Archives

Henry Gassaway Davis (left) and his son-in-law, Stephen B. Elkins (above), were partners in West Virginia mining, railroads, banking, and other enterprises.

WV State Archives

West Virginia Collection, WVU Library

Founded by Ernest Weir in the early part of the twentieth century, the Weirton Steel Corporation became known as the largest worker-owned manufacturing enterprise in the United States.

ing Steel Corporation. It was organized in 1920 and remained based in Wheeling until 1968, when it merged with a Pennsylvania steel company and moved to Pittsburgh. The headquarters of Wheeling-Pittsburgh Steel returned to Wheeling in 1987.

Weir's Weirton steel mill was bought and operated for many years by a Cleveland-based company. Then, in 1984, Weirton Steel was sold to the workers who ran it. Since that time, the managers of the worker-owned steel company reorganized and modernized the mill. They made Weirton Steel the largest worker-owned manufacturing enterprise in the United States.

The contrast between Weirton Steel's success and the earlier failures of absentee owners further illustrates a point about management. Businessmen who lived in the communities where their businesses operated seem to have been more concerned with the general welfare of their communities - and their state. Other examples can be seen in the work of Davis, Elkins, Camden, Watson and Fleming. All of these men became political leaders - Fleming served as governor and the others were U.S. senators. In the meantime, the mining companies owned by these men had reputations of being less exploitative of their workers than the average West Virginia coal company. Their operations were also larger, better-financed and more independent than others. This may have been because these men had to answer to the public - not only as employers and members of the community, but as political candidates.

Similarly, southern West Virginia mine owners who actually lived in the coal camps also had a reputation of being more fair and humane toward their workers than absentee owners. Two well-known examples were William H. Edwards of Coalburg (Kanawha County) and William P. Tams of Tams (Raleigh County).

It also seems important to note that West Virginia's leading **philanthropists** - people who invest in human resources - came from among these entrepreneurs. Davis established hospitals in

Charleston and Elkins. He also joined with Stephen B. Elkins in establishing Davis and Elkins College. Michael L. Benedum established a foundation that built buildings and continues to support higher education across West Virginia. Oglebay and August Reymann, a wealthy Wheeling brewer, funded agricultural experimentation and research. Oglebay also donated the land which became the center of Wheeling's outstanding park and recreation facilities. His gifts encouraged other Wheeling business leaders to provide money for even more public facilities. As a result, Wheeling boasted the largest and finest array of civic cultural institutions of any city in the state.

By the time the twentieth century began, control of West Virginia's locally-owned business firms was passing rapidly into the hands of large corporations. Thus, the state's basic decisions about its economic system - as well as control of its natural resources - were passing out-of-state too.

In order to regain a share of control over the system, people turned to other large organizations. Workers, for example, turned to national labor unions. Small-business entrepreneurs, workers and middle-class citizens increasingly asked government agencies to assert more control over their economic system. It was hoped that these large organizations could deal with the corporations on more equal terms. The development of these organizations is the subject of the following chapter.

Study Questions - Chapter 8

1. Apply what you have learned about the "boom and bust" cycles of economic growth and economic depression to answer the following questions:

    a) Why is economic growth in our society uneven?

    b) What are some ways in which business owners coped with the boom-and-bust swings in economic growth?

    c) How did workers cope with the boom-and-bust cycles?

2. How many of the following problems of West Virginia's economy are related to "absentee landowners?" Justify your choices.

a) Farms were usually too small for farmers to save much capital.

b) Federal banking laws made it difficult for West Virginia's small banks to gather much capital.

c) The state of Virginia had granted so much land in present West Virginia to speculators that there was little government land left for economic development.

d) West Virginia's Constitution did not permit the government to finance economic development.

e) Some developers are interested only in profit and do not care how much damage is done to the land.

f) Much of the profit from West Virginia's fuel resources went to such places as Baltimore, Philadelphia, Pittsburgh and New York.

g) Legal hassles caused by arguments over land titles and ownership tied up much West Virginia land.

h) Poor farmers had no money to extract oil, natural gas, and timber from their land, so they often sold mineral rights for these resources to large land companies, and often for a small price.

3. Mine owner Justus Collins managed to gain some control over transportation costs and markets for his coal. How did he do this?

4. West Virginia's population grew rapidly during the Industrial Period. Give some reasons for this. Where did the new people come from? (Give more than one source.)

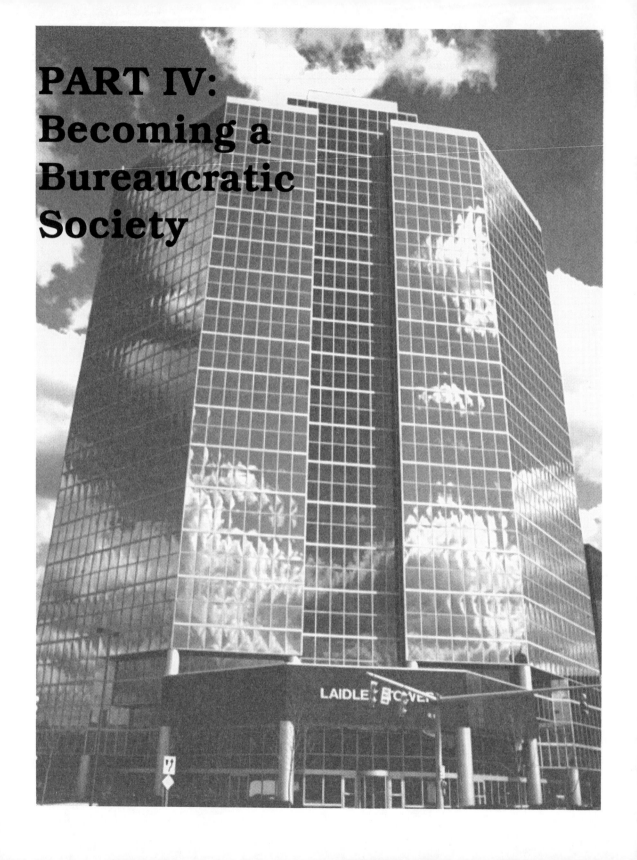

PART IV:
Becoming a Bureaucratic Society

Chapter 9:
The Age of Large Organizations

The twentieth century is an age of large organizations. This is true of West Virginia. It is also true of the United States - and of most industrial societies. That is why we call the last two-thirds of this century "the Bureaucratic Period," from the word **bureaucracy**, a term for large organizations. You can realize the importance of such organizations if you think for a moment about the roles they play in your own life.

Your own county school system is a good example. In most West Virginia counties today, the school system is a bigger organization than the entire state government was in 1880. After school, you might go out someplace for a snack. If you live in a small town, the most popular place - a restaurant or store - might be one-of-a-kind. You might even know the people who own it. But, if you live in a large town, chances are that the place to go is part of a "chain." The chain might own similar stores or restaurants in locations all over the country, and sometimes in other parts of the world.

Another example: At home tonight you will probably watch television. Your TV set was manufactured by a large organization with dozens of factories. The programs you watch are created and broadcast by still other large organizations. The sponsoring car company has more employees than the population of any single town in West Virginia. If you watch the news, you will probably hear something about at least one agency of the government - another big organization. On most evenings, you can watch the representatives of one large organization criticizing the activities of another.

In short, large organizations are the basis of much of modern life. This chapter will discuss the origin and growth of such organizations in West Virginia. It identifies some concepts that social scientists have used to describe the activities of large organizations. It also identifies and discusses other forms of group life that help to make up our modern social system.

Armies were the first large organizations to play a significant role in West Virginia life. Frontier warfare generally took the form of small groups of Indians and whites fighting each other. But the most decisive battles were fought by large numbers of people.

It required careful organization to supply, equip and move large armies under frontier conditions. Virginians had to learn this the hard way. Poor organization was partly behind the military disasters suffered by General Braddock in 1755 and the 1756 Sandy Creek expedition, both discussed in Section 3.8. on page 50.

The well-organized march of frontiersmen to the Battle of Point Pleasant in 1774, however, showed that settlers had learned from their early defeats. General Andrew Lewis's army numbered more than one thousand soldiers. Each man needed more food than he could carry or kill by hunting along the way. There was also a need for ammunition, medical supplies, tents and other equipment. So the army built a road across the mountains. This was so that large numbers of men and wagons carrying supplies could cross the mountains relatively quickly.

The army's leaders also sent men ahead - to the area of modern Charleston - to build flatboats. By the time the main body of troops reached the Kanawha River, the boats were ready to float men and supplies down to Point Pleasant. A herd of cattle was also driven along with the army to provide food.

This movement of a military organization across West Virginia involved four important procedures:

1.) It brought together large numbers of people, many of whom were strangers to each other.
2.) It divided the soldiers into smaller groups and assigned them specialized tasks.
3.) It assembled and distributed the supplies that were necessary to accomplish those tasks.
4.) It had a well-understood structure of authority, identifying those people who were entitled to give orders to others.

Each of these procedures can be found in the activities of other large organizations as well. In these organizations, as with Lewis's army, a leader's authority didn't necessarily depend upon his personal character or social position. When an officer was killed early in the battle at Point Pleasant, for example, another officer promptly stepped in to take his place. This rarely happened among Indian warriors, who chose their leaders according to their strength of character or social standing. If an Indian leader was killed, his followers often abandoned the battlefield. This was one of the reasons why the Indians lost control of their territory to the whites.

The above example shows how important military organization was in taking control of West Virginia from the Indians. Military organization was also important in the Union army's process of conquering northwestern Virginia and defending it during the Civil War. Otherwise, the influence of the military on later kinds of organization was indirect. The military's indirect influence took several forms.

First of all, military organizations provided a model for other large organizations. Most later organizations featured a structure of authority similar to an army's. Top officials had authority to issue orders to lower members of the organization. Large organizations also adopted the military practice of requiring lesser officers to make written reports to top officials. Modern organizations followed the military model by assembling large numbers of people who were generally unknown to one another. And they divided members into groups with specialized tasks while supplying them with appropriate materials to do their jobs.

The second indirect effect of the military was as a supplier of trained personnel for newer organizations, especially business corporations. For much of the nineteenth century, military schools were the only source of trained engineers. Armies needed specialists to build roads, bridges and other structures to move

West Virginia Collection-WVU Library

Military organization played a major role in organizing large numbers of people. These West Virginia University cadets are drilling before Woodburn Hall, which still stands today. This photograph was taken around 1876.

and house troops. Thus, the military pioneered in training people for these tasks. As a result, army-trained engineers supervised construction on many of West Virginia's early railroads, including the Baltimore & Ohio. After 1820, a French military engineer - Claudius Crozet - supervised the construction of many Western Virginia turnpikes. In 1839, Crozet helped establish the Virginia Military Institute (VMI), partly as a school for training engineers.

Eventually, VMI became a place where many West Virginia coal operators sent their sons to learn engineering. The term "civil engineering" grew to mean the construction of highways, bridges and other public projects. The word "civil" distinguished the profession from its military origins. West Virginia University began its civil-engineering program in 1888.

Military engineering remained important in developing West Virginia's transportation facilities. Beginning in the late nineteenth century, the U.S. Army Corps of Engineers began turning the Ohio, Monongahela and Kanawha rivers into canals. This project stimulated a revival of river traffic on these rivers. During the 1930s, the Corps of Engineers began construction of a series of flood-control dams on West Virginia's smaller rivers including the Cheat, Tygart Valley, Guyandotte, Gauley, Elk and Little Kanawha. Unlike the canalization of rivers, some flood-control dams were controversial. Public protests against destroying farmlands and natural river recreational areas blocked construction of the Stonewall Jackson Dam in Lewis County for several years, for example. But the lakes created behind the existing dams became popular recreation facilities.

In addition to producing engineers, military organizations had another indirect effect. They introduced hundreds of thousands of men and women to the rules and conduct of a large organization. For some people, joining the Army (or the Navy, Air Force, or Marines) was a way of seeing the world, perhaps of finding a job, a spouse, or a home in some distant part of the nation. For others, it was a means of escaping the economic swings that caused the severe depressions and unemployment in West Virginia from 1929 to 1940 and from 1953 to 1969. But for many - probably the majority - military experience offered the skills and attitudes they needed to cope with other large organizations.

Soldiers learned how to follow instructions, to work together in groups and to perform specialized tasks. It seems logical to suppose that all of these lessons contributed to general industrial discipline during peacetime conditions. Thus, the experience of military life prepared people for working and living within large business and government organizations. In fact, some experts would argue that the military taught more people how to get along in industrial society than any other institution except schools.

It should be added that military life did not usually teach people to *like* a highly organized life. It merely taught them to accept it. Moreover, this was not the main goal of the military. The military mission was to fight wars in the most efficient and successful way possible. This was why the U.S. Army had encouraged John H. Hall to perfect his principle of interchangeable parts in weapons manufacture at Harpers Ferry during the nineteenth century. This was also why the armed services drew hundreds of thousands of men and boys - and thousands of women - from West Virginia during the twentieth century. Not all of these people came back. More than 750 West Virginians died while serving in the military during the First World War. For the Second World War, the figure was about 4,700. About eight hundred West Virginians died in Korea, and more than seven hundred were reported killed in Vietnam. But - living or dead, in war and in peace - the numbers show that West Virginians have given more than their share of service to the military.

A third indirect effect of military organizations in West Virginia has to do with organized veterans' activities. After the Civil War, ex-soldiers of the Union Army created the Grand Army of the Republic (GAR). For the next thirty years the GAR was one of the most powerful organizations in the country. It was one of the first examples of what is called a **pressure group**. Its purpose was to pressure political leaders and government agencies to pay benefits to veterans and their families. These benefits included pensions to disabled soldiers and to the widows of men who had been killed. Later, the benefits programs were expanded to include pensions for *all* Union veterans and their widows. Eventually, these benefits cost the United States treasury more than the Civil War itself.

The GAR was closely allied with the Republican Party. It was influential in many counties around northern and western West Virginia, where Union veterans were the most numerous. Ex-Confederates tended to vote for Democrats. There was no hope of persuading the United States government to pay benefits to Confederate veterans. Nor would the state of West Virginia pay such benefits. Even Virginia limited the benefits it paid to its Civil War veterans. Thus, the Confederate veterans' organization, the

National Park Service - Steve Trail Collection

Civil War veterans met for years after the end of the war. This group of Confederate veterans gathered in 1907. Most of the men here served in the New River Regiment, Army of Northern Virginia.

United Confederate Veterans, tended to be a purely social organization. The GAR was a social organization too - but it also had political "clout."

The veterans' organizations that appeared after the twentieth-century wars tended to be similar to the GAR. That is, they were both social organizations and pressure groups. But they were even more effective than the GAR because they did not side with one particular political party. Instead, they simply backed the politicians who promised the largest veterans' benefits. This method was very productive. Benefits won by twentieth-century veterans included free college education, health care, programs that helped them borrow money to build or buy homes, and pensions for disabled veterans and their widows. These benefits were paid for by the federal government, which also built four veterans' hospitals in West Virginia - at Huntington, Martinsburg, Clarksburg and Beckley. In addition, the state government paid cash bonuses to West Virginia veterans of the two World Wars, the Korean War and Vietnam.

9.2 Business Organizations

Business corporations were the next type of large organization to appear in West Virginia. The "corporate" form of organization was developed hundreds of years ago to organize hospitals, colleges and other non-profit activities. It began to be used for business purposes in the 1700s. Banks started to form corporations during the 1780s, followed by steamboat lines and railroads in the 1820s.

Except for these examples, however, businesses generally did not use the corporate form until the late nineteenth century. This was because the corporation is best suited to large enterprises. Most West Virginia businesses remained too small to benefit from incorporating until the 1890s.

Corporations must be compared with two other forms of

business organization: the **proprietorship** and the **partnership**. A proprietor is the sole owner of a business. A partnership consists of two or more owners. These forms of business organization have many advantages. They are small, independent and quick to take advantage of new business opportunities. But they have important disadvantages. Small businesses have limited resources. They are often the first to fail during depressions. Proprietors and partners also have difficulty supervising large numbers of employees, particularly if the employees are scattered in several locations.

Most of all, small businesses have a hard time raising large amounts of capital. Modern businesses usually have to be started by borrowing money. In the case of railroads or fully-mechanized manufacturing operations, the necessary capital is more than most individuals or partnerships could ever afford. Small businesses have **unlimited liability**. That is, the proprietor or partners are responsible for all the debts of their business. This means that they have to repay everything the business borrows, even if it means selling their homes and other personal property to do it. Thus, proprietors or partners normally can't borrow money in amounts much greater than their own personal worth. But in most economic areas before 1900, they didn't need to.

The railroads were the first to create the type of large corporations that are common today. They did so because they required lots of money to construct the tracks, buildings, bridges and other equipment they needed to operate. The generic term for these things is **capital goods**. Since a railroad needed all its capital goods before it could earn any money, it had to begin by raising capital. The corporate form of organization permitted railroads to raise money in larger amounts than ever before. It raised capital by borrowing and by selling stock and bonds.

Stocks are shares of ownership in a business. Selling **bonds** is a way that corporations borrow money from banks and individuals. Unlike proprietors or partners, stock holders cannot be held personally liable for a corporate business's debts. A stock holder's liability is limited to the amount of money he or she invests in the stock.

Another advantage of the corporate form of organization had to do with work relations. The corporation provided a structure of authority for organizing thousands of employees in many different locations. Before the railroads came along, businesses rarely had more than a few dozen employees, all of whom could be supervised personally by the owner. If a business operated in more than one location (as merchants frequently did), the owner could choose someone else (a relative, perhaps) to handle things at the second location.

A railroad could not operate this way. Thousands of railroad employees worked at dozens of specialized tasks in numerous locations. A railroad could not very well start up a train in Baltimore and then ask the relatives of its stock holders to maintain it when it reached Grafton, Parkersburg, or Wheeling. Everything had to be well organized, right from the start. There had to be a railroad headquarters, with other departments organized around the corporation's particular functions. There was usually a department devoted to the passenger business, one to freight, and a department to handle the corporation's legal and financial affairs. There was also a "field" staff to handle these functions in each of the locations where the railroad did business. In other words, a clear structure of authority was created to establish who gave orders, who made reports to whom, who performed what tasks and so on. The Baltimore & Ohio Railroad was one of the railroads that pioneered this new form of organization during the 1850s.

Another feature of the corporate form had to do with legal and political matters. Railroads were in a special class of businesses that became known as "public utilities." Such businesses have two characteristics: they perform vital public services, and they have little or no competition in the places which they serve. Some examples of public utilities are telephone companies and suppliers of gas, water, waste disposal and electricity. Transportation services such as pipelines, airlines and buslines are also public utilities. The railroads were the first businesses of this type to appear.

The fact that public utilities had little or no competition made some people afraid that they would charge too high a price for their services. The railroads were the first to arouse this fear in West Virginia. Apart from Wheeling, Charleston and Huntington, no West Virginia locality had service from more than one railroad. Railroad prices (called rates) for agricultural freight shipments were generally higher in West Virginia than elsewhere. They were generally lower, on the other hand, for coal and other extractive products - businesses that the railroads wished to encourage. This led to demands by farm and small-business spokesmen that railroad rates be **regulated** or controlled by the state government. There was also a great deal of controversy over railroad taxation. This was due to the belief among small property owners that railroads and other public utilities avoided paying their fair share of taxes.

Controversy over railroad rates and taxation continued from the 1860s through the 1920s. In 1869, the West Virginia state government took over the job of levying taxes on railroads. This measure introduced the practice of taxing railroad property at a uniform level, statewide. But the railroads used their political influence to keep the state from regulating their rates.

The federal government took this step in 1887, however, when Congress created the **Interstate Commerce Commission**. In 1913, West Virginia created a state **Public Service Commission** (PSC) to supervise the activities and rates of all public utilities. The PSC still exists. But it has more influence over utilities such as electric, natural gas and telephone companies than it does over transportation services. This is because the transportation companies operate in several states and, thus, are regulated by the federal government.

9.3 Corporate Influence

Because they were public utilities, railroads became more involved with politics and government than most other businesses in the Industrial Period. This led them to build up their political influence. One way for railroad officials to increase their influence was to hold public office themselves. Henry G. Davis, Johnson N. Camden and Stephen B. Elkins were all railroad builders. They were also prominent politicians, as we have seen.

A more typical way to raise a railroad's influence in politics was to do favors for politicians. One method was to offer railroad "passes," entitling the recipient to free train rides. These became very popular among West Virginia politicians in the late nineteenth century. Numerous bills were introduced in the legislature to outlaw railroad passes, but they were usually defeated.

Still another way of adding to corporate political power was to employ attorneys who were active in politics to do part-time legal work for the corporation. This method was particularly effective for railroads. Since they usually had legal business in every county where their lines were located, they could spread their legal patronage around quite effectively. The major trunklines also developed the practice of employing Charleston-based lawyers as **lobbyists**. A lobbyist is the representative of a special-interest group or organization that wishes to influence legislation or some other government activity. According to tradition, the

172   West Virginia: A History for Beginners

lobbyist hangs around the lobbies of government buildings and waits for the chance to deliver his message to legislators or other officials.

Actually, lobbying assumes a variety of forms. But there is little doubt that the railroads were the first to deploy lobbyists effectively. The B&O's chief lobbyist in the late nineteenth century, for example, was said to be one of the most powerful men in West Virginia. During the 1920s, the most prominent lobbyist worked for the C&O. Along with pressure groups, lobbying is one of the most important political institutions of the Bureaucratic Period. Both pressure groups and lobbying are informal political institutions. Both are part of the impact of large organizations.

Small businesses often disappear when their proprietors or partners die or leave. But a corporation can outlive its original owners indefinitely. Corporations also have the capacity for growth. They can grow by reinvesting their profits in more capital goods - which, in turn, can create more output and profits. They can also grow by acquiring or combining with other corporations. The term for this last type of corporate growth is **merger**.

The Pennsylvania Railroad's acquisition, around 1900, of the stock of the B&O, C&O and N&W railroads threatened to produce a merger of West Virginia's largest corporations and public utilities. Political opposition to this merger grew so intense that the federal government acted in 1906 to make the Pennsylvania give up its attempt. Before too long, however, there were new forms of mechanized transportation: automobiles, trucks, buslines and airlines. Railroad mergers no longer seemed as threatening as they once did.

During the 1920s, state and federal regulators approved mergers that enlarged the Chesapeake and Ohio. The C&O, along with the Baltimore & Ohio, had acquired most of West Virginia's feeder rail systems after 1910. In 1959, Norfolk & Western absorbed the Virginian Railway and became the Norfolk Southern Corporation. In 1963, the C&O Railway and B&O merged to form the Chessie System, later renamed CSX. Because of their lucrative coal traffic from West Virginia, Norfolk Southern and CSX have become two of the strongest and best-managed rail transportation systems in the country.

Toward the end of the nineteenth century, corporations became important in other industries. The Standard Oil Company - based originally in Cleveland, Ohio, and later in New York - acquired control of West Virginia's largest oil refinery in 1875. In 1892, large steel and glass corporations, primarily based in

Pittsburgh, began acquiring plants in the Northern Panhandle. In 1902, the Western Maryland Railroad, a Baltimore firm, bought the Davis and Elkins railroad and coal companies. The following year, Fairmont Coal Company, West Virginia's largest, was acquired by Consolidation Coal Company, also based in Baltimore at the time. Wheeling Steel Corporation absorbed the remaining independent local steel producers in 1920.

The appearance of large manufacturing and mining corporations around the turn of the century is called the **consolidation movement**. Like railroad mergers, this movement was controversial. It aroused public fears of **monopolies**, or unified control over the prices and output of industrial products. This was not always the intention of corporate growth. But corporate goals were similar enough to the building of monopolies to make public fears reasonable.

From the corporations' standpoint, the basic reason for growth was **rationalization**. The exact meaning of this term changed from industry to industry. Usually it meant modernizing production facilities, phasing out obsolete equipment and plants, and improving the corporation's ability to control the volume and prices of its output. "Administered prices" were nearly always a goal of rationalization. This means that the prices of goods are set on the basis of the actual costs of production instead of the changing prices offered by buyers. This was a rational goal from a manager's point of view.

Rationalization challenged basic beliefs about the nature of capitalism. According to capitalist theory, prices are supposed to be set in the open, competitive market. The price is supposed to be a kind of compromise between the buyer and seller, not something "administered" by the seller on the basis of his costs.

John D. Rockefeller, founder of the Standard Oil Company, was one of the most controversial business rationalizers of the Industrial Period. In creating his oil company, Rockefeller's objective was to end competition between dozens of small oil refineries. Consequently, he bought up many refineries and forced others out of business. He closed down inefficient refineries and built new ones in urban locations.

Rockefeller's companies acquired control of most of West Virginia's crude oil production and much of its natural gas. Not all of this was done through the Standard Oil Company. Other Rockefeller companies that were active in West Virginia included

9.4 Corporate Consolidation

South Penn Oil Company and Hope Natural Gas. Rockefeller's reorganization of the oil industry caused all but one of the state's refineries to be closed down. His chief West Virginia agents in carrying out his plans were Johnson N. Camden and A. Brooks Fleming, both important political leaders.

Corporations like Standard Oil and business leaders like Rockefeller aroused intense controversy in the early twentieth century - both in West Virginia and the nation. There were three reasons for the controversy. One was the very size of the new corporations. They were larger than any other non-government organization in the nation's history. Another was their impersonality. Corporate managers were remote from their workers, from their consumers and even from their corporations' stockholders. Managers did things in the corporation's name which would have been shocking and unethical if done by individual proprietors and partners.

A third reason for controversy was that many of the new corporations introduced drastic changes in familiar areas of

National Park Service Photo

business and commerce. Consolidation put hundreds of small coal, oil and steel firms out of business in West Virginia and elsewhere. Most of the businessmen who sold out to larger firms were usually well paid. But people were shocked by the disappearance of local firms or their absorption by giant corporations with headquarters in Pittsburgh, Baltimore, Cleveland, Philadelphia or New York.

Oil companies were controversial before the popularity of the automobile enabled them to create thousands of local businesses like this Fayette County gas station, photographed in 1923.

Significantly, however, some turn-of-the-century corporate giants were not controversial at all. These were the companies that introduced new products or *created* local outlets for their products instead of merely absorbing once-independent local businesses. Neither automobile manufacturers nor telephone companies, for example, generated as much controversy as the railroads did. Thomas A. Edison and George Westinghouse were famous as human benefactors while people like Rockefeller were seen more often as evil geniuses. Actually, the companies which Edison and Westinghouse founded in the electrical industry were just as much monopolies as Rockefeller's firms. But they were based on **inventions**, whereas Standard Oil was the product of **innovation**.

Standard Oil and other oil companies became less controversial after gasoline (for automobile fuel) replaced kerosene (for home lighting) as their principal oil product. The increasing popularity of the automobile led oil companies to create thou-

sands of new local businesses in the form of service stations. Along with heavy advertising, this new development made these companies more popular than they had ever been before 1910.

Corporations also appeared in businesses that produced services - with similar results. Beginning around 1890, nationwide retailing companies - Montgomery Ward and Sears, Roebuck and Company, for example - began competing with local merchants by selling goods through the mail. Later, during the 1920s, these retailing corporations challenged local merchants right on their own main streets. National or regional firms opened branches all across West Virginia. Ward's, Sears and Woolworth's operated in dry goods, while Kroger and A&P dealt in food sales.

Library of Congress

Welch (McDowell County) in 1946. What signs or products can you see that reflect "economies of scale?"

The operation of these firms illustrated another advantage of large corporations. They enjoyed **economies of scale**, as economists call it. This means that large firms can buy, produce and distribute goods more cheaply. This is because they deal in larger volumes and, thus, have a lower cost per unit. In other words: the more of something they made, the cheaper the cost to make and distribute it.

Economies of scale allowed large corporations to offer lower prices and a larger selection of goods than local merchants. In West Virginia, merchants fought back with political pressure. They opposed cheap postal service, for example, because it helped the mail-order companies. And they supported chain store legislation, designed to cancel out the advantages of bigger firms. None of these measures worked. Large corporations continued to grow in every area of economic life.

After World War II, corporations appeared in the hotel and restaurant business. They created nationwide chains of motels and "fast food" stands, with units in most of West Virginia's cities and larger towns. Corporations also influenced professional workers, employing doctors and dentists, accountants, architects, engineers and lawyers.

National communications corporations bought control of local newspapers and radio and television stations. For example, West Virginia's best-known radio station, Wheeling's WWVA, became a subsidiary of Columbia Pictures, a Los Angeles-based motion-picture company. Later, Columbia itself was acquired by a Japanese corporation. Mergers reduced the number of daily newspapers, but the number of radio and TV stations increased. Even those stations that remained locally owned were linked to nationwide wire services and networks, which supplied most of the information and entertainment they distributed.

Thus, the spread of large corporations influenced nearly every aspect of West Virginia's economic system in the twentieth century. Further, the anxieties that this process created in people gave rise to the growth of other large organizations. These included labor unions, private associations and, most of all, government agencies of every kind.

9.5 Labor Unions

Labor unions offered the same general advantages to workers that corporations offered to capitalists. Unions were a means by which workers could pool their strengths and work together for their own benefit. Together, they achieved goals that were beyond the grasp of individual men and women working alone. Unions were similar to corporations also in that they attempted to operate on a national scale. Local union organizations, or "locals," were linked together into national organizations through a formal structure. Like corporations, labor unions contributed significantly to West Virginians' experience with large organizations. Both unions and corporations have come to be accepted as a standard feature of the state's modern economic life.

The differences between unions and corporations are more important than their similarities. Corporations were able to grow peacefully and steadily in West Virginia. Their growth aroused political opposition, but their political friends generally outnumbered their enemies. Throughout the Industrial Period, corporations enjoyed friendly protection from state and federal courts. It was just the opposite for labor unions. Their organizers had to fight continuous struggles to establish union locals. Scenes of union struggle often were repeated within every industry that was unionized. In some cases, a union struggle was repeated several times within the same industry - sometimes for generations. And such struggles were often far from peaceful.

The effort to establish labor unions set off violent opposition on the part of business and political leaders. Labor organizers and their union members frequently responded to corporate opposition with violence of their own. Four times between 1912 and 1927, West Virginia was the scene of bloody **"mine wars."** These wars pitted coal miners and their union leaders

WV State Archives

against coal mine owners, state and local officials and, in one instance, against federal troops. These incidents attracted nationwide attention. They gave West Virginia a reputation for labor violence that persisted through most of the twentieth century.

The mine wars were only the most dramatic confrontation between labor and business. Many less-dramatic incidents marked the history of coal and other industries, including railroads, iron and steel, glass and chemicals. The impact of labor struggles on West Virginia history has been as great as the struggle between whites and Indians during the Frontier Period

State soldiers occupied Paint Creek, in Kanawha County, during the winter of 1912 and 1913. The soldiers arrested, tried and jailed striking miners under martial law.

or the struggle between North and South during the Civil War.

Union organization in West Virginia began with the railroad workers. The national "brotherhoods," as the railroad unions are called, were organized on a **crafts** basis. That is, workers with different specialties or skills joined different unions. Thus, the railroad workers had separate unions for engineers, firemen, conductors, clerks, telegraphers, trainmen and trackmen. Some early non-railroad craft unions in West Virginia included carpenters, plumbers, painters, barbers, blacksmiths, cigar-makers and glass-blowers.

In addition to forming national organizations, craft-union locals also joined together in the larger cities and towns to form **central labor councils**. West Virginia's pioneer central labor council was the Ohio Valley Trades and Labor Assembly, organized in the Wheeling area in 1885. By 1903, central councils were also operating in Huntington, Clarksburg, Fairmont and Charleston; but Wheeling had more than 40 percent of West Virginia's craft-union membership at this time. In 1903, the craft unions and central labor councils organized a statewide labor federation.

The focal point of labor struggles in West Virginia was the coal industry. The **United Mine Workers of America** (UMWA) was organized in the Central or Midwestern coal fields of the United States in 1890. In West Virginia, the UMWA was organized officially in 1897. Unlike the craft unions, the United Mineworkers is an **industrial union**. This means that its membership is drawn from all workers in the industry, regardless of their individual jobs or skills. During the 1930s, industrial unions developed in West Virginia's steel, chemical, textile, electrical and communications industries. Between 1935 and 1957, industrial and craft unions formed state and national organizations, and competed among each other for members. But the leadership in all these labor developments belonged to the coal miners. Few organizations have played as important a role in West Virginia history as the UMWA.

The most dramatic events of labor history occurred during strikes. But the strikes that marked the growth of the UMWA differed somewhat from the strikes discussed in Chapter 7. Two kinds of strikes, you will remember, were discussed then: wage strikes, in which workers attempted to increase or preserve a certain level of income; and "wildcat" strikes, which usually developed in sudden protest against a change in working conditions.

Wage strikes had taken place in West Virginia before labor unions were organized. But they were usually more successful in cases where the union was securely in place. Success in a wage strike usually resulted in the union's **recognition.** This meant that business leaders who had opposed unionization during the strike recognized its right to speak for workers in future wage negotiations. For example, the UMWA won recognition in the Kanawha coal field after a strike in 1902. Then, in 1912, mine owners in the Paint Creek and Cabin Creek districts of this coal field withdrew their recognition of the union. This led to the first and bloodiest mine war - the Paint Creek-Cabin Creek Mine War of 1912-1913.

During World War I, mine operators in northern West Virginia and the Kanawha Valley recognized the union. The second and third mine wars took place in 1919 and 1921. On both occasions, armed miners tried to extend the UMWA's influence into the "unorganized" coal fields of Logan and Mingo counties, where coal operators refused to recognize the union. The fourth mine war took place in the Monongahela Valley coal towns around Morgantown and Fairmont. This mine war lasted from 1924 through 1927 and was caused when coal companies began paying lower wages than they had promised in their contracts with the UMWA.

The term "mine war" is a drastic but fair description of these incidents. Mine owners were fiercely determined to limit the union's influence among their employees. They hired private police called "mine guards," who patrolled the company towns with the most advanced weapons, including machine guns. The guards frequently beat up and sometimes killed - or were killed by - union organizers. The companies also hired spies to infiltrate the union and report on the activities of its members. Union miners were evicted from company-owned houses. Deputy sheriffs would pile up their belongings on the roadside. During long strikes, the miners and their families lived in tents or in wooden barracks furnished by the UMWA.

One reason why the operators fought the union so fiercely has been discussed in Section 8.4. West Virginia coal companies were at a disadvantage when they competed with coal producers in other states. They sought to make up for these disadvantages by paying lower wages and making profits on company houses

National Park Service Photo

Coal companies hired "mine guards" to patrol company towns and limit the union's influence among employees.

Courtesy of Eastern Regional Coal Archives

Excerpt from report of operative #9, dated June 14th.

"I heard Jesse Stafford say he saw the Matewan shooting and just before it started the detective was talking to Sid Hatfield, and Isaac Brewer called to Hatfield to come over to the hardware store, and A.C. [Felts] let him go, and then followed him over there. Stafford said just as the shooting started, Brewer told A.C., 'You are not going to take him [Hatfield]', and then the shooting started.

Bill Bowman had told me that he was in the door of the hardware store and bullets [were] flying all around him. But Stafford works in the store and says they only found traces of one bullet in the store.

Old J.W. Chambers told me he saw his brother Reese shoot Lee [Felts], so did Bill Bowman."

This is the text of a report made by an undercover company detective investigating the shootings of other company agents in Matewan, Mingo County, on May 19, 1920. The report was sent to Thomas Felts, director of the Baldwin-Felts Detective Agency. Felts's brothers, Albert C. and Lee, were among the ten detectives who were killed after evicting striking miners and their families from company homes.

and company stores. But another reason has to do with the nature of large organizations. Corporations generally saw labor unions as a threat to their structure of authority.

Labor unions were potentially as powerful as the corporations themselves. The two organizations competed with each other for the loyalty of employees. The unions' goals of higher wages for their members usually meant lower profits for the companies and their stock holders. As corporations grew larger and technology grew more complicated, it became both more difficult and more necessary to plan carefully how to combine human and natural resources in production processes. From the standpoint of corporate leaders, labor unions added another set of complications. The unions gave voice to workers' desires for safer and steadier jobs and a higher share of the company profits. This was a complication that corporation managers would rather have done without if they could have.

As the twentieth century continued, however, it became apparent that corporations would have to come to terms with labor unions. One reason was politics. Initially, political leaders gave little encouragement to union organizers. Between 1880 and 1910, both the Democratic and Republican parties were led by rich industrialists. At that time, many labor leaders favored establishing political parties of their own. The **Union Labor**, the **Populist** and the **Socialist** parties all won support from workers during this period, especially in the mining districts of the Kanawha Valley. Eventually, politicians in the two major parties realized that workers were voters too. In West Virginia, they discovered that there were many more working voters than there were corporation stock holders.

West Virginia Collection-WVU Library

At first, the Republican Party benefitted more from labor support than the Democrats. Nationally, the Republicans had backed trade and economic policies that appealed more to working people. In West Virginia, the party also had the early edge among black voters. These voters actually had little choice, since the Democratic Party, oriented to the old South, was still officially pledged to a program of racial segregation. The Republicans also tended to be favored by new voters. This included both immigrants and men moving from agricultural areas to new industrial districts.

All these factors helped West Virginia's Republicans win elections for state offices in 1894 - their first such victory since 1868. Significantly, their largest gains at the polls appeared in railroad towns, industrial areas and in the new coal fields. Except for one legislature elected in 1910, a governor in 1916, a U.S. senator in 1922, and the occasional congressman, the Republicans retained their control of West Virginia until 1932.

In the long run, however, the Democratic Party made the most effective bid for labor support. Beginning around 1910, Democratic leaders began to adopt pro-labor positions and to advocate stronger government regulation of the economic system. This was happening in West Virginia and across the nation. Eventually, these views prevailed among Democrats at the national level, but only after economic hard times had affected the entire country.

President Franklin D. Roosevelt took office in 1933, at the worst point of the Great Depression. He immediately began to

After being evicted from company houses, union miners moved their families into camps they built themselves. These union barracks were located in Lewiston, Kanawha County.

advocate a program of legislation known as the **New Deal**. Among its other features, the New Deal included programs that encouraged union membership. It also established a federal agency, the **National Labor Relations Board** (NLRB) whose purpose was to insure fairness in strikes and wage negotiations. The NLRB also set up rules for union-organizing campaigns.

9.6 Business and Labor Strategies

Thus, unions grew rapidly during the 1930s - especially industrial unions like the United Mine Workers. West Virginia membership in the UMWA rose from 16,000 to 107,000 in just two years, between 1933 and 1935. Even with the split between craft and industrial unions, labor became increasingly powerful in state and national politics. Cooperation between labor leaders and voters created a successful "liberal" wing of the state Democratic Party, headed by Matthew M. Neely of Fairmont. Neely won the governorship in 1940. His administration marked the first time in West Virginia history that the state government was genuinely neutral in business-labor disputes.

WV State Archives

The political success of unions forced businesses to adopt new strategies for handling work relations. These new strategies often were designed to limit the appeal of unions among employees. Some corporations, for example, created **company unions** which included only the workers of a single firm. Others adopted a program called **welfare capitalism**. This program limited the appeal of unions by offering high wages and other benefits to employees. Such benefits included retirement plans, health-care programs and recreation facilities. West Virginia corporations that adopted company-union and welfare-capitalism policies included Union Carbide Corporation and Weirton Steel, the state's largest producers of chemicals and steel.

Some businesses realized that labor unions could help them create a more stable and productive work force. But this was true only if workers would give up certain traditional goals. As discussed in Chapter 7, workers did not necessarily like all the jobs and working conditions that industrialization had created. Where possible, they tried to hold on to control of the pace of their work and of other working conditions. They also resisted the introduction of machines that eliminated or reduced the importance of their jobs.

John L. Lewis was president of the United Mine Workers Union from 1919 to 1960.

Some managers reasoned that labor unions might give up the goal of controlling working conditions in return for higher wages. That way, unions could contribute to more efficient production. They would become another means of promoting industrial discipline and higher productivity. Higher productivity made it possible to pay higher wages without lowering profits.

During the 1920s, the national leadership of the UMWA accepted this strategy of tying higher wages to productivity. The principal advocate of adopting this strategy was John L. Lewis, the union's national president from 1919 to 1960. Lewis advocated the mechanization of coal mining. He also worked for a reduction in the number of miners and coal companies. This would raise the wages and profits of those that remained. Not all union leaders agreed with Lewis on these goals. But he was successful in defeating opposition within his union. By 1933, the UMWA had a structure of authority as rigid and as tightly controlled as any business corporation in the world.

It took a long series of bitter strikes before business leaders

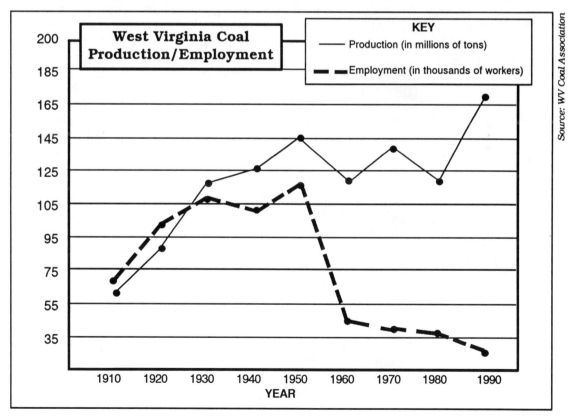

Source: WV Coal Association

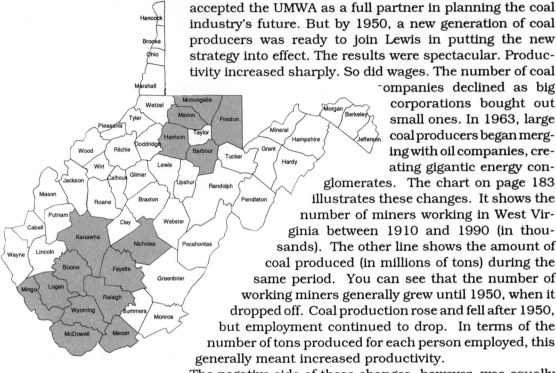

accepted the UMWA as a full partner in planning the coal industry's future. But by 1950, a new generation of coal producers was ready to join Lewis in putting the new strategy into effect. The results were spectacular. Productivity increased sharply. So did wages. The number of coal companies declined as big corporations bought out small ones. In 1963, large coal producers began merging with oil companies, creating gigantic energy conglomerates. The chart on page 183 illustrates these changes. It shows the number of miners working in West Virginia between 1910 and 1990 (in thousands). The other line shows the amount of coal produced (in millions of tons) during the same period. You can see that the number of working miners generally grew until 1950, when it dropped off. Coal production rose and fell after 1950, but employment continued to drop. In terms of the number of tons produced for each person employed, this generally meant increased productivity.

The negative side of these changes, however, was equally spectacular. The employment decline had a devastating impact on mining communities. It also hurt bigger towns and cities such as Welch, Logan, Beckley, Bluefield, Fairmont and Williamson, whose economies were geared to providing services linked to the coal fields. After World War II, at a time when the national economy was expanding, West Virginia experienced a deep economic depression. Thousands of workers left the state to find new jobs and homes elsewhere. The state's population declined by 13 percent between 1950 and 1970. The chart on the next page shows population changes in the fifteen counties that produced the most coal in 1950. You can see that in many communities where mining had been the main occupation, the drop in population was significant. By 1990, most counties had recovered to some degree. But only one had a larger population in 1990 than in 1950.

Increased productivity, therefore, came at a higher price than the miners had expected to pay - in more ways than one. Even though the number of mining jobs declined, coal-mine accidents and fatalities remained high. Work-related illnesses

WV COAL COUNTIES POPULATION 1950-1990			
COUNTY	1950	1970	1990
Barbour	19,745	14,030	15,699
Boone	33,173	25,118	25,870
Fayette	82,443	49,332	47,952
Harrison	85,296	73,028	69,371
Kanawha	239,629	229,515	207,619
Logan	77,391	46,269	43,032
Marion	71,521	61,356	57,249
McDowell	98,887	50,666	35,323
Mercer	75,013	63,206	64,980
Mingo	47,409	32,780	33,739
Monongalia	60,797	63,714	75,509
Nicholas	27,696	22,552	26,775
Preston	31,399	25,455	29,037
Raleigh	96,273	70,080	76,819
Wyoming	37,540	30,095	28,990
West Virginia	**2,005,552**	**1,744,237**	**1,793,477**
United States	**151,325,798**	**203,302,031**	**248,709,873**

Source: US Census; 1992 World Almanac

may actually have increased during these years. This was partially because the new mining machinery threw more coal dust into the air for miners to breathe. Lewis had promised generous pensions and health benefits for the union's old, sick and disabled miners. But the sudden drop in dues-paying working miners depleted the UMWA treasury. The union could not afford to keep these promises. Corruption and fraud among UMWA leaders made these matters even worse after Lewis retired in 1960.

Beginning in 1969, a new generation of union leaders attempted to reverse these conditions. The new leaders were drawn mainly from working "rank-and-file" miners from West Virginia. Under their leadership, the UMWA tried to regain control over working conditions and re-emphasize health and safety matters instead of productivity. The union used wildcat strikes, wage strikes and political pressure to fight these battles.

At the same time, other factors were working against the union. National and state government officials were pressing for increased coal production. The new energy conglomerates wanted to apply the industrial discipline that prevailed in less-dangerous industries. Once again, powerful forces with conflicting goals had found their principal battlefields in West Virginia.

9.7 Government Regulation

The largest organization of all in twentieth-century life is government. There is not just one government, but many. Or, better, there are different levels of government - federal, state and local (city and county). Each level has a bewildering variety of agencies, and some agencies are jointly operated by two or more levels. But, regardless of which level we talk about, government operations have grown more numerous, more influential and more complex with the passage of time.

A basic reason for this growth in government was economic growth. It's easy to understand when you think of the earlier discussions about the rise of industrialization, corporations and labor unions. Severance taxes, railroad regulation, chain-store laws, labor-relations laws: all of these government activities - and many others - were stimulated by economic change.

Generally speaking, governments have taken on three kinds of activity in relation to economic change. First, government agencies were developed to **regulate** - or control - economic activities. Two examples are the federal Interstate Commerce Commission and the state Public Service Commission, mentioned in Section 9.2. In addition to public utilities, state agencies regulate banks, insurance companies and other professions and businesses.

Secondly, agencies and programs have been created for the purpose of **developing human resources**. The growth of public education provides one example. Others include the many welfare programs set up to protect workers from the effects of accidents, illness, unemployment and old age.

Thirdly, governments have become providers of **capital** and of **capital goods**. A large number of federal programs and some state programs make loans (or give credit against taxes). They have made loans for a variety of uses, ranging from college education to building shopping malls. Corporations, local governments and individuals have benefitted from these loans. Government has also provided capital goods in the form of highways, bridges, dams, recreation facilities, public buildings and other costly products. Such capital goods enhance the possibility of the nation's economic growth. They are generally provided by government because private investors either lack the capital to build such facilities or they are unwilling to build them in a way that benefits the largest number of people.

In addition to providing goods, loans, human services and regulatory control, governments greatly expanded all the other things they had been doing before industrialization began. For example, in 1870, the state of West Virginia operated three institutions - a mental hospital, a penitentiary and a university. By 1991, there were eleven penal and mental institutions, along with sixteen state colleges and universities. The number of state trial judges increased from about thirty-five in 1918 to sixty such judges in 1991. The number of opinions written by the state Supreme Court increased from 110 in 1890 to 271 in 1990.

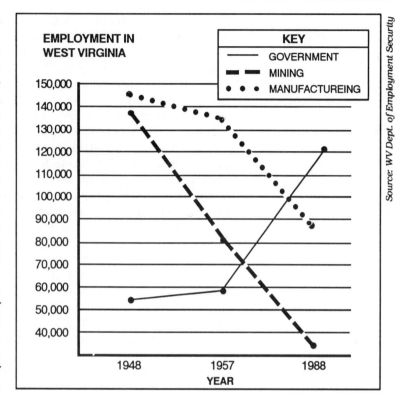

EMPLOYMENT IN WEST VIRGINIA

KEY
—— GOVERNMENT
— — MINING
• • • MANUFACTUREING

YEAR

Source: WV Dept. of Employment Security

Law enforcement had always been the responsibility of local governments. But, generally speaking, this had been only an occasional need in earlier times. Industrialization and the growth of cities brought strangers together in larger and larger numbers. The need for law enforcement increased steadily, until it became a full-time concern for both state and local governments. The West Virginia State Police force, for example, was founded in 1919 - mainly for the purpose of preserving order during labor disputes. It quickly became involved in enforcing liquor laws, regulating automobile traffic, and conducting criminal investigations. Thus, the number of state police officers increased from 120 in 1919 to 511 in 1990.

One general point needs to be made about this growth of government activity. Growth affected all levels of government, in terms of the *amount* of government activity. Also in terms of the *purpose* of these activities, the federal government became steadily more important. More and more in the twentieth century, the power to make or change government policies became a federal function. This was especially true after World War I, and it was true even though many of the policies made in Washington had to be carried out by state or local agencies. State and local governments grew more rapidly after 1920 than the federal government did - at least in terms of the total number of government employees. But, frequently, this growth took place along lines that were determined at the national level.

During the nineteenth century, for example, the federal government provided funds for programs to be carried out by state governments. (The establishment of "land grant colleges," such as West Virginia University, embodies this principle.) Important changes in this practice were made in 1916, however, when Congress passed the Federal Highways Act.

First, the act began the practice of issuing **federal matching grants**. Under these grants, each dollar spent by an individual state for a specific purpose was matched by a certain amount of federal money. In this case, the purpose was building highways. Aside from the funding change, the Highways Act established the United States Bureau of Public Roads. This bureau was to make certain that the highways were built to the same standards in all parts of the nation. It was set up to do research and to determine **federal guidelines** for highway builders in every state. This was the beginning of our huge modern investment in interstate highways. As time passed, the federal guidelines for road building became more demanding and the federal matching grants increased. During the 1960s, '70s and '80s, federal highways were built across the country, each with the same specifications. In West Virginia - as in every other state - these rigid guidelines were followed. But the Mountain State's rugged terrain made construction very costly. Still, federal funds paid 90 percent of the costs. (At the same time, other Appalachian highways or "development corridors" were being built under different grants and less-rigid guidelines.)

This matching grant/federal guidelines formula was followed in many other areas of government activity. It was particularly important in the area of developing human resources. During the 1930s, Congress established programs that were designed to protect people against the expansion and contraction of the economic system. Some of these programs were to be run entirely by the federal government, such as the Social Security system. Others were set up as joint federal/state programs, with federal guidelines and matching grants. Examples of these include unemployment insurance, which makes payments to unemployed workers, and programs that assist people who are unable to work.

National Park Service Photo

The New Deal of President Franklin D. Roosevelt also introduced a new type of intergovernment cooperation: federal/local joint programs. These programs initially targeted housing problems in U.S. cities. As urban growth increased in West Virginia and the nation, so did the number and variety of federal/local programs. One of the more controversial federal programs created new settlements to house unemployed workers during the Depression. Three of these were built in West Virginia, at Arthurdale (Preston County), Eleanor (Putnam County) and Tygart Valley (Randolph County).

Imagine the amount of bureaucracy it took to operate this Fayette County school around 1920, compared with your own.

State and local governments developed other joint programs, particularly in the area of education. In addition, there continued to be programs operated mainly or entirely by each of the traditional levels of government.

Naturally, the steady growth of government activity introduced changes to West Virginia's political system. One change was to strengthen the office of governor. This was done both formally and informally. Formally, a number of federal and federal-state programs were administered through the governor's office. This gave the governor power over budgets and employees that were not directly controlled by the legislature. Another formal change was to make the governor responsible for preparing and submitting an annual budget to the legislature. A related constitutional change made governors eligible for re-election to a second four-year term, beginning in 1972. These changes strengthened a governor's formal political power in relation to the other branches of government.

Informally, the governor's power grew because of all the new state government jobs. The amount of patronage (see Section 6.3) available to West Virginia governors increased dramatically during the 1930s and '40s. This trend was countered, however,

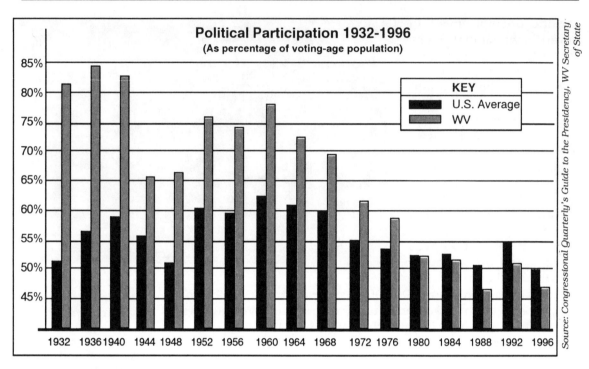

Political Participation 1932-1996
(As percentage of voting-age population)

KEY
- U.S. Average
- WV

Source: Congressional Quarterly's Guide to the Presidency, WV Secretary of State

Political Participation 1932-1996 (percent of voting-age population)

by federal guidelines that accompanied some federal funds. The guidelines increasingly directed state governments to employ program workers on the basis of their qualifications, instead of their political connections. This practice was called "merit appointment."

In 1940, a state Merit System Council was set up to administer merit appointments. Increasingly, this new merit-standards system included other state agencies. In 1961, the system was administered by a state Civil Service Commission and then, in 1989, by the state Personnel Board. Through all these changes, the number of state employees covered by merit standards has grown steadily.

The number of **elected** officials remained roughly the same between 1900 and 1990. But there was a steady increase in the number of state officials who owed their power to **appointment**, rather than election. This increase in appointed officials was, perhaps, the most sweeping change in the state's political system during the Bureaucratic Period. Whether these officials were appointed on a "merit" or patronage basis, they were usually several steps removed from the election process that was supposed to provide people with control of their government.

Impatience with government operations and "red tape" grew as a result of these changes, while participation in elections and electoral campaigns declined. In 1936 West Virginia had one of the highest rates of political participation in the nation. Almost 85 percent of the eligible voters in the state voted in that year. By 1988, this had declined to 46.7 percent.

Like other trends in this age of large organizations, the long-range meaning of this remains to be seen.

9.8 Interest Groups

What happens to ordinary people in an age of large organizations? For one thing, individuals can form organizations of their own. A whole range of **voluntary associations** appeared in West Virginia during the Industrial Period. These included fraternal organizations, service organizations, ethnic organizations, religious organizations and a great variety of special-interest groups.

Occupational and special-interest groups, in particular, learned to use the lobbying and pressure tactics that had been pioneered by veterans and business organizations. The West Virginia Education Association, an organization of public school teachers, provides an example of an occupational group that has effectively used such tactics to advance the interests of its members.

Direct action provides another tactic open to groups that find themselves unable to pursue their goals through conventional means. This method consists of public demonstrations, parades, rallies, strikes and symbolic protests. The purpose of such actions is to dramatize the goals of the group and win broader public support.

One of the most effective proponents of direct action in West Virginia history was Mary Harris "Mother" Jones. She was an organizer for the UMWA who worked in West Virginia off and on between 1897 and 1921. She was in her 60s at the time of her first campaign here. Partly for this reason, Mother Jones was very successful in generating publicity for the miners' cause. Her dramatic speeches and marches helped bring

David Corbin

*Mary Harris
"Mother" Jones*

Mother Jones organized rallies and gave speeches to generate publicity for the United Mine Workers union. Here, she is speaking before a crowd in Star City, Monongalia County, in June 1918.

in more members for the union. She also inspired a congressional investigation of the West Virginia coal fields in 1911. The UMWA and other labor unions also employed direct-action strategies during the 1930s.

During the 1960s, the same direct-action techniques were employed by African-American students who protested racial segregation in cities such as Huntington, Charleston and Bluefield. In 1990, West Virginia school teachers combined a strike with demonstrations and lobbying in Charleston to force politicians to deal with their demand for higher wages.

The environmental movement of the 1970s, '80s and '90s represents a combination of voluntary associations and direct action. This movement included a variety of special-interest groups seeking to preserve wilderness areas, to protect scenic and historic areas, to conserve natural resources, and to limit or prevent air and water pollution. Beginning in the early '70s, the environmental movement used public demonstrations and symbolic protests to call attention to the problem of strip mining. During that time, West Virginia became a major battlefield in the struggle to protect the environment.

In that battle - and others since - the beauty of the state's mountains and rivers is balanced against its abundant reserves of energy, especially coal. Choices between environmental and economic values have occurred frequently in the state's history. No doubt, they will continue to play a role in West Virginia's future development. It is yet to be seen whether corporations, government agencies, or voluntary organizations of citizens will have the most decisive influence in making these choices. It's safe to say, however, that each of these forms of organization has played an important role.

In spite of all the large organizations in public life, there was still room in the twentieth century for individual achievement. The most famous individuals in the nation excelled in entertainment and the arts, national politics, or in certain branches of professional athletics. West Virginia produced its share of leaders in each of these fields. They included Pearl Buck, Davis Grubb and John Knowles - all novelists; Phyllis Curtin, an opera singer; George Crumb, a music composer; Sam Huff, a football player; Jerry West, a basketball player; and Senator Robert Byrd, who served as majority leader of the U.S. Senate from 1976 to 1989.

None of these individuals achieved their national prominence while living and working in West Virginia, however. In an age dominated by large organizations, ambitious individuals were often drawn toward the centers of power and communications in the nation's big cities.

During the 1960s, a reaction against this process developed among many people, especially young people. Life in big cities and work for large organizations lost their appeal. People began searching for simpler ways of life in quieter, more rural places. West Virginia became one of the places that young people most frequently considered for new ways of living and building new homes. A new type of settler began moving into West Virginia communities, especially into small towns and farming areas. These "back-to-the-land" settlers included artists, writers, craftsmen and a variety of other former urban people. Many of these people struggled - with mixed results - to turn themselves into subsistence farmers.

Other kinds of people were migrating to the hills of the Mountain State during the 1970s. These included the native West Virginia workers who had left during the 1950s and 1960s to find jobs in the big industrial cities. After 1969, the state's economy expanded and many of these people were able to return home. Also coming into West Virginia were professional people, eager to create a new life for themselves in the mountains - lawyers, doctors, teachers, architects and engineers. Among these was a nationally prominent politician, John D. Rockefeller IV, who moved from Washington, D.C. to West Virginia in 1964, and was elected the state's governor in 1976.

Thus, West Virginia experienced a modest increase in population growth during the 1970s. Its per-capita (per-person) income and share of the nation's overall economic growth increased even more rapidly. But these gains turned into losses

9.9 Individual Achievement in a Bureaucratic Age

again during the 1980s, as another depression settled over the coal industry and spread into the state's manufacturing industries as well. By 1990, the state population figures showed a decline of about 6 percent.

We can see, then, two different kinds of trends during the Bureaucratic Period. First, the arrival of new settlers has shown that life in our state is very good in many respects - especially in the areas of life that do not depend on economic factors. But the continued loss of jobs and people to other states shows that West Virginia's economic problems have been as severe as ever, maybe worse. It remains to be seen which of these two trends will have the greatest impact on the future of the state and our quality of life.

Study Questions - Chapter 9

1. If your local drug store, shoe store, or flower shop decides to charge more money for a product, it does not need government permission to do so. If your local electric, gas, or telephone company wants to raise the price of its products and services to customers, it must get permission from the Public Service Commission, a government agency. Explain why this is so.

2. Pressure groups, lobbyists, and regulatory agencies are three political institutions mentioned in the text. All three developed as a response to the growth of large organizations. Two of the three are informal political institutions. One is a formal political institution. Which is which? What is the difference between them?

3. What advantages do corporations have over small businesses? Can you think of advantages that small businesses would have over large ones?

4. Explain each of the following:
   a) a "wildcat" strike.
   b) a wage strike.
Which type of strike had more to do with employers "recognizing" their workers' union?

5. In what ways could "welfare capitalism" take the place of labor union membership for workers?

6. In order to get higher wages for miners, UMWA President John L. Lewis agreed to support higher productivity in the mines. In doing this, he gave up one of the union's goals of preventing the introduction of machines into the mines. Since machines took jobs from people, why would Lewis support such a policy? Explain the economic reasons for his decision to accept the introduction of machines?

7. In 1906, the federal government prevented a merger between the Pennsylvania Railroad and all smaller railroads in the state. Why would the government oppose such a merger? Why were such mergers permitted during the 1970s and '80s?

Chapter 10:
Bureaucracy and the Social System

In every society, people join together in groups for a variety of reasons. Groups are important in work, play and in the concerns of everyday life. A society's groups and organizations are part of its **social system**. The social system determines how people become members of groups, and how groups relate to each other. The social system also determines how groups make decisions, how they settle disputes, and which groups are most important within the overall society.

This chapter discusses four concepts for describing and classifying some of the groups that have played important roles in West Virginia life. These concepts are **family**, **bureaucracy**, **ethnicity** and **religion**. The chapter identifies differences and similarities between different types of groups. It also discusses the changes in the relative importance of groups over time. The last part of the chapter discusses two more concepts that are sometimes applied to the analysis of West Virginia life. These are the concepts of **social class** and **region**.

Ideas & Issues:
Contrasting
Bureaucracies and
Families

Perhaps the most important differences between groups are the reasons why people become members of them. You are born into some groups. Others you make a conscious decision to join. This basic difference can explain many other differences. For example, a group which people are born into tends to instill a stronger sense of mutual obligation among its members. Members also have a stronger sense of being different from non-members - a sense of difference, in other words, between "insiders" and "outsiders." Voluntary groups - groups you join as a matter of conscious decision - tend to be more adaptable to the demands of an industrial economic system. In our history, such groups tended to become more important as industrialization advanced.

In any society, the family is the most important social group. It is a group that *everyone* is born into. Even adopted children are "born" into their families in the sense that their parents generally choose to have them, instead of vice versa. One important point must be noted: Throughout history, family groups have been the most important economic unit in all societies. But today, the family shares this role with many other groups and institutions.

If you compare the role of the family in economic and social life during the Frontier Period with similar activities today, you can see how the family's position has changed. The first column in the chart below lists activities that an average West Virginia family in 1800 would have carried out entirely or mainly on its own. The last column lists groups and institutions besides the family that are likely to be involved in the same activities today.

At the other extreme from families are the large organizations discussed in Chapter 9. No one is born into an army, a corporation, a labor union or a government agency. People become members of these organizations as a matter of choice. In some cases, someone other than the member makes the choice. This is true of children who are required by law to attend school or men who are drafted into the Army. But in all of these cases, the act of joining is still a matter of conscious decision on somebody's part.

	FRONTIER	STATEHOOD	INDUSTRIAL	BUREAUCRATIC
SCHOOLING	Family	Family Neighborhood	Local Government	County/ State/Federal Governments
FOOD PRODUCTION	Family	Family	Family & Commercial Growers	Commercial Growers
FOOD PROCESSING	Family	Family Neighborhood, Mill	Packers/Canners	Factories
FOOD DISTRIBUTING	Family	Small Stores	Small Stores/Chains	Mostly Chains
CLOTHING	Family	Family, Small Stores	Small Stores/Chains	Mostly Chains
HOUSING	Family	Family	Family/Builders	Builders, Factories
TRANSPORTATION	Family	Canal, Railroad, Turnpike	Railroads/ Highways	Railroads/Air/ Highways
LAW ENFORCEMENT (CRIME)	Family/Neighbors	Neighborhood, County	County/State Governments	Local/State/U.S. Governments
DEFENSE (WAR)	Family/Neighbors	County/State	Federal	Federal/ International

Bureaucracy is a word often used to describe the kinds of large organizations in which most people participate today. It is a controversial word with several meanings. Some people use it to describe only government organizations. Others use it to refer to any organization that operates according to a rational plan. Still another definition uses the term to mean something negative. According to this definition, a bureaucracy is inefficient and irrational; a "giant power wielded by pygmies," in the words of one nineteenth-century critic. However it is used, the term usually refers to a large organization. (The word "bureaucracy" comes from the French word "bureau," which means both "office" and "desk.")

Bureaucracies have the four characteristics of large organizations that were discussed earlier. They bring together a large number of employees and officials who are divided according to specialized tasks. They command a volume of supplies or other resources necessary to accomplish these tasks, and they have a structure of authority. Bureaucracies also generate a lot of paper work, which is known in popular language as "red tape."

The contrast between bureaucracies and families is instructive. Families are bound together by a general sense of mutual obligation. The obligation has no specific limits. Parents are supposed to do everything they can to meet a child's needs. If the parents live to a very old age the obligation is reversed, but it is still unlimited. People may not live up to these ideals, but the ideals are still part of our society's values.

Members of bureaucratic organizations, on the other hand, have a relatively limited sense of obligation toward one another. Usually the obligation is confined to the specific purposes for which the organization was created. After work, after school, or after the meeting, those obligations generally cease to exist - unless organization members are also bound by ties of family, personal friendship, religion, or ethnicity.

The same difference exists in terms of group identity. Families often have a strong sense of identity. They believe they have characteristics that set them apart from outsiders. But bureaucratic organizations generally do not inspire a strong sense of group identity. People who work for Union Carbide, for example, generally do not think of themselves as being very different from those who work for Montgomery Ward. Democrats get along fine with non-Democrats, Kiwanis with non-Kiwanis, and so on.

Ethnic and religious groups are somewhere between families and bureaucracies. People are born into ethnic or racial groups. But it is sometimes a matter of personal choice whether or not they share the sense of obligation and identity that ethnicity involves. For their part, religious groups frequently require a declaration of choice from new members. Some groups even require some proof of conversion to their beliefs. But, in practice, most people join the religious organizations of their parents. Even in cases where proof of conversion is expected, the act of conversion becomes an intensely personal or emotional one. It is quite different from the sort of decision a person makes in joining a bureaucratic group.

10.1 Ethnicity

Ethnic and racial groups have played a very important role in West Virginia history. Black West Virginians have been the most consistently distinctive group. This was partly because of racial prejudice on the part of whites. After slavery was abolished in 1865, racial segregation - or separation - took its place as a means of maintaining white supremacy over African-Americans. Both the 1863 and 1872 state constitutions required separate school systems for African-American children. In theory, the two systems were supposed to be equal - at least in terms of buildings, equipment and supplies. In fact, they rarely were equal. In terms of their teachers, the black schools were sometimes superior. This is because racial prejudice limited the kinds of jobs that talented African-Americans could hold, so many outstanding individuals turned to teaching. **Booker T. Washington** and **Carter Woodson**, two of America's greatest educators during the Industrial Period, started out teaching in segregated West Virginia schools.

Booker T. Washington, born into slavery before the Civil War, became internationally known as a consultant on industrial education. He gained notoriety as principal of the Tuskegee Institute, an industrial school for blacks in Alabama. Washington built Tuskegee into the finest institution of its kind. After 1895, he became a nationally-known speaker, emphasizing the need for Americans to put aside their sectional and racial differences. He had spent his youth in Malden, Kanawha County, and returned there after college to serve as a schoolmaster.

The original centers of African-American population in West Virginia were the Kanawha salt-making district and the Shenandoah, South Branch and Greenbrier valleys, where the best agricultural lands were situated. Industrialization changed this pattern. African-American miners and construction workers began to move north from Virginia and the Carolinas and east from Kentucky. McDowell County, which had no blacks in 1860, had a black population of nearly 15,000 by 1910, representing 31 percent of the county's total. Jefferson County had the second-largest proportion of African-Americans, followed by Fayette and Kanawha counties.

West Virginia had never been as segregated as Kentucky, Virginia and other Southern states. The state, in fact, made some progress toward racial equality while its Southern neighbors were still moving backward. But racial segregation remained in force in West Virginia until the 1960s, when the state's African-Americans joined people from other parts of the country in a combination of lawsuits and direct-action campaigns. The national civil rights campaign and pressure from the federal government began to limit segregation's effects. As the external pressure of segregation declined, African-Americans found that they had a sense of identity based on their common heritage and culture. This discovery helped stimulate a revival of interest within other ethnic groups in recent years.

Like African-Americans, Euro-American ethnic groups were present in West Virginia from the very beginning of the Settlement Period. For many years, it was thought that a Welsh Quaker named Morgan Morgan was West Virginia's first settler. It is now believed that he was preceded by the German families who settled Shepherdstown. Germans remained the most distinctive ethnic group on the Virginia frontier, partly because they spoke a different language. Later, an urban German colony developed in Wheeling, where German-language newspapers were published, beginning in the 1830s. German accents remained common in Wheeling - and in parts of rural West Virginia - throughout the nineteenth century. One of the more noted rural German settlements was the Aurora area of Preston County.

English-speaking British ethnic groups were more prominent than English settlers on the Virginia frontier. These included the Welsh, Scots, Irish and Scotch-Irish. But the sense of group identity did not persist very long among these West Virginia immigrants for a couple of reasons. First, the British ethnics made up a majority of white settlers. Secondly, they were not set apart by language (like the Germans) or by race and a history of slavery (like the blacks).

I r i s h Catholics were an exception to this rule, however. They spoke English, but were otherwise set apart from other English-speaking communities by their religion. There was almost as much prejudice against Catholics in early West Vir-

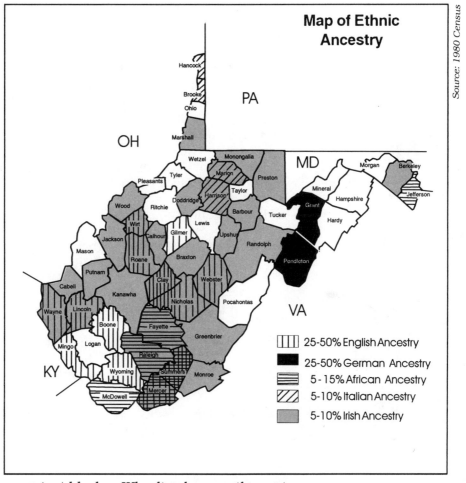

Map of Ethnic Ancestry

Source: 1980 Census

IIII 25-50% English Ancestry

■ 25-50% German Ancestry

≡ 5-15% African Ancestry

▨ 5-10% Italian Ancestry

▦ 5-10% Irish Ancestry

ginia as there was against blacks. Wheeling became the center of Irish-Catholic settlement. But there were also smaller centers in most of the railroad towns of the state. Rural Irish-Catholic colonies also could be found in Lewis and Braxton counties.

After 1880, the European immigrants who came to America tended to come largely from southern or eastern Europe. West Virginia was no exception. Local coal companies hired labor agents to meet arriving immigrants in New York and bring them to the Mountain State.

Italians were among the first to respond to this lure. More than 14,000 Italian-born people were living in West Virginia in 1920, mostly in the Monongahela Valley and the southern coal fields. One of the talents that Italian immigrants brought was the ability to build with stone. Many West Virginia communities, especially in the coal fields, are full of the beautifully constructed stone walls and buildings they made.

Sometimes West Virginia employers went to Europe to recruit specific types of workers. For example, a zinc-smelting company near Clarksburg recruited zinc workers from Galicia in northern Spain. The result was the tiny Spanish-speaking community of Spelter, in Harrison County. The town is known to its inhabitants as "Zizi," which is easier for Spanish-speaking people to pronounce.

But most immigrants came to West Virginia on their own and traveled to places where they were told that work could be found. During the decade from 1910-1920, for example, Weirton - in Hancock County - had a reputation of being a good place to work. Members of twenty-two different nationalities settled in the county during these years, when immigration from southern and eastern Europe was at its peak.

How the first member of a particular group decided to settle in a particular spot would make a fascinating story. But, in most cases, that person and his or her reasons for coming to a particular place are unknown. We do know that, once a few members of a group became well-established somewhere, other members followed.

Can immigrants and their children, who value the language and culture of their old-country heritage, make good Americans? Today we know that the answer is *yes*. We know that someone's ethnicity is not the same thing as his or her loyalty to a particular nation. But during the time around World War I (1914-1919), this question worried American leaders. Hostility among ethnic peoples and nations was tearing Europe apart. Some Americans feared that ethnic identity here would lead to a lack of unity within the United States. The public schools in particular became an instrument to "Americanize" immigrants and their children, who were pressured to abandon

West Virginia Division of Tourism

Ethnicity has been an important influence in West Virginia history. Events like the Italian Heritage Festival in Clarksburg serve as annual reminders of West Virginians' ethnic "roots."

their native languages and cultural values.

Partly as a means of resisting this pressure, Roman-Catholic ethnic groups founded their own schools. Eventually, there were Catholic high schools in Wheeling, Weirton, McMechen, Fairmont, Clarksburg, Morgantown, Charleston and Huntington. Elementary schools were found in these cities and several smaller ones. Thus, ethnicity refused to disappear. Instead, ethnic groups founded American-style voluntary associations such as the German Turnvereins, the Italian-American Sons of Italy, the Polish-American Polish National Alliance and the Irish-Catholic Knights of Columbus. Ethnic organizations served several purposes. They served as a means of socializing. Meetings were settings where immigrants, their children and their grandchildren felt comfortable. Ethnic organizations also reinforced the group's sense of identity and provided ways of meeting the mutual needs of its members, such as insurance programs. Finally, ethnic organizations were places where the values of American industrial society could be taught and explained.

National Park Service Photo

A one-room school in a Greenbrier County community founded by Irish immigrants. This photo was taken sometime between 1915 and 1920.

10.2 Religion

Religion was often one of the most powerful ways in which ethnic groups expressed and maintained their identity. At the same time, religious organizations also served as a means of breaking down ethnic differences.

Almost every ethnic group in West Virginia was originally associated with a particular church or religious tradition. The early ethnic/religious groups included Lutherans, Evangelicals and Pietists from Germany; Quakers and Methodists from Wales; Scottish and Scotch-Irish Presbyterians; and Baptists, Methodists and Episcopalians from England and Ireland.

In the early nineteenth century, a great revival of religious enthusiasm, called the "Great Awakening," went a long way toward breaking down ethnic and religious barriers within these groups. The Methodist and Baptist churches, in particular, became very broad-based organizations, with effective means of recruiting new members. Protestants from different ethnic backgrounds joined these churches. Gradually, people's religious identity became more important than their ethnicity.

Later, something similar happened within the Catholic Church. Originally, the Irish held most positions of authority within American Catholicism. The first Catholic bishops of Wheeling, for example, were Irish. Then Germans, Italians, Polish, Hungarians and other Catholic groups joined the church in greater numbers, each expressing its own religious customs and values. At first, there was tension - especially between the Irish and the later-arriving Catholic immigrants. The Irish-Catholic leadership tended to treat Italians and other non-Irish Catholics as a "problem." Eventually, however, these barriers gave way to a general sense of Catholic religious identity, embracing all of the Catholic ethnic groups.

The core of any religious group's identity, then, remained its belief in a certain set of convictions. Beginning in the Statehood Period, the Catholics and the larger Protestant churches created new organizations and strengthened their identities. Protestant churches, for example, founded Sunday schools, special clubs for young people, missionary organizations, athletic teams, musical groups and social-service organizations. Catholics created similar institutions in addition to their existing network of schools. They also founded hospitals in Wheeling, Morgantown and Clarksburg.

Some Protestants, however, found the "worldliness" of such activities to be unsatisfactory. Many Baptist churches in southern West Virginia retained their loyalty to what they called "primitive" principles. Members of such churches practiced their beliefs within their own congregations, with few if any links to other organizations. Other Protestants withdrew into smaller churches, which stressed the importance of "fundamental" Christian doctrine. Many of these placed a high value on shared religious experiences. These fundamentalist churches, such as Pentecostal Holiness and the Church of God, have become an important part of West Virginia life in the twentieth century.

The importance of ethnicity and religion to a group's identity varies from group to group. Jews, for example, have been able to maintain their identity in West Virginia without a large religious establishment. This has been partly due, perhaps, to prejudice against Jews (anti-Semitism) on the part of non-Jews.

Nevertheless, in the larger cities, Jewish communities built synagogues and established Hebrew schools as soon as they were able, which in Wheeling was in 1849 and in Charleston in 1858. For the small Greek and Russian Orthodox and Byzantine Catholic communities of northern West Virginia, the establishment of a church meant the preservation of both religious and ethnic identity against great odds.

The church played a particularly vital role in African-American communities. After the Civil War, for example, white authorities - in defiance of state law - refused to establish a school for African-American children in the Kanawha salt district. The schools were established by African-American preachers, who used funds collected from their desperately poor congregations. Booker T. Washington attended such a school. Later, churches became one of the most effective means of preaching the doctrine of self-improvement that Washington developed. As with other ethnic groups, African-American churches were effective tools of maintaining group ties. They provided means by which church members could take care of each other and establish a sense of group solidarity. As with other ethnic groups, churches also helped African-Americans learn and practice the values that helped them get along in the larger society.

Library of Congress

African-American institutions like this McDowell County church promoted self-improvement during the Industrial Period.

One of the worldly activities of religious groups has been their adoption of pressure-group tactics to advance religious values through government action. The most successful example was the prohibition campaign of the Methodist, Baptist and other Protestant churches. The movement favored banning the manufacture, sale and consumption of alcohol. It appeared in West Virginia during the 1850s and again in the 1880s.

These early campaigns were not successful, despite widespread support among Protestant church members. It was not until the churches founded a pressure group together that the "temperance" campaign succeeded. Their interdenominational pressure group was called the Anti-Saloon League. It was supported by funds collected from church congregations. The league worked steadily and systematically to establish prohibition, first on a county-by-county basis, then on a statewide basis

WV State Archives

SAVE THE YOUNG MEN. VOTE

GOD SEES EVERY VOTE.

A parade float promoting "Christian temperence" in Clarksburg. The temperence movement was successful in getting a statewide ban on the manufacture, sale, and consumption of alcohol in 1912.

in 1912 - seven years before it became national law. Although the measure was opposed by most Catholics and many Episcopalians and Lutherans, prohibition remained in effect in West Virginia until 1933, when it was repealed nationally.

Similarly, Catholics and other religious organizations began adopting pressure-group tactics on another issue during the 1970s. Their hope was to reverse certain court decisions that allowed pregnant women to have abortions. As it gathered momentum in the '80s and early '90s, the anti-abortion campaign adopted direct-action tactics. The campaign eventually forced federal officials to review laws legalizing abortion.

A direct-action campaign also was used in 1974 and 1975, when fundamentalist churches in Kanawha County attempted to remove English textbooks from the public schools. This campaign included demonstrations, rallies and wildcat strikes by coal miners who supported the cause. The conflict also led to violence, including shootings and bombings. These events drew nationwide attention to West Virginia but did not result in the removal of the books. Significantly, religious leaders from other Protestant churches opposed the fundamentalist "anti-textbook" campaign. Thus, the controversy demonstrated that, while religion has been an important force in West Virginia life, it is by no means a unified one.

10.3 Social Class

Social scientists have used two other concepts to describe West Virginia's group life, **region** and **social class**. Anyone who looks at any modern society can see that there is social inequality. By "social inequality" we mean differences in levels of wealth, power, or in social prestige that individuals enjoy. The concept of social class is based upon the perception of these different levels.

Determining which individuals belong to which class is a complicated problem. It depends upon what you are measuring and where you draw the line. People can be ranked differently in terms of their income, power, family prestige, or job title. But in everyday language, we generally speak in terms of "upper," "middle," and "lower" classes. "Upper class" carries the image of people who have lots of money, prestigious families and jobs, and a great deal of power to make other people carry out their wishes. "Lower class" summons the image of people who work with their hands, have a limited income and very little power. The middle class is everyone in between, including - in the United States - some upper-class and many lower-class people who think of themselves as being middle-class.

There is nothing new about social inequality. It is often a feature of traditional societies as well as of industrial societies today. Think back to the world of the Mound Builders, where a few people were given fancy burials and everyone else presumably got plain ones. But social inequality stands out more in an industrial society. Inequality in industrial societies seems to contrast distinctly with that of traditional societies for at least three reasons.

First, political democracy rested on the belief that everyone is created equal. Second, modern mass production - say, along an automobile assembly line - depended upon the cooperation of many people. This seemed to imply that the wealth created by production should be distributed more evenly. Thirdly, a belief in industrial progress inspired many people to work harder and turn out more goods. But it also inspired a belief in prosperity for all. People thought that the Industrial Age would weaken or destroy the barriers between them, including the barrier of social inequality.

During the early twentieth century, several groups proposed to end social inequality by taking political action. Of these political-reform groups working in West Virginia, the **Socialist Party** was perhaps the most significant. The Socialists' idea was that all members of the lower or "working" class should vote together. Then they would out-number everyone else. Once it was in control of the government, the lower class (or the Socialist Party) could use its new political power to take over the economic system. The Socialists argued that an economic system operated by the state would be fairer and more efficient. Factories that belonged to the public instead of private owners would lead to lower prices and less waste, they said. Everyone would be able to buy everything they really needed under the socialist system, at least in theory. No one would be better off than other citizens just because they were rich.

The Socialists published these views in labor newspapers in Wheeling, Huntington and Charleston. But their party won only limited support in West Virginia and the nation. Party members were elected to some city and county offices around Wheeling and Charleston, along with other offices in a few small industrial communities. They were also elected to leadership positions in the United Mine Workers and other unions and to the leadership of the state Federation of Labor in 1912.

Many reformers did not agree with the party's entire program but supported parts of it. For example, a coalition of middle- and upper-class reformers in Wheeling tried to get the city to buy its privately-owned electric company. The reformers suggested that industrial facilities should remain privately owned. But, they said, public utilities were best owned and operated by the government.

In terms of their ambitions, the Socialists' successes were disappointing. One basic problem was people's rejection of the "social class" concept. People might be part of the working class, but they don't necessarily feel any sense of identity with this group. Socialists believed that it was their responsibility to arouse this sense of identity, which they called **class consciousness**. They were not very successful in this effort. Class consciousness often developed among workers who were engaged in labor struggles. But non-Socialist labor leaders, such as John L. Lewis, channeled these feelings into demands for higher wages and shorter working hours.

Another consideration is that Socialists found it difficult to obtain a fair hearing for their views. During World War I, socialism came to be identified with pacifism and with foreign revolutionary movements. In this climate, it was considered unpatriotic to advance any socialist views. Even before the war, in 1913, West Virginia Governor Henry D. Hatfield forced two socialist newspapers to close down and had their presses destroyed.

10.4 Regional
Culture

The concept of *region* is similar to the concept of social class. Both originate in social analysis. This means that the concepts can be used to describe groups of people. But, at the same time, people are not necessarily conscious of belonging to these groups.

Region started out as a concept used by geologists and geographers to classify differences in the surface of the earth. Late in the nineteenth century, the term began to be used to classify cultural differences. The concept of a **regional culture**, then, refers to a geographic concentration of cultural patterns within a larger national culture. By 1920, there was a large body of social analysis that described the Southern Appalachian region as the home of one of the most distinctive regional cultures in the United States. The discoverers of this cultural region gave it the name "Appalachia," a term originally used by geologists. These discoverers included fiction and travel writers, such as West Virginia's David Hunter Strother (who wrote under the name of "Porte Crayon"). They also included teachers and clergymen, nearly all of whom came to the southern mountains from cities in the north or in England.

Appalachia seemed distinctive to these people because of the survival of a **folk culture**. A folk culture is one in which customs, skills and values are transmitted from generation to generation on an informal, face-to-face basis. It contrasted with twentieth-century American culture, transmitted largely through organized schooling and mass communication.

Topper Sherwood

The best-known feature of Appalachian regional culture is folk music. Some Appalachian folk songs have been traced back to seventeenth-century England and Scotland. Others originated as spontaneous forms of entertainment or commentary on current events. Besides folk music, the discoverers of Appalachia also found a great variety of folk-art forms, such as stories and regional speech dialects. Another discovery was handicrafts - especially needlework and wood-working.

What made Appalachian culture remarkable was the contrast between it and the culture of America's industrial society.

Old-fashioned quilting patterns were part of a major revival of regional culture, which the Mountain State experienced in the 1970s.

Originally, it was thought that industrialization would destroy folk culture. It was thought that mass entertainment would drive out folk tales and folk music. It was thought that machine-made products would eliminate handicrafts, and that schools and mass communications would erase all evidence of regional speech.

The discoverers of Appalachia hoped to prevent this. They set about finding ways to preserve regional cultures. They founded folk schools to transmit traditional skills, and festivals where folk-music performers could demonstrate their talent. Arts and crafts fairs were created where people displayed and sold hand-made products, such as musical instruments and patchwork quilts.

The earliest folk schools and festivals were established in Kentucky, North Carolina and Tennessee. Many folk-culture experts originally thought that West Virginia had already been "spoiled" by industrialization. But during the 1920s and 1930s, university and government researchers found a wealth of folk-life resources in West Virginia. Glenville State College established the first folk-music festival in 1950. The state Department of Commerce established arts and crafts fairs at Cedar Lakes, near Ripley, in 1963 and at Harpers Ferry in 1972. All three endeavors became great commercial successes, attracting thousands of tourists and inspiring dozens of additional fairs and festivals in other parts of the state.

Meanwhile, the radio and the recording industry helped to create a nationwide audience for folk music and for various blends of folk with commercial popular music, including "country," "old-time" and "bluegrass." The revival in Appalachian music, arts and crafts helped draw attention to West Virginia. These movements were partially behind the state's attraction for new "settlers," especially young white people from the nation's large urban areas.

By the mid-1970s, the Mountain State was undergoing a major cultural revival, with new artisans, musical groups and crafts organizations emerging in every corner of the state. Patchwork designs, based on old-fashioned quilting patterns, became an unofficial symbol for the cultural revival. In 1977, for example, huge colorful patchwork banners decorated the marble walls of the state Capitol for the inauguration of Governor John D. Rockefeller IV. A newly-formed state Department of Culture and History took over the fairs and festivals that year, and designed a kit of patchwork quilting materials to be distributed to school children.

There are other aspects of regional culture besides music and folklife. Consider the matter of crime. During the 1980s, people living in big cities became more and more concerned about an increased level of violent crime. The number of murders soared in cities such as Detroit, Houston and Washington, D.C., the nation's capital. Other forms of violent crime - such as rape, robbery, burglary and car theft - grew more common also. Yet throughout this decade, West Virginia had one of the lowest violent crime rates in the country. In fact, a 1985 survey of crime rates in 300 cities found that Wheeling was the most crime-free city in the country. To put it a little differently, the average American in another city was twice as likely to be murdered than the average Wheeling resident. The average American elsewhere was five times more likely to be robbed than a Wheeling resident, and four times more likely to have a car stolen. Cumberland, Maryland, with its West Virginia suburbs, ranked third in terms of safety from crime. Ten of the nation's twenty safest cities were found in Appalachia.

West Virginia's overall crime rate was the lowest of all the states from 1973 to 1991. The overall rate concealed different rates for different types of crime, however. West Virginia's 1990 murder rate was higher than twenty-two other states, although it was still lower than the national average. But the rate for other types of violent crime - that is, crimes which hurt or threaten to hurt people - was lower than all but six states. The rates for property crimes - robbery and car theft, for example - were even lower. Here, West Virginia had the lowest rate in the nation. Altogether, West Virginia was one of the safest places that an American could live.

The fact that West Virginia, one of the poorest states, was also one of the most crime-free, puzzled some experts. In large cities, crime is often linked with poverty. In West Virginia this link seems to be broken. Why? While experts have no firm answers, it seems reasonable to believe that the low crime rates of Appalachia are partly explained by its regional culture.

10.5 Region and Bureaucracy

In one form or another, the concept of "region" came to be used by various bureaucracies. In fact, the concept led to the creation of new levels of bureaucracy. New federal agencies were created to deal with *regional* problems of economic development. In order to benefit from these programs, federal law required local governments to create "regional planning districts." Eleven of these districts were established in West Virginia, embracing every county in the state.

In 1965, Congress established the **Appalachian Regional Commission** (ARC) to deal with the economic depression that had affected West Virginia and parts of nearby states. The ARC's creators wanted it to eliminate the *economic* differences between the Appalachian region and the rest of the nation. They were less concerned with preserving the *cultural* differences that had come to be admired. The ARC thus spent millions of dollars of state and federal funds on capital goods, all in the hope of bringing West Virginia's economy up to the national level. ARC projects included parks, libraries, sanitation and water systems, rural trash collection and a system of high-speed freeways. Its best-known project was a breathtaking bridge over the New River Gorge, in Fayette County.

WV Division of Tourism & Parks

The contrast between these two applications of the regional concept is instructive. In economic terms, "region" stood for a method of administration, the continued development of bureaucracy and standardization, and the continuous growth of a more prosperous - and complex - way of life. The greatest projects of regional bureaucracy, then, were symbols of the conquest of nature. This type of regionalist faced the difficult economic challenges posed by West Virginia's mountainous terrain.

Construction of the New River Bridge was largely financed by the federal Appalachian Regional Commission.

In cultural terms, the "regional" concept implied just the opposite. Regional culture symbolized a reaction *against* the impersonality, uniformity and large scale of modern life. Cultural regionalism expressed distaste for mass production and mass media. It expressed a preference for hand-made goods, home-made entertainment, and for dealing with people face-to-face. Most of all, regional culture implied an *acceptance* of - not a battle against - the limits that nature imposes on people who live in the mountains.

Thus, while the first type of regionalist celebrated soaring bridges and highways, the second kind sang about country roads. Which song is the right song? Your generation of West Virginians will soon have its own chance to decide.

Study Questions - Chapter 10

1. What do religious groups and ethnic groups have in common? How are they different? Can you join an ethnic group you are not born into? What if someone marries "into" the group?

2. What do the concepts of **region** and **social class** have in common? How are they different? Could a regional political party ever get going comparable to the Socialist Party? What sort of issues might such a regional party address?

3. How does the *bureaucratic* idea of region differ from the *cultural* idea?

4. Compare the African-American experience of ethnicity with the British-American. How much does outside pressure - or its absence - have to do with a group's sense of identity?

5. Racial segregation as it existed in the West Virginia school system from 1863 to 1954 was a formal institution. That is, it was required by law. What types of informal segregation did black people confront in West Virginia during and after this period? Be sure to consult the pictures as well as the text.

6. Examine the two sides of West Virginia's state seal. In what ways do you see the idea of "region" expressed in terms of economic development? In what ways is "region" expressed in terms of culture?

WV State Archives

PART V:
Living in
West Virginia

Chapter 11:
Biography and Autobiography

Pearl Buck's mother never learned how to dance. In her old age, this became a source of regret to her. Her name was Carrie Stulting, and dancing seemed like such a beautiful and enjoyable thing to her. But Carrie had grown up in the Greenbrier Valley during the troubled years just after the Civil War. At a time of so much hardship and grief, it seemed foolish to spend time on amusements such as dancing.

Instead, Carrie busied herself with religious pursuits. She turned down an offer of marriage from a fun-loving man she knew, and instead married a stern and solemn preacher. The preacher took Carrie away to China, where he served as a missionary. Thus Carrie's daughter, Pearl, grew up thousands of miles from her West Virginia birthplace. During the 1920s, Pearl Buck became a world-famous writer. She interpreted Chinese life and culture to millions of readers in the United States and Europe.

This story is worth telling for a good reason. It makes a point about the relationship between great historical events and the lives of ordinary people. Up until now, this book has been primarily concerned with important events and social trends. These are relatively remote from the lives of ordinary people, or so it seems.

Most of us are interested mainly in the day-to-day events of our lives. We rarely see ourselves as the participants in historical events. This has been true even for people who are swept up in great disasters, such as economic depression or war. Soldiers and refugees in the Civil War and unemployed workers in the Great Depression were concerned, first of all, with surviving from day to day. It is only later that people look back and see that they had a role in making history.

People seldom feel that they are part of historical processes and events, but those events actually help shape their lives. If you had asked young Carrie Stulting why she never learned to dance, she might have given you any number of reasons. But at the end

Ideas and Issues:
Everyday History

WV Division of Culture & History

Pearl S. Buck's birthplace near Hillsboro, in Pocahantas County.

Jim Comstock

Pearl S. Buck

of her life, she looked back and saw that the reason was an historical event - the Civil War and its aftermath.

Of course such events influence more aspects of life than a young girl's decision about dancing. In one way or another, great events and processes of history shape all of the aspects of day-to-day life for ordinary people. This includes the ways people meet their needs for food, shelter, and clothing, as well as the ways they learn, work and play.

The rest of this book describes the lives of ordinary people in West Virginia. It will concentrate on the needs of everyday life: food, clothing and housing. The following chapters will explain how changes in these needs are related to the historical processes and events described in previous chapters.

11.1 The Lives of Not-So-Famous West Virginians

A second point to be made from the story of why Pearl Buck's mother never learned to dance is this: Much of the information we have today - information concerning the daily lives of people in the past - comes from studying the lives of famous people. We can study people's lives in several ways. If a person writes his or her own life history, that history is called **autobiography**. If it is written by someone else, it is called **biography**. **Reminiscences** and **memoirs** are forms of autobiography that describe particular episodes in someone's life. There are many biographies or autobiographies about famous people. But there are very few about ordinary people. This is true for two reasons. First, readers are naturally much more curious about famous people than about ordinary folks like themselves. Secondly, ordinary people are likely to believe that there was nothing in their lives worth writing about. And so historians often must turn to the life histories of famous people to find out about everyday life in the past.

Thus, we know about Carrie Stulting's decision about dancing because she was Pearl Buck's mother. She told the story to her daughter, who became a famous writer and told it to one of *her* biographers. Carrie probably could have told us a lot more about life in West Virginia when she was a girl. But this information is lost to us, because biographies concentrate on her famous daughter. Pearl Buck, unlike her mother, spent very little time in West Virginia and was not much involved with its daily patterns of life.

The chart on the next page lists and describes ten of the most famous historical figures associated with West Virginia

NAME	BORN-DIED	LIVED OR VISITED IN WEST VIRGINIA	IS FAMOUS AS
Daniel Boone	1734-1820	1791	explorer, hunter, Indian fighter
George Washington	1732-1799	1740s-1750s, 1770, 1784	land speculator, soldier, U.S. president
Aaron Burr	1756-1836	1805	soldier, politician, adventurer
Stonewall Jackson	1824-1863	1824-1851, 1861-1862	soldier
Robert E. Lee	1807-1870	1861, 1868	soldier
John Brown	1800-1859	1859	abolitionist
Booker T. Washington	1859?-1915	1866-1873	educator
Mother Jones	1830-1930	1902, 1912-1921	labor union organizer
John W. Davis	1873-1955	1873-1915, 1924	politician, diplomat, presidential candidate
Pearl S. Buck	1892-1973	1892	writer, Nobel Prize winner

These are ten of the most famous people associated with West Virginia. In some cases, the biographies of famous people provide important sources of information about everyday life in West Virginia. For example, Booker T. Washington wrote one of the greatest American autobiographies of the nineteenth century, a time when black people created relatively few autobiographies. A study of Washington's life provides scarce and valuable information about the everyday experiences of other African-Americans who lived here at that time.

history. They are Daniel Boone, George Washington, Aaron Burr, Stonewall Jackson, Robert E. Lee, John Brown, Booker T. Washington, Mother Jones, John W. Davis and Pearl Buck. These people are famous because each of them played an important role in the history of the nation. Each of them also had an important connection with West Virginia. Yet not one of them lived an entire lifetime here. John W. Davis spent more time here than any of the others, yet he left his home in Clarksburg permanently at the age of thirty-eight in 1911. Stonewall Jackson spent the first eighteen years of his life in various West Virginia locations. The other eight people lived here for much shorter periods, ranging from a few weeks to a few years.

Still, the stories of less-famous people usually tell us the most about everyday life in West Virginia. What follows are the stories of eleven people who were *not* famous, or at least they were much less famous than the ten people listed in the chart on page 217:

Joseph Doddridge (1769-1826) was a minister and doctor who lived in western Pennsylvania and West Virginia's Northern Panhandle during the Frontier Period. In 1824 he published a book called *Notes on the Settlement and Indian Wars of the Western Parts of Virginia and Pennsylvania.* "Doddridge's Notes" is the informal title of this book. It contains the best single account of daily life on the Virginia frontier during the Frontier Period.

Mary Jane (Mollie) Hansford was born near Paint Creek in eastern Kanawha County in 1828. She lived there and at Coalsmouth (now called St. Albans) until 1853, when she married and moved to Winchester, Virginia. After her first husband died, she returned to the Kanawha Valley. She married again and lived there until her death in 1900. She wrote her autobiography near the end of her life, but it was not published until 1975. It is one of the liveliest accounts of everyday life during the Statehood Period.

Rebecca Harding moved to Wheeling with her parents in 1836, when she was five years old. Except for a brief period when she was sent to school in nearby Washington, Pennsylvania, she lived in Wheeling until 1863. Then she moved away to be married. This made her an eyewitness to many of the historical events of her day, such as the achievement of West Virginia statehood. But she witnessed much more. Her story, *Life in the Iron Mills*, was published in 1861. It was the first literary work by a West Virginian to capture nationwide attention. It was also the first attempt to portray in American literature the lives of workers in the new industrial society. Her description of immigrant iron workers in Wheeling was harsh and gloomy but factual. Her reminiscence, *Bits of Gossip*, was published in 1904. It gives a view of the more cheerful side of life in Wheeling during Rebecca Harding's youth.

George McIntosh was born in Fayette County in 1868. He grew up in Huntington. George lived in Huntington, Fayetteville, and Hinton as an adult. He became a newspaper editor and participated in political events. But his autobiography is more interesting for his account of growing up in the Industrial Period than for his inside view of politics. The autobiography was written for his family and was never published. But the family placed a copy in the West Virginia University Library, where George McIntosh's story will be preserved.

Fred Mooney was born in a remote part of Kanawha County in 1888. He grew up to become a coal miner and a leader of the United Mine Workers of America. His autobiography, like 'George McIntosh's, found its way into the West Virginia University Library. The library published Fred Mooney's story in 1967 under the title *Struggle in the Coal Fields*. It gives a first-hand account of the mine wars in the West Virginia coal fields between 1912 and 1927.

Julia Davis was born in Clarksburg in 1900. Her mother died when she was born. Because her father, John W. Davis, was busy with his career as a lawyer and politician, Julia was raised by her grandparents. She spent the school year with the Davises in a large and solemn house in the center of Clarksburg. She spent her summers with her mother's parents, the MacDonalds, on a lively and fun-filled farm in the Shenandoah Valley near Charles Town. The contrast between these two homes, plus Julia Davis's talent as a writer, makes for one of the liveliest of West Virginia autobiographies. It is called *Legacy of Love*, and was published in 1961.

Ted Arrington was born in southwestern Virginia, but he moved to Huntington and spent almost forty years as a West Virginia businessman. Arrington was a salesman, selling tobacco products to small stores throughout southern and central West Virginia. His career extended from 1925 to 1964. His memoirs, *Salesman of Appalachia*, contain tales that he swapped with the storekeepers he visited and descriptions of the towns and people he encountered. Ted Arrington's fondness for people and his understanding of them shine through every page of the book.

Lizzie Grant told her story in a somewhat different way. She told it through **oral history**. That is, she answered questions by an interviewer, who wrote her answers down. In this way, we now have a narrative of her life as an African-American slave in the Kanawha Valley during the years just before the Civil War. The oral history also tells us about her experience as a free adult working in West Virginia and in Texas where she moved a few years after the war.

Bridget ("Biddie") Greene and **J. Ross Tennant** were two other West Virginians who showed us how daily life is related to historical events and processes. Greene and Tennant were two people who did research and created their genealogies or "family trees." They wrote them for their friends and their relatives, but went beyond the typically lifeless branches showing births, deaths and marriages. Greene's and Tennant's trees were colored with lively character sketches of the family members they knew. Thus, their work is of interest to people outside of their own families.

Joseph Doddridge, Mollie Hansford, Rebecca Harding, George McIntosh, Fred Mooney, Julia Davis, Ted Arrington, Lizzie Grant, Biddie Greene and J. Ross Tennant were not ordinary West Virginians in the strictest sense. After all, it isn't an ordinary thing to write your autobiography. But these people created, out of their own life experiences, something larger than themselves. They created stories showing how day-to-day life is related to historical events and processes.

In addition to these eleven not-so-famous (but not quite typical) people, many other West Virginians wrote autobiographies, reminiscences or memoirs. The lives of millions of others are revealed in documents and newspapers or in the objects they made and used which have survived after them. There is no way to be sure that any one person was typical. But many people probably lived as these eleven did. In the chapters that follow, their stories provide many examples of how West Virginians lived at different times in our history.

The rest of this book should help you apply the concepts you learned in previous chapters. In particular, review the the concepts of social change, evidence, inference, environment and culture in the Introduction and Chapter 1 of this book. See if you can identify some effects of environment, culture and social change on everyday life in West Virginia from the Frontier Period to the days of your grandparents. Do you think that your parents' and grandparents' stories would enable you to see how developments continued from the 1930s to the present time?

Library of Congress

This photo shows a group of children living in Monongalia County during the early 1930s.

Study Questions - Chapter 11

1. What is the difference between **biography** and **autobiography**? Which, in your opinion, is most likely to provide the most accurate evidence about an individual's life?

2. What are some advantages of studying the lives of famous people who were born in our state? What are some of the disadvantages?

3. Look at the photograph on this page. In what way might these children be witnesses to history?

Chapter 12:
Food

12.1 Food from the Forest

During the Frontier Period "it was no uncommon thing for families to live several months without a mouthful of bread." So wrote Joseph Doddridge. The same was true of vegetables. Believe it or not, children could hardly wait for the first vegetables to appear in the garden each summer. They went out every day to the "truck patch," as family gardens were called. They checked on the progress of the potatoes, squash, corn and beans. Late summer or early fall was a wonderful season of fresh vegetables and fruits. This was true, at least, for the settlements that were old enough to have orchards and gardens. There were also wild fruits, nuts and berries to be gathered in the forest.

At other times of the year people depended upon three types of food. First, there were vegetables that could be dried and stored: beans, pumpkins, or squashes, for example. Secondly, there were grains that could be ground into flour or meal. For pioneer West Virginians, corn was the most important staple - just as it had been for the Indians. In fact, a common name for the crudest form of ground corn was "Indian meal." Finally, there was fresh-killed meat. Hunting was the most important type of meat-producing activity during the Frontier Period. Joseph Doddridge wrote, "It frequently happened that there was no breakfast until it was obtained from the woods."

West Virginia Collection- WVU Library

A Frontier Period kitchen.

Despite the abundance of game in the forest, getting the meat on the table called for careful planning and organization. Hunting was best in middle or late fall. This was after the leaves were down but before the time of heavy snows. The deep snow of mid-winter made animals easier to track. But it also made life hard for the hunter. Winter's cold provided natural refrigeration, however. This meant that meat stored up in the fall months could last through the winter into the early spring. At least, it would last if the hunter had been lucky and skillful enough. The same was true of meat obtained from domestic animals. November, the prime month for hunting, was also the time for butchering hogs.

During the Frontier Period, people lived very close to nature. This did not make for very comfortable living. But they learned to recognize the resources of each season of the year and to make the most of them. The first fruit to ripen, Doddridge recalled, was the wild strawberry. Then came the service berries, which ripened in June. In mid-summer there were blackberries and wild raspberries. These were found in open places in the forest during the Frontier Period. Later these blackberry and raspberry bushes spread out along the fences of farms. There were also wild plums, cherries and grapes to be harvested, and the fruit of the hawthorn bushes. Doddridge recalled that the hawthorns were special favorites of children.

Besides late-ripening fruits, the fall brought hickory nuts, walnuts, hazelnuts and chestnuts. These were added to the food and meat stored up during the fall harvests and hunts. In late winter and early spring came the time when maple trees could be tapped for their "sugar." Most of the maple sap was made into syrup. But some was spilled out on the snow to provide a kind of instant candy for children.

After the sugaring time came the time of hunger and waiting for spring. For people who depended upon the rhythms of nature, spring was a time of hardship as well as a time of renewal. The food stored up from the previous fall was gone. The new crops of the fields and the berries and fruits of the forest had not yet matured. There was only meat to depend on. Meat without vegetables or grains caused nutritional problems. This diet left children with an unsatisfied feeling that Joseph Doddridge never forgot. Ramps or wild leeks are wild vegetables that appear in the forest in the early springtime. They have a bad odor when cooked but are otherwise wholesome. You can see why ramps became a traditional West Virginia food. *Stop*

The shift from a forest to a farming economy occurred at different places at different times. In districts with good transportation and good land, it took place soon after settlement. This was true of the Shenandoah Valley or along the Ohio River, for

12.2 Farming and Food

example. In the remotest parts of central and southern West Virginia, the shift was never complete. Some people in these places were still following pioneer ways in the early twentieth century. But in most parts of West Virginia, the shift from a forest to a farming economy began around 1800 and continued through the Statehood Period.

The spread of farming brought about several types of changes in West Virginia's food. First, the variety and quality of food increased. Vegetables continued to be grown in "truck patches," but farmers also planted large fields of corn, hay and grain crops. These provided food for animals as well as people. Farmers also created pasture land on hillsides that were too steep to plow and in bottom lands that were subject to flooding. These pastures also provided food for animals. This meant that the animals provided more and better food for people. Animals provided food directly, as in the case of cattle and hogs. They also provided food indirectly, as with the oxen, mules and horses, which provided much of the muscle power for farm work.

Farmers also planted orchards. In fact, orchards were one sign of a mature and well-settled district because fruit trees took a long time to grow and produce. Joseph Doddridge's father planted and cultivated peach trees, apple trees, pear trees and cherry trees, all of which eventually bore fruit. Joseph described the wild fruits of his childhood as "inferior in size and flavor" to the cultivated varieties he tasted later.

Pasture lands and orchards brought another benefit in the blossoms of clover and fruit trees. Blossoms provided the nectar from which bees made honey. Tame honeybees were not native to West Virginia. They came with the settlers. Bees made a different-flavored honey after each particular tree or flower bloomed. The most delicious honey was made after the bees visited the blossoms of locust trees, which bloom in late spring. In fact, these trees became known as honey locusts.

Farming also brought improvements in the preservation of food. Consider the example of salt. During the Frontier Period, salt was scarce and expensive. Joseph Doddridge's father had to go back east across the mountains to obtain his family's supply. The small amount of salt he obtained in this way was too valuable to be used as a preservative.

The Kanawha Valley salt industry made salt available cheaply and in large amounts after 1800, however. This made it possible for farm families to preserve some of the meat they butchered each fall. Kanawha salt also made possible the rise of a meat-packing industry. This industry was centered in Cincinnati. Commercial meat-packers preserved beef and pork by packing it in barrels. This product was sold through merchants and stores. This source made meat available to town-dwelling families and to others who didn't farm or hunt.

Another traditional method of preserving food was drying. Every mature farm had facilities for dry storage. Smokehouses, for example, were used to preserve meat, especially pork, which had been dried in the smoke of a hickory-wood fire. Winterhouses or root cellars were usually dug into a hillside. They provided a place where potatoes, cabbages, onions, turnips and other root crops could be kept cool and dry without freezing. Springhouses were for summer storage. Here milk, butter and eggs could be kept in containers floating in cool spring water right at the place where it emerged from a hillside.

People like Lizzie Grant, who were held as slaves on other people's farms, had no control over the products of their labor. Her owner kept a large garden and, Lizzie recalled, "he gave the slaves what he wanted them to have out of his garden," which usually meant some greens "and a few potatoes." Many other ex-slaves recalled being hungry much of the time, or only getting cheap and fatty foods. Lizzie, however, remembered being well-fed:

> Yes we had plenty to eat such as it was. We had cornbread gathered right out of the field as we ate it grated by hand, nothing in it but water and salt. We had pork and beef cooked on the open fireplace and...it sure was good. We had plenty rabbit, possum and fish, but I never did care anything about such except fish. I sure did like fish fried good and brown on a big flat iron skillet in plenty [of] hog grease. That was all the kind of grease we had back there in those early days.

12.3 The Industrialization of Food Processing

The Industrial Period brought still other forms of storage. The spread of railroads made it possible to ship ice harvested from lakes in New York, New England and the Great Lakes region to towns in West Virginia.

Icehouses in the towns distributed the ice to consumers (usually town dwellers, since farm families had spring houses). "Ice boxes," designed to hold ice obtained in this manner, became

Topper Sherwood

Two examples of early food preservation. A cloth or waxed paper was pulled over the jar's lip and tied with string.

the first step toward refrigerated food storage in the home.

Today we think of "canning" as an old-fashioned method of preserving and storing food. But it was the very latest thing in the late nineteenth century. Canning involves sealing cooked food in airtight containers. It did not become a widespread method of storing food until cheap containers became available. Hand-blown glass bottles were no good for preserving food because they were too expensive and could not always be made airtight. Metal containers made from iron or steel would rust and spoil the food. Pottery was no better. The photograph at the top of this page shows the kind of preserve jars made by West Virginia potters between 1790 and 1850. These jars had no lids. They were closed by a bit of oiled paper tied with a string. Several of these jars might be used to preserve food for a family. But they would not keep bacteria out of the food for very long. Something else was needed to preserve large amounts of food for longer periods.

Topper Sherwood

Four nineteenth-century canning methods (from left)
1) A Globe jar - 1886
2) Jar with screw-on top and glass liners - 1858
3) "The Weir" jar - 1892
4) Metal can sealed with melted lead - 1869.

That something else was tin cans. Cans were made by "tinplating." This process placed a thin coating of tin on steel cans. The tin would not rust. The steel was strong and durable. The combination was thus ideal for storing cooked food for long periods of time.

Tinplating did not become widely practiced in the United States until after 1890. Between 1890 and 1910, tinplate factories were set up in Clarksburg, Morgantown, Follansbee, Wheeling and Weirton. (Not all of these factories made tin cans, however. Some made building materials.) Sealing tin cans was best done by machines. Thus, a new industry had begun to process food in factories. However, not all canned food came from factories. Businessmen in small towns all over West Virginia rented food-processing machines every summer. They set up canneries where local farmers and gardeners could bring their food to be canned. The cannery owners either charged a fee for this service, or they kept a share of the canned food to sell to stores. Either way, these small canneries greatly increased the food-storage abilities of West Virginia farm families. There was also canning done at home. Despite its name, home canning did not use tin cans. It used glass jars. Like tin cans, machine-made glass jars first became available in large amounts at the end of the nineteenth century. This was another development which gave a big boost to the industrialization of food-processing.

12.4 The Development of Stores

Another big change affecting food after the Settlement Period came in the area of distribution. Pioneer families were not completely self-sufficient. But they came as close to self-sufficiency as anyone in West Virginia, except perhaps the Indians. Stores appeared soon after settlement to make available the things that pioneer families could not make for themselves. These stores sold bullets, knives, kettles, nails and other molded iron products or they sold tropical foods, such as coffee, sugar and tea, which Americans had learned to enjoy.

These first stores were usually small affairs which did not last very long. What happened was this: a traveling merchant or local settler obtained a stock of goods. He then opened a store in a corner of a cabin or building and kept it open until the stock of goods was all sold. Later the stores became permanent establishments. They remained open most of the year and for several years instead of a few weeks or months.

During the early Settlement Period, storekeepers handled very little cash. Their customers bartered (traded) forest products or whiskey for store goods: furs for nails, ginseng for coffee, whiskey for knives or kettles or bullets, for example. But later, cash trading became the rule, not the exception. In 1784, for example, a Greenbrier Valley storekeeper did most of his trade through barter. Only 2 percent of his business was in cash. Ten years later he and other Greenbrier merchants were doing much more business in cash. Barter was still important. But customers offered farm products rather than forest products in exchange for store goods. They also bartered services such as spinning, shoemaking, land-clearing, blacksmithing and so on.

A cash basis for store trading was established in most parts of West Virginia within ten or fifteen years of permanent settlements. Yet barter never entirely disappeared during the Statehood and Industrial periods. In Ross Tennant's neighborhood in Monongalia County, farm families traded butter and eggs for store products during the 1890s. In the early twentieth century, people in Logan and other southern West Virginia communities still bartered forest products such as pelts, nuts, ginseng, wild honey and beeswax. Barter enjoyed a revival in popularity during the Great Depression of the 1930s, when many West Virginians found cash very scarce.

A different sort of barter took place in coal field communities. When coal companies opened new mining operations in unpopulated districts, they usually built houses to rent to their workers. They also built stores to sell workers the food and household products they needed. These company houses and company stores often made a good profit. But they involved very little cash trading.

Instead of cash, the coal companies paid their miners in "scrip." This consisted of metal tokens. Each token stood for a certain value in regular money. The scrip could be traded for

Topper Sherwood

goods in the company store. However, the scrip issued by each individual company was different from the scrip of other companies. The miner was usually forced to trade only at his company's store in order to obtain full value for the scrip. "Independent" storekeepers would take the scrip only at two-thirds or three-fourths of its value, if they took it at all. The practice of issuing scrip made it hard for miners to obtain cash. Yet they some-

Coal companies in rural areas often paid miners in "scrip," metal tokens that were traded in company stores.

times found ways around the problem. Ted Arrington remembers that miners during the 1920s and '30s used scrip to obtain cigarettes at the company stores. They would take the cigarettes to Williamson or other towns to trade for things like meals in a restaurant or even cash.

The stores of the Statehood and Industrial periods were small compared to the large supermarkets of our day. In rural areas, storekeeping was often a part-time job. Usually it was combined with farming or some other occupation, such as postmaster. A store in a rural district or coal town often served as the local post office. The salary which the storekeeper earned as postmaster added to the money earned in the store.

A coal company store in Fayette County around 1929.

National Park Service photo

Most of these stores sold what were known as "dry goods." These included cloth, clothing, household products such as pots and pans, patent medicines and drugs. But specifically the term referred to foods that were sold according to their dry weights and could be stored for a long time without spoiling. This included such things as flour, corn meal, sugar, molasses, salt, spices, baking powder, lard, beans, preserved meats and tobacco. "Wet goods" meant liquor and beer. These were available legally in saloons before 1914 and illegally from makers of moonshine. The legal sale of liquor and beer was prohibited in West Virginia between 1914 and 1933. Between 1933 and 1990, liquor could be legally sold only in liquor stores ("state stores") operated by the state government. Beer came to be sold by storekeepers. Sometimes a small tavern or "beer joint" was combined with a small rural dry-goods store. Another combination that was popular in the early twentieth century was dry goods and gasoline.

Even after food began to be processed in factories by large companies, dry goods remained the principal product of small country stores. Ted Arrington, for example, sold tobacco products to rural and company stores in southern West Virginia from 1925 to 1963. Most of the other salesmen he encountered there before 1950 also represented dry-goods companies: flour manufacturers, for example, or drug companies. Rural and company stores also sold canned goods, such as processed vegetables and condensed milk. But such products made up less of the stores' business than they would today.

Fresh vegetables, fruit and dairy products were things

National Park Service photo

Rural stores in the early twentieth century, like this one in Summers County, sold canned vegetables, biscuits, tobacco and other dry goods.

which most West Virginians provided for themselves during the Statehood and Industrial periods. This was true even for people who did not live on farms. Rebecca Harding's house was in the center of Wheeling during the Statehood Period. Yet her family had a garden which produced melons and vegetables. There was also a cherry tree which was Rebecca's favorite place to hide and sit by herself.

Though she didn't mention it, her family probably had other fruit trees. They may also have had chickens and a cow. Most middle-class urban families did before 1920. There were milk cows in a stable behind Julia Davis's home in downtown Clarksburg. Her aunts made apple butter in a big kettle over a campfire in the backyard, just as farm women did. However, Julia doesn't say whether the apples came from their own trees or were purchased from farmers nearby. Usually farmers drove into town in late summer or early fall, their wagons loaded with apples or peaches for town families to buy. Farmers continued to do this in Greenbrier Valley towns as late as the 1950s, except that they changed from wagons to old Model T trucks whose horns called customers out to the street to make purchases.

In the coal towns where Fred Mooney lived, miners' families created small truck patches where they grew vegetables and corn. Farmers also visited the towns with wagon-loads of vegetables and fruit, fresh butter, eggs and milk. However, not all coal companies supplied residents of their towns with space to grow vegetables. Some companies kept farmers from selling produce in their towns because this competed with the company stores.

Not all West Virginians had enough to eat. The Wheeling mill workers in Rebecca Harding's stories had nothing to eat besides bread, potatoes, molasses and "flitch." Flitch was a kind of salt pork that was mostly fat and slightly spoiled or "rank." There were people in coal towns who lived on similar diets. During the first years of the Great Depression, unemployed workers and their families rarely had enough to eat. Investigators from the Red Cross and other charity organizations found cases of actual starvation in the West Virginia coal fields.

12.5 Food in the Age of Bureaucracy

The growth of large organizations in the twentieth century brought about many changes in the ways that West Virginians obtained and consumed their food. There were three particularly important types of changes. First, people became much less dependent upon (or aware of) the forces of nature in obtaining their food supply. A second change was the growth of **mass merchandising**. Mass merchandising brought cheaper and more efficient ways to distribute food. And it created pressure, through advertising, for people to consume more food than they actually needed. Thirdly, governments became more involved in regulating the amount and content of the food supply.

When Biddie Greene was a little girl in the 1890s, an orange was something that most children saw only at Christmas time. Oranges were too rare and expensive to obtain at other times of the year. Twenty years later, they were common items in the stores of West Virginia's cities and larger towns. By 1950, West Virginians everywhere expected to see oranges in their supermarkets every week, all year long. Orange juice became a standard item in the daily menu of most families. Unless a family was very poor or a victim of unemployment, it could enjoy other tropical products as well. These included bananas, pineapples, apricots, lemons, grapefruits and limes.

Topper Sherwood

Tropical fruits cannot be grown in West Virginia or in any nearby state. The fact that West Virginians could obtain them easily and cheaply shows that they no longer depended on their local environment for all of their food. Products that couldn't be grown in West Virginia's climate (such as

Food in a modern supermarket.

tropical fruits) could be shipped in from places thousands of miles away such as California, Texas or Florida, or even New Zealand or Chile. This meant that consumers were no longer dependent upon their local climate's growing season. Fresh strawberries are available in February as well as in June; apples are as common in April as they are in October; tomatoes, lettuce, cucumbers, peppers and other garden vegetables are available all year round, not just in the summer. When it's winter here, these vegetables are grown in Florida or Latin America and then shipped north to our stores.

These changes are not confined to fruits and vegetables. Consider the matter of seafood. Occasionally, store keepers who lived near the Baltimore & Ohio Railroad ordered fresh oysters, crabs, shad and rockfish shipped in ice-packed barrels from Baltimore. This happened once a week in Harrisville, in Ritchie County, for example. But communities that did not have a railroad, or whose railroads did not lead directly to a saltwater port, were out of luck. Their seafood came canned, dried or salted, if it came at all. Today, however, it is common to find in West Virginia stores seafood from all over the world, not just from the nearest arm of the ocean, the Chesapeake Bay.

What made these changes possible? First, modern transportation and refrigeration make it possible for food to be moved quickly over great distances. Secondly, the invention of new food-preservation techniques (such as freezing and freeze-drying) make it possible to preserve more types of food over longer periods of time. Thirdly, there is the growth of mass merchandising, through chain stores and supermarkets. These are usually large bureaucratic organizations that distribute food from producers to consumers. But mass merchandising also includes the modern practice of advertising, which makes it possible to persuade consumers to accept strange new foods. Advertising also makes it possible to tell large numbers of people about special food values or quantities that become available. The Harrisville storekeeper who ordered oysters from Baltimore first had to be sure that there were enough oyster lovers in town to make the order profitable. He also had to make certain that they would come to his store to get the oysters when the train brought them. Mass merchandising solves these problems through advertising.

Advertising does more than inform, however. It also persuades. It is capable of persuading people to consume things that are not healthy - and sometimes even harmful to them. This problem first appeared in the area of patent medicines and drugs. Patent medicines are remedies that are developed and sold under a brand name rather than a scientific name, based on the ingredients. These medicines can be bought without a doctor's prescription. During the late nineteenth and early twentieth centuries, manufacturers sold a great variety of these medicines. Many of them were mostly alcohol. They made sick people feel good by making them a little drunk. They were marketed through newspaper advertising. The ads put forward all sorts of untrue claims about the medicines, including claims that they would cure all sorts of diseases - even serious diseases such as cancer or tuberculosis. These claims threatened the health of consumers. The ads persuaded people to consume these worthless drugs instead of seeking medical help for their health problems.

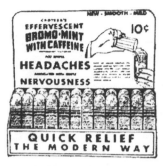

PATENT MEDICINE

Today, a lot of advertising concerns food products. This is particularly true of television advertising. Some of this advertising also concerns products that are harmful to consumers. For example, manufacturers have learned that children like pleasing tastes and interesting colors. They have learned to use chemicals to create these tastes and colors. Then they use television ads to persuade children to consume products that may in fact cause tooth decay and other health problems. Two examples of this type of food are breakfast cereals and candies with large quantities of sugar in them.

Industrialization has made possible the invention of a variety of foodlike products which have no food value to consumers. The popular term for such products is "junk food." Such products usually begin with some sort of natural food base. But their flavor is enhanced by chemicals. Health experts are concerned that, by taking the place of real food, junk food may cause health problems, particularly for children. Because of this, the West Virginia Department of Education put limits on the sale of junk food in schools in 1975.

Government agencies have become involved in managing the food supply in three ways. First, the federal government began in 1906 to try to prevent false advertising about food and drugs. It also tries to identify disease-causing chemicals and to stop their use. State and local governments have undertaken similar programs. The West Virginia Department of Health, for example, supervises the manufacture and marketing of dairy and meat products. It also inspects restaurants to make sure that they use sanitary food-preparation methods. This type of management is called **regulation**.

Secondly, the federal government has given **subsidies** to growers of certain food crops. A subsidy is money given by the government in order to encourage production or use of a particular product. Peanuts and peanut butter provide a good example of how food subsidies work. Beginning in the 1930s, government crop subsidies and education programs encouraged the growing of peanuts in the southern United States. (The peanut plant originally came from Africa.) The idea was to create a larger variety of crops in places that formerly had grown mostly cotton. Government-financed research also led to the development of new products, one of which was peanut butter. Advertising helped to introduce the new product to American consumers. Today West Virginians - along with other Americans - consume large amounts of peanut butter. They are usually unaware that this product was unknown before 1920 or that it is still unknown in most of the world. West Virginians of the Statehood or Industrial periods would probably have thought that peanut butter was a weird thing to eat, just as Europeans and Asians do today.

Besides regulation and subsidies, government agencies have also created welfare programs based on food. These programs supply food to needy people. Usually the programs are run by state agencies operating under federal guidelines. This practice began during the Great Depression. From 1933 to 1964, food was made available directly to the people who needed it. The food came in the form of "surplus commodities." This means that the food came from extra supplies of crops that had been grown with federal subsidies. Since only certain foods were subsidized, only certain foods were available to be given out. Some examples were flour, corn products and peanut butter. These commodities made for a dull diet. But they were better than nothing. In 1961, the federal government tested the first "food stamp" program in West Virginia. Food stamps were issued to people who were part of the program. The stamps could be used to buy food from stores. This made a greater variety of food products available than the surplus-commodities program had done.

Study Questions - Chapter 12

1. During the Frontier Period, fresh vegetables were a treat for children. Explain why this was true. What did people eat when there were no fresh vegetables?

2. What advantages for the seller does cash buying of goods have over bartering?

3. Why was the use of scrip an advantage for the coal companies?

4. Would you like to have "flitch" to eat at your dinner today? Why or why not? Why is flitch not a common food for us?

5. Honey, apples, and pizza have all been considered treats by children at different times in West Virginia history. Which one of these foods could be found in the state at every period of its history? Which one in only one period?

<table>
<tr><td colspan="2" align="center">Chapter 13:
Clothing</td></tr>
</table>

13.1 Clothes from the Forest

West Virginians of the Frontier Period obtained much of their clothing from the same place where they got much of their food: the forest. Animal pelts provided fur for hats and cloaks. Deerskins gave material for men's leggings and breeches. Shirts were also made from skins, although cloth shirts were more popular. Deerskin shirts "were very cold and uncomfortable in wet weather," Joseph Doddridge recalled. So were deerskin shoes or "shoepacks." These were simple moccasins. The settlers learned how to make them from the Indians. Young men sometimes adopted a complete Indian style of dress. This included leggings and a hunting shirt, with only a breech clout in between. This left the upper thigh and part of the hips naked. "The young warrior...was proud of his Indian-like dress," according to Doddridge. A few times he saw young men dressed this way in church.

Apart from their shoes, women and girls did not dress in skins. Their simple dresses were made from cloth. So were most of the men's hunting shirts. Since sheep were relatively scarce on the frontier, woolen fabrics were not easily available. Neither was cotton, since this sub-tropical plant could not be grown in West Virginia's climate. This left linen, which was woven from the fibers of the flax plant, or linsey, a mixture of the fibers of flax and wool. Linen also provided the bonnets or caps that women wore. The settlers had to prepare the materials from which they made their garments. Skins had to be dressed. Leather had to be tanned. Thread had to be spun, and fabric had to be woven. Both men and women worked at these tasks. Joseph Doddridge's father, for example, considered himself to be his neighborhood's best spinner of shoe thread. He also tanned his own leather. Sometimes groups came together to help with the harder jobs.

13.2 Textiles

Homespun cloth was warm and strong. But it was not very stylish or comfortable. Thus, people welcomed the chance to get "store bought" cloth. The coming of stores meant that silk, cotton, woolen and linen cloth could be bought by consumers who could afford them. These textiles generally became cheaper as the

**A WEST VIRGINIA FRONTIERSMAN
(OR "LONGHUNTER")**

Timothy Truman ©

A tri-cornered military hat of heavy felt. Broad-brimmed felt hats and even simple cloth head-sashes were also common. Contrary to typical stereo types, "coonskin" or fur hats were rare!

Long hair bound by ribbon in back.

Sometimes trade-beads were worn, as were "Asephedity" poultice bags, thought to ward off colds.

Sometimes called "The Kentucky Rifle," most of these single-shot, muzzle loaded flintlocks were actually hand-made by craftsmen in Pennsylvania.

A fringed "hunting frock" of thick linen or animal hide was worn over a cotton pullover shirt.

Powderhorn, hunting bag, and small "patch knife."

Other items of survival included a small hatchet or tomahawk, a heavy butcher's knife, and an awl for punching holes in leather and cloth.

TYPICAL DRESS OF A FRONTIER WOMAN

"Mobcap" of white linen or cotton muslin (sometimes worn under a straw hat).

Laced-front bodice made of wool, linen or cotton.

Chemise or "shift" of fine white linen or muslin-also worn as a nightshirt.

Apron of fine linen or muslin, usually white, but also gray, blue, tan, striped or checked.

Ankle-length skirt, usually made of cotton, wool or linen.

Leather shoes or, often, Indian-style moccasins.

Timothy Truman ©

Statehood Period wore on. They became cheaper because textiles were the first product of large-scale industrial production. Wheeling had two cotton and two woolen factories by 1830, for example. The city also had two tailors who made up men's clothes on special orders from customers, plus five hatters. There were probably some dressmakers who made women's clothes also. Most West Virginia families still made their own cloth, however. Only people with cash incomes and access to one of the larger towns could own tailor-made clothes.

Many people continued to wear homespun clothing during the Statehood and Industrial periods. Slaves, for example, had little choice in what to wear. They had to wear what their owners gave them. Booker T. Washington never forgot the rough shirt of flax that his owner gave him when he was six years old. It was made of leftover fibers. "It was stiff and coarse. Until it had been worn for about six weeks it made one feel as if a thousand needle points were pricking his flesh." Booker could not stand to wear it. But his older brother John "did me a kindness which I shall never forget. He volunteered to wear my new shirt for me until it was 'broken in.' " For the rest of his life, Booker could never look at a new shirt without remembering this.

A nineteenth-century dress made from fine, "store bought" cloth.

Lizzie Grant's owner gave his slaves clothes made of good material, however. Their summer clothes were homespun and "dyed with poke root berries," Lizzie recalled. (Poke is a kind of wild vegetable.) In winter, Lizzie had warm wool clothes. But her owner gave the slaves no shoes. "All the shoes we had was just rags that we wrapped our feet up in cold weather."

The slaves owned by Mollie Hansford's family were always well-dressed in clothes made from good cloth. At least this was how Mollie remembered it. One of the slaves, Tildy Bowles, was the family's seamstress. She taught Mollie to sew.

Mollie turned out to be a good pupil. She made many of her family's clothes as she grew older. Mollie's mother died when Mollie was a baby. But her father and stepmother saved many of Mollie's mother's clothes. Mollie got patterns for her own clothes by taking her mother's clothes apart and copying them. She also cut up some of her mother's dresses to get fabric to make new clothes for herself.

Mollie went to Cincinnati, however, to buy her wedding dress. She went there with another young woman who also was going to be married. They traveled by steamboat on the Kanawha and Ohio rivers. Mollie and her friend each bought three other dresses besides their wedding gowns. Mollie also bought a cape and three hats. All these clothes were made by a dressmaker. "You could not buy many ready-made things at that time," she explained. These were the most new clothes Mollie had ever had. Before this, she had generally only had two "nice" dresses. Of course she had some others to wear around her house.

Mollie Hansford was a member of a large and wealthy family. Her father kept eight slaves. If finding and making and taking care of clothes was such a tough job for Mollie, you can imagine what it was like for families who were poor. Lizzie Grant, for example, was married at about the same time Mollie was. She wore home-made clothes to her wedding, as she did every day of her life in West Virginia. "I had on a plain white dress trimmed with some cloth," she remembered. But she still didn't have any shoes. Even on her wedding day, she had no choice but to go barefoot.

Poorer people in the Statehood and Industrial periods dressed mostly in cheap cottons and woolens. The coarse cotton cloth we call denim made a strong fabric for men's work clothes. Denim jeans were almost a uniform for miners and farmers. Fred Mooney remembered wearing nothing but jeans in his days as a young miner. His wife made her dresses out of a cheap cotton print called **calico**. Sixty years earlier, when Mollie Hansford was young, calico cloth had been fashionable. The first dress Mollie made all by herself was made of pink calico. When she was thirteen, she had a calico dress that cost thirty-seven and a half cents a yard. This was a lot of money in 1841. The dress was tea green. "I thought I was very fine" in that dress, Mollie wrote.

By the end of the nineteenth century, calico was no longer fashionable. It had become a standard dress for farm women. In fact, chicken-feed manufacturers packaged their product in calico bags. This was done to get farm women to buy this product. The calico could be washed and made into clothes when the feed was used up. In this way calico came to be thought of as poor people's clothing. This was because families who could afford store-bought cloth would not make clothes out of feedsacking. But for many West Virginians calico and denim were great bargains. Thus, calico dresses and bonnets and denim jeans became the symbolic clothing on nineteenth-century West Virginia mountaineers, just as buckskin and homespun clothes remind us of the eighteenth-century frontier people.

Good cloth was hard to come by for most West Virginians. It was thus important to use it as efficiently as possible. Eventually clothes got so badly worn that they no longer could be mended. Then they could be cut into scraps or "patches." The scraps were sewn together to make "patchwork" quilts. Quilting was a social occasion for rural women. It was a task that was easily adapted to cooperative work. While their hands were busy, the women were still free to laugh and exchange stories. Quilting also became an art form. The scraps were sewn into intricate patterns based on geometric designs. For some quilters, the design was more important than the economical use of cloth. When the quilter could afford it, expensive and beautifully patterned fabrics could be used in quilts. Still the art form began as a practical necessity. It was a thrifty way to use cloth.

A turn-of-the-century washing machine.

Taking care of clothes and household fabrics was not very easy. Electrical household appliances, including laundry appliances, were not available before 1920. Automatic washers and dryers were not widely used before 1950. Thus, laundry days meant hard work. Clothes had to be scrubbed by hand against a washboard or other hard surface. They had to be wrung out by hand, a practice that developed strong forearm muscles for many women. Then they had to be rinsed and wrung out again. Mechanical wringers were developed in the late nineteenth century. So were galvanized steel tubs, which were much lighter than wooden tubs. There were few such improvements in ironing, however. Heavy metal irons had to be heated on a stove or in front of a fireplace. Then they were run over the clothes until the iron cooled. Usually the ironer worked with two or more irons. In this way, one iron could be used while the other was reheating. Ironing was another task that developed strong arms.

Families who could afford it employed servants to take care of such hard tasks as doing the laundry. But even where there were servants, family members sometimes needed to help. Julia Davis remembered her aunts stretching lace curtains to dry on racks in the back yard of her grandparents' house in Clarksburg. Machine-made lace curtains were very popular with middle- and upper-class families during the Industrial Period. They had to be dried on special racks. The racks folded for storage but on laundry days opened to six- or eight-foot lengths. The curtains were stretched between rows of little nails along the edge of the rack. Anyone who participated in this task never forgot it.

Handling the heavy wet curtains made a person's fingertips puckered and sensitive. This made pinpricks from the little nails painful but there was no way to avoid it.

13.3 Changes in Clothing and Values

Clothing in every period of history reflects the values of a society. This was true of the Statehood and Industrial periods in West Virginia. There were four important changes that affected the way that middle- and upper-class West Virginians dressed. First, men's clothing became much simpler and less colorful than it had been before 1800. Secondly, changes in women's fashion began to affect more people. Thirdly, both of these changes contributed to the introduction of machine-made clothing. Finally, special styles of children's clothing were developed.

Before the American and French revolutions, prosperous men dressed in the same colorful and fancy fabrics that women wore. Men's clothes were cut differently, of course. Men wore trousers so that they could ride horses easily. Men's coats had slits or vents in the back so that they could carry swords. Riding horses and wearing swords were habits left over from the days when most men were soldiers. Otherwise, fashionable men were just as likely to wear laces, silks, brocades, satins or velvets as their ladies were. They also wore wigs.

The two revolutions changed all this. During the 1790s, some French leaders began wearing simple costumes of black jackets and trousers and white shirts. They also gave up wigs and cut their hair short. These changes became symbols of "Republican simplicity." This meant that men who believed in democracy and in a republican form of government wore these clothes in protest against the fashions of European monarchies. For this reason the new clothing styles became popular in the United States. During the Statehood Period, American men shocked European royalty by wearing only black and white clothes on formal occasions.

By the beginning of the Industrial Period, the new simple clothes had developed into the modern business suit. The fancy lace or silk cravats of earlier years gave way to simple modern ties. Lace and ruffles disappeared from men's shirts. The jacket and trousers became loose-fitting, better for sitting at desks or walking on city streets, though not for riding horses. In fact, this loose-fitting business suit became known as the "sack suit." This was because the basic shape of the jacket was like a sack. The loose fit of these clothes recognized the fact that men no longer needed to dress like soldiers. But it also made it much easier to make men's clothing with machines.

Women's clothing underwent a different type of change. The first fashion designer established his business in Paris in 1860. It is doubtful that many West Virginia women wore Paris-made clothes. But the practice of copying Paris designs soon spread to West Virginia dressmakers, as it did to dressmakers all over America and Europe. The innovation of fashion design meant that changes in women's clothing could be introduced swiftly. This innovation helps explain the rapid adoption of shorter skirts and machine-made dresses after World War I.

The earliest fashion designers did not design simple clothing, however. On the contrary - women's fine clothing was very fancy between 1860 and 1910. During the Civil War years, women wore huge skirts over steel hoops and layers of petticoats. During the 1870s, the "bustle" was introduced, along with an uncomfortable forward-leaning posture known as the "Grecian bend." Bustles were layers of padding and cloth shaped like a bun and worn at the base of the spine. They provided tempting targets for boys who wanted to get into trouble or make smart remarks. Ross Tennant used to steal his sister's bustle and hang it up in a tree or use it for target practice. In his old age, he asked his sister to forgive him for being so mean. After 1880, women straightened their posture but continued wearing tight corsets and bustles. Between 1900 and World War I, women's clothes became more flowing in outline and the bustle disappeared. But a single dress still used many yards of cloth. In fact, that was the point of fashion. It was the fashion for middle-aged men to have huge bellies during these years, while their wives had huge skirts. Both the bellies and the skirts were a way of showing off the wealth of the owner. Both also were a result of industrialization.

Industrialization had helped make possible cheap and abundant food and cheap cloth. And both were unhealthy. The fatness of the men caused heart disease. The tight corsets of the women caused fainting and dizziness, while the big skirts were a fire hazard. A well-dressed woman who was careless around a fire could easily be burned to death before she could get free of her clothes. Hard-working men who did not get fat and women who could afford only one layer of petticoats were probably better off than they knew.

The practice of making clothing using machines in factories began during the 1850s. Men's shirts and jeans were among the first store-bought clothing items, along with shoes and boots. Factory production of military uniforms and boots during the Civil War got millions of men used to wearing machine-made clothing. Wealthy men continued to have their clothes made by tailors. But by 1900 most other men were accustomed to buying clothes in stores (or from mail-order companies).

It took longer for women to adopt ready-made clothing. As with men's clothing, manufacturers began with cheaper clothing and simpler items, such as petticoats, underwear, aprons and blouses. After 1920, women's dresses became much simpler. They used much less fabric. Only then did it become common for well-dressed women to buy their clothes "off the rack."

Another change in the nineteenth century was the development of special clothing styles for children. Before 1800, children had worn smaller versions of the clothes that adults wore. This continued to be the case for poorer children. But middle- and upper-class children had to wear special garments. One example was "pantalets," which little girls wore through much of the nineteenth century. Pantalets were lace-trimmed leggings that extended from above the knee to the top of the shoe. They stuck out from beneath girl's dresses, which came down halfway between the knee and shoe. Mollie Hansford hated them. She started school in Charleston, where pantalets were fashionable. But then she moved to a country school near St. Albans. None of the other girls wore pantalets at this school. But Mollie's stepmother made her wear them anyway. This made her "the laughing stock of the school" until she started hiding the pantalets under a log on her way to school. On her way home, she would put them back on. Her aunt found out about this but did not tell her stepmother.

Julia Davis remembered that her clothes seemed to be made of nothing but buttons when she was a little girl. Her underdrawers and stockings were buttoned on, "also the flannel petticoat." Then came a starched slip and a ruffled dress. Both had pearl buttons down the back. Shoes, leggings and gloves had to be buttoned also, plus outer coats during cold weather, of course. Her grandmother used buttons to teach Julia the multiplication table. The box held enough spare buttons to take Julia to 12 x 12.

At least buttons had the advantage of security. When Biddie Greene was seven years old, she snuck downstairs and watched some of her teen-aged cousins dancing at a party. The drawstring on one girl's underwear broke and her drawers fell down on the dance floor. This led to a fight between the victim's boyfriend and

Pantalets

another boy who had laughed at the sight.

The most common special clothing for boys were short pants and knickers, which were pants that came down to just below the knee. Knickers were the common dress of young boys throughout the Industrial Period. A boy usually got his first set of long pants when he was 13 or 14. This was an occasion for celebration. Poor boys got to wear long pants at an early age, however. This was because they started to work then. Middle- and upper-class mothers would have been shocked to see their boys wearing blue jeans. This was because denim was used only for work clothes. After World War II, however, boys began wearing jeans for play and school time. Girls wore them at home, also. Only after numerous court battles during the 1960s, however, were girls permitted to wear jeans or any other form of trousers to school.

Examples of late-nineteenth-century childrens' clothes. Note the multi-layered dress on the older girl, and the boys' knickers and button shoes.

The Bureaucratic Period brought about many changes in the clothes that people wore. Two of these changes were caused directly by the rise of large business organizations. Large corporations developed mechanical and, later, automatic laundry equipment. Large corporations also organized the research that resulted in the development of man-made fibers and textiles. These human-made (or "synthetic") fabrics began with celluloid. This was used in shirt collars in the early twentieth century. Then came rayon, which used wood fibers as a raw material. Nylon, made from chemicals derived from coal, was introduced to the public in 1939. After World War II, chemical companies, oil companies, plastics and film manufactures began making dozens of varieties of synthetic fibers. These developments have led to a much larger variety of household textiles. It has made clothing easier to clean and care for. This would not have been possible without the large and complex research activities that bureaucratic organizations have been able to maintain.

Mass communications and mass merchandising have also led to changes in the way we dress. Films and television are as likely to lead to changes in clothing styles today as the fashions of Paris designers. The way in which people began to use swimwear is a good example. People in West Virginia did not wear special clothes for swimming in the late nineteenth century. George McIntosh and his friends went swimming naked in the Ohio River at Huntington during the 1870s. Twenty years later, Ross Tennant and his friends did the same thing in Dunkard's Creek in rural Monongalia County. They also covered themselves with mud and ran nude foot races in the road nearby. The adults did not seem to mind, Ross remembered. This was an activity that was expected of children.

If West Virginia adults had the urge to go swimming, they hung their clothes on a bush near some secluded stream or took vacations at beach resorts along the Atlantic Ocean or Lake Erie. People wore swimsuits at the beach, of course. But even there, prosperous people avoided direct exposure to the sun. Suntanned skin was considered a symbol of poverty, especially on women. Except for children, a suntan was evidence that you had to work outdoors.

After World War I, the movies popularized the lifestyle of dry, sunny southern California. This led fashionable people all over the country to develop an interest in swimwear and swimming pools. This included people in West Virginia. During the 1930s and '40s, progressive city governments built outdoor swimming pools in West Virginia. After World War II the federal and West Virginia governments built artificial lakes and beaches in every part of the state. Thus, swimming came to be a popular adult activity, and special clothing came with it. Suntans came to be thought of as a sign of health rather than poverty. (Since medical research has identified sunbathing as a potential cause of skin cancer, suntans might look much healthier than they actually are.)

Mass merchandising led to frequent changes in swimwear fashion. Similar developments created other types of "sportswear" for modern West Virginians. During the nineteenth century, many sports inspired special costumes: baseball, football, horseback riding and hunting, for example. Except for certain types of hunting jackets, these costumes were worn only while engaged in the sport. During the Bureaucratic Period, however, mass communications have made heroes of champions in golf, tennis, and skiing. The special costumes of these sports also became popular. During the 1950s, people began wearing sports costumes or clothing inspired by them in everyday life. This is another outcome of mass communications and mass merchan-

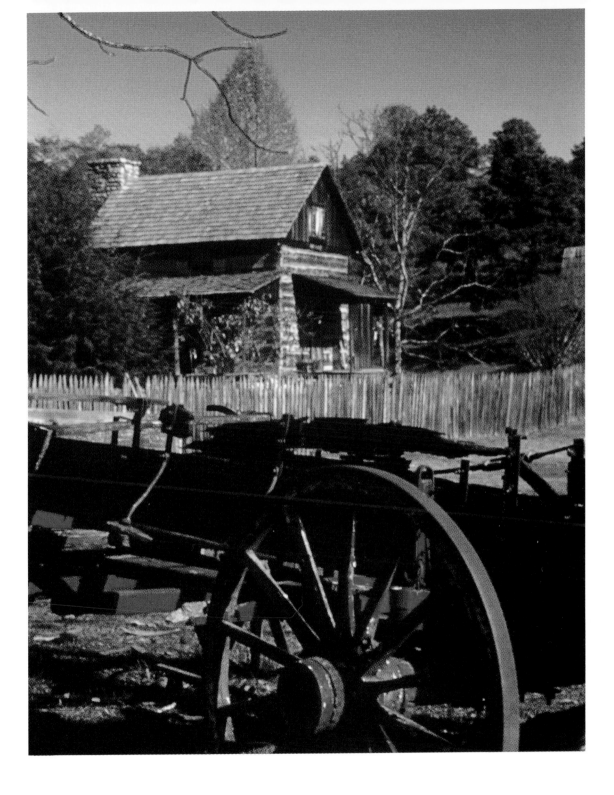

Pioneer Farm, Twin Falls State Park
Wyoming County

dising.

Under these circumstances, there are no types of modern clothing that can be identified as belonging to West Virginia. When people want to dress up in a special West Virginia costume, they put on buckskins from the Frontier Period or jeans or calico work clothes from the nineteenth century. (Actually, the buckskin and calico worn today are likely to be synthetic "look-alike" fabrics.) There is nothing in modern everyday dress to distinguish West Virginians from people in any other state - or, for that matter, from those in any other modern country.

Study Questions - Chapter 13

1. At one time in our state's history, the kind of fabric used in clothing indicated whether the wearer was rich or poor.

> a) Write a paragraph describing how you might have recognized poor people in one particular period by their clothing.

> b) Name as many kinds of clothing as you can that are popular with almost all people today.

2. Describe how the following customs began.

> a) making quilts of pieces of different kinds of fabric.

> b) men wearing black suits and white shirts on formal occasions.

> c) wearing denim jeans.

> d) packing chicken feed in bags made of calico.

> e) wearing a baseball cap or jogging clothes clothes around town.

Chapter 14:
Housing

Ideas and Issues:
Design and
Structure in
Traditional Houses

If you compare houses built in West Virginia before 1900, you can see that most of them look somewhat alike. This is not just because they were built of local materials. There are two other reasons why they look alike. One is their **design**, the other is their **structure**. The design means the way that the parts of a house fit together. The structure means the way a house is built. Traditional West Virginia houses are like one another both in design and in structure.

The design of West Virginia houses was part of the cultural traditions brought by American colonists from Europe. These were Scottish, Irish, German, Scandinavian, and English housing traditions, plus the Georgian architectural style brought over from England in the eighteenth century.

This does not explain everything about the similarities of traditional houses, however. Design traditions tell us why houses looked alike. They tell us why doors and windows were arranged similarly, why rooms were arranged in a certain way, and so on. Traditional houses also resemble one another in structure, as well as design. This means that they were *built* along similar principles. Structural similarities are noticeable in the sizes and shapes of the houses.

14.1 Log Cabins
and Log Houses

West Virginians' first shelters, like their food and clothing, came from the natural environment. This is true no matter which people we consider to be the first West Virginians. The forested and hilly land of the state provided two kinds of natural shelters. One consisted of the space under overhanging rock ledges. The pioneers of the Frontier Period called these places "rock camps." They used them for hunting camps. But the white settlers were not the first to use these shelters. The oldest Paleo-Indian site near West Virginia was a rock shelter. This is the 13,000-year-old Meadowcroft site in western Pennsylvania. Archeological sites have been found in rock shelters for other prehistoric periods as well. An example is an Archaic Period site near Rohr, in Monongalia County.

Another kind of natural shelter for hunters was provided by

hollow trees. Sycamore trees, some of which were more than ten feet in diameter, were particularly good for this purpose. Stephen Sewell moved into a hollow tree when he quarreled with his hunting partner, Jacob Marlin, at the site of modern Marlinton in 1749. The Pringle brothers lived in a hollow tree near the present site of Buckhannon in 1764. Hollow tree or log shelters figure in many stories of frontier adventure and romance.

Natural shelters are temporary housing at best, however. Since Archaic times, West Virginia residents have generally wished to live in human-made structures. During the Prehistoric, Frontier and Statehood periods, many different types of housing were built. However, all West Virginia houses had one thing in common. They were constructed from materials available in the state's natural environment. This began to change with industrialization. Since the Industrial Period, the trend for housing has been the same as the trends for clothing and food. West Virginia housing styles and building materials have become identical with those found in every other part of the United States.

When we think of housing during the Frontier Period, we think of log cabins. This thought is correct. Yet it is also misleading, in two ways. First of all, pioneer settlers built two kinds of log cabins. One type was crude and temporary. It was constructed of untrimmed logs, with shallow "saddle notches" at the corners where the logs fitted together. It usually also had a dirt floor and chimney made

Topper Sherwood

from sticks daubed with mud. These cabins were cold and drafty. The saddle notches caught rainwater and rotted the corners out. Chimneys caught fire or eroded after a few winters. Most of the cabins of this type disappeared after a generation.

This log house was built in Kanawha County around 1797.

The second type of cabin was more finished and permanent. The logs were trimmed and hewn to fit snugly together. The walls were raised on stone posts or foundations, with a wood floor inside. The corners were notched in such a way as to prevent the collection of rainwater. Chimneys were built of carefully cut and fitted stone. Houses of this type were comfortable and durable. In fact, many of them were large enough to be called log houses rather than cabins. Or if they started out as cabins, they soon "grew" into houses with the addition of one or more rooms. Many log cabins and houses of this type are still standing in West Virginia today.

The slave cabin where Lizzie Grant lived was somewhere in between the first and second type. It was built out of unpeeled logs, that is, logs with the bark left on. As Lizzie described it:

> All the cracks were daubed with mud to keep out the cold and rain. Our beds were built down on the ground in one corner of our quarters out of moss, shucks and grass. Yes, we kept real warm in there all the time as we had a big rock fireplace. ...We kept plenty of wood as that and water was about all we got free.

The second misleading thing about identifying log cabins with the Frontier Period is this: Log cabins and houses continued to be built in West Virginia long after the Frontier Period. The slave cabin Lizzie Grant lived in is only one example. George McIntosh was born in 1868 in a "one-room hewed log cabin" (that is, a cabin of the second type). It stood near the headwaters of Big Creek in Fayette County. His father had built the cabin a couple of years before. This was just after he returned from service in the Union Army and got married. His wife's brothers and father helped him build the house. This was a "house raising" party.

Topper Sherwood

The corners of early log cabins were cut with saddle-type notches, which allowed water to settle in the joints. Later log houses like this one, were cut to keep the water out of the joints.

Traditional log cabin construction probably continued in remote parts of West Virginia into the 1930s. George McIntosh's description of the cabin in which he was born is probably a good general picture of the better log cabin type. At one end of the house stood a large stone chimney, which was built of roughly dressed stone. Of course, the fireplace - an open one, built into the chimney - afforded warmth for the room and a place to do the cooking. A window with a single frame was in the back of the room, directly opposite the cabin door. There was no porch in front, as was usual with country cabins, but a shed covered the door to protect the room from the hot sun of summer days.

"However, the sun had not much chance in the narrow valley where stood the house of my birth," George remembered.

> The cabin had been built at the foot of a huge mountain, which was a full thousand feet in the air. The opposite mountain started its rise...a hundred yards away. The rays of the sun did not reach the spot where the cabin stood until about nine o'clock in the morning. It was behind the other hill by four in the afternoon. A narrow stretch of flat land in front of the house afforded a garden spot, which was supplemented by an additional garden arranged on the opposite side of the creek. Each was surrounded by the old fashioned worm fences, built of oak and chestnut and rails, crossed at the ends.

The cabin, George added, was built of poplar logs. These grew abundantly near his home "five or six feet in diameter, and maybe 40 or 50 feet to the first limb." During the Frontier Period, cabins were built in more accessible locations, close to the big rivers. Otherwise there was probably little difference between the McIntosh cabin and others built earlier or later.

George McIntosh did not describe any outbuildings around his parents' cabin. Since his family moved away in 1873, perhaps his father and uncles didn't have time to build many buildings. However, most log houses came to be surrounded by other buildings. There were smokehouses, springhouses, corn cribs, root cellars and barns. All of these structures could be built out of logs.

So were the first churches and school houses of most neighborhoods. Mollie Hansford attended both school and church in a large log structure near St. Albans. Biddie Greene attended church in a log chapel in the Knawls Creek section of Braxton County during the 1890s. This church was probably built during the 1880s. It was unusual in that it was a Roman Catholic chapel. Catholic churches were more common in cities like Wheeling. But Biddie's family was one of a number of Irish Catholic families who settled along the Lewis-Braxton county border. The log chapel was built for those families who lived too far from the brick churches in Orlando or Weston. It was the same type of building as the log Protestant churches that were found in every part of the state.

Topper Sherwood

Log structures were still popular in the mid-1930s, when this Greenbrier County house was built.

When people outgrew a log cabin or house, they often built another right beside it. Then they connected the two by a doorway or porch. The log house in Kanawha County where Fred Mooney's family lived was evidently built in this way. There were two separate rooms divided by a porch. A low second story covered all three and provided three bedrooms upstairs. The covered porch between the two downstairs rooms became a breezeway or "dog trot." This was a pleasant sheltered place to sit during hot weather or summer rains.

A log house that began growing in this way could continue to grow with each generation. Julia Davis's mother's home in the Shenandoah Valley grew in this way. They called their house "Media." It began as a two-story log house and a smokehouse, possibly before 1750. Around the time of the American Revolution, a wing was added. This wing was built out of stone, as are many late eighteenth-century houses in the Shenandoah Valley. Later, in 1869, Julia's great-grandfather had oak siding cut from nearby trees. Some of this siding went to cover up the old logs. The rest went to build a new frame addition. The result was a large, friendly house. It was not a very elegant or comfortable home by our standards today. There were nine bedrooms when Julia visited there in the early 1900s. But there was still no electricity, indoor plumbing or heating except for fireplaces. The old log smokehouse still stood nearby.

14.2 The "White House"

Many West Virginia log cabins and houses "disappeared" in this way. They became parts of larger houses. Eventually, sawed siding ("clapboards" or "weather boards") covered the logs. It isn't unusual today to find that an old farm house conceals an even older log house inside it. But it was probably just as common for people to start all over when they wanted a larger house. Mollie Hansford's grandfather built the first frame house in the Kanawha Valley in 1796. One hundred and three years later, Biddie

Greene's parents built a frame house next to their log house on Fletcher's Run near Burnsville. Apparently these two houses were quite similar: two rooms wide, two stories high and one room deep, with a central hallway and one-story front porch. The porch was added later to the Hansford house. But by the time the Greene house was built in 1899, porches were nearly always built on West Virginia homes.

The technical term for this type of frame house is **I-house**. This derives from its long, narrow rectangular shape, which resembles the letter 'I'. Actually many such houses grew into L- or T-shaped houses, with the addition of wings. Even without wings, the 'I' shape of the house was disguised by front and back porches, or by kitchens built as "lean-to" additions on the side or rear. Biddie Greene's family had another name for their house. They called it "the white house," which is a good general name for it. This type of frame farm house became the typical shelter of West Virginians during the nineteenth century. The house was built from sawed lumber and covered with oak or poplar siding. The siding and window frames and trim were nearly always painted white. This color offered a contrast to the dark earthy colors of the log house that the white house replaced. The white color also contrasted the house with the surrounding trees, hillsides and fields. Like

An I-house

the log house, the white house was built from native materials taken from the West Virginia environment. But the house's bright white color and its many windows and doorways showed much more clearly than hewn logs that human hands had been at work.

Brick and stone houses were also built during the Statehood and Industrial periods. They were especially common in cities and towns such as Wheeling or Harpers Ferry. Brick or stone farm houses were most common in the richest agricultural districts - the Shenandoah, South Branch and Greenbrier valleys and in the Ohio and Kanawha river bottomlands. Such houses were usually larger than frame or log houses. But they had the same 'I' or 'L' or 'T' shapes. Windows and porches were placed on the house in the same way. And the same type of frame or log outbuildings surrounded them. The large brick and stone houses were also built of local materials. The bricks for mansions built along the Kanawha River were generally made by the wealthy homeowners' slaves, for example.

Julia Davis wrote of Media that "it may truly be said to have grown out of the earth on which it stands." This was true of all of the traditional housing of West Virginia - large and small, log, frame, brick or stone.

14.3 Traditional Designs of West Virginia Homes

Why are West Virginia's traditional houses so much alike in design and structure? That is a hard question to answer. The state's traditional housing has not been investigated in detail, except for a few houses lived in by famous people, such as Pearl Buck. However, the farm houses of two counties in Eastern Virginia have been investigated. So have mountain log cabins in many parts of the Appalachian region. Since many West Virginia settlers came from Eastern Virginia, and since many of them lived like the mountaineers in other Appalachian states, these investigations may tell us something about the design and structure of West Virginia houses.

If this is true, then the design of West Virginia houses came originally from Germany and the British Isles. Many German settlers were familiar with log houses in Central Europe. Small houses, similar to log houses in shape and design but built of different materials, were also common in Scotland and Ireland. Both German and Scotch-Irish immigrants entered the American colonies mainly through the seaport of Philadelphia. The earliest settlers of the Philadelphia region came from Sweden and Finland. Log buildings were common in these countries also. Thus, German and Scotch-Irish settlers may have borrowed from the material culture of these Scandinavian ethnic groups as well as from each other.

Germans and Scotch-Irish had different languages and religions. But they seem to have carried the designs for similar types of houses from eastern Pennsylvania south through the Appalachian mountains. They also carried these designs westward through the Ohio Valley. This is how the log house came to West Virginia.

The design of the white house seems to have come from

English settlers in Eastern Virginia. Log structures were not common in Virginia east of the Blue Ridge. Instead, the early settlers built frame houses there. The shape of these houses was similar to the shape of English houses, although stone houses were more common in England because wood was scarce there. During the eighteenth century, Eastern Virginia frame houses were influenced by a style of English architecture called "Georgian." It was named after the eighteenth-century kings of England, Kings George I, II, and III.

Historic Preservation-Dept. of Culture & History

Design symmetry can be seen in Harewood, built in the 1760s by George Washington's brother.

A principal idea of Georgian architecture was **symmetry**. This is an idea that is hard to explain. But it is easy to see. The photo on this page shows the front wall of "Harewood." This house was built by George Washington's brother Samuel near Charles Town in the 1760s. It is a rich man's house. But it shows the symmetry, which was also found in thousands of small and middle-sized houses throughout the state. Imagine a line running through the center of Harewood, right through the middle of the front porch. Notice that the two halves of the house are alike. This makes it a "symmetrical" design. Symmetry means placing the openings in a wall in such a way that the two halves of the wall are identical. In other words, each half is a "mirror image" of the other half. This is symmetry.

Symmetry is what the designers of West Virginia houses aimed for during the Statehood and Industrial periods. They did

WV State Archives

The Mansion House, in Mason County, was built in 1796 as a tavern.

not always reach their goal. But they came close enough that we can see what they were aiming for. Look at the photo of the Mansion House at Point Pleasant on page 255. It is a log house built as a tavern in 1796. It is almost symmetrical. But not quite. Notice the little window next to the right-hand door. There is nothing like it on the left half of the wall. This little window spoils the symmetry of the wall. Still we can see that the man who designed the house used the concept of symmetry. Otherwise he would not have placed the other doorways and windows as he did.

The Mansion House is more typical of West Virginia houses than Harewood. Perfect symmetry like Harewood's is rare. In fact, a closer look shows that not all of Harewood's walls are perfectly symmetrical. When you study the design of old houses, you sometimes have to use your "mind's eye" to "see" what the builder had in mind. You have to ignore non-symmetrical features that the builder added. Or you have to "see" symmetrical features he left out.

According to the rules of symmetry in Georgian architecture, an even number of windows should be arranged on each side of a doorway. There should be an upstairs door or window for each one downstairs. The openings should be arranged in pairs, one directly above the other. Doors, windows and fireplaces should also be placed symmetrically on inside walls. They were placed in the centers of rooms where possible. Or sometimes a door or window was placed on each side of a fireplace. In Eastern Virginia, these rules were copied from rich men's homes into the building of frame farm houses. This type of house was most likely an ancestor of the West Virginia white house.

If you look at the old farm houses of your neighborhood, you might notice that their windows and doors follow Georgian rules of symmetry. (You will have to "look" beneath the aluminum siding or colored paint or added rooms which may have changed the old house's original shape.) A large house may have five windows across the top, with four windows downstairs, two on either side of a central doorway. A medium-size house may have three windows up, and two windows plus a central door down. The smallest house may have only one story, with two windows and a central door. But there are also two-doors-and-no-windows small houses; or two-doors-and-two-windows. There are a lot of variations, in fact. The point is that the arrangements of doors, windows, stairways and chimneys will have some sort of symmetrical relationship. The same thing applied to L's, T's or shed additions which may have been added later to the house.

To sum up: there seems to have been a general system of housing design in effect in Eastern Virginia. This system probably spread to West Virginia during and after the Frontier Period. The system provided patterns for very small houses, very large houses and everything in between. It had patterns for log, brick and stone houses as well as for white frame houses. It had patterns for town houses as well as rural houses. For example, the most common type of rural house was the two story, four-room I-house with a central hall. In towns, however, carpenters built only two-thirds or so of this house. They built the hall and one set of rooms, but did not place rooms on the other side of the hall. Probably this was because of the narrow width of urban building lots. Often urban house-builders made deeper or taller houses to make up for the narrow width. But there were small, medium and large versions of the townhouse. There were also frame, brick and stone versions. Wheeling today is a treasure trove of old town houses built between 1830 and 1880. They range in size from small workingmen's cottages to rich merchant's houses, such as the one in which Rebecca Harding grew up. These houses are symmetrical, also. But to "see" the symmetry you have to picture in your mind the missing one-third, which the house-builder left off.

14.4 Housing and Culture

Similarities of structure in traditional houses are easier to picture if you think about a row of cereal boxes or fruit juice cans on a supermarket shelf. Cans and boxes produced by the same manufacturer will have the same general design. That is, they will be the same shape and color. They have the same style of letter on their labels. But the boxes and cans will also resemble each other in their structure. Their sizes will be proportionate to each other. The proportions are not necessarily the same as they would be if a large box was twice as large as a small box. Instead, a large box may be one-and-a-half times larger than a small box. The "giant size" may be two-and-a-half times larger than the small box. Different sizes of cans may be obtained by multiplying a unit of weight, such as one ounce. You could have 16-ounce, 24-ounce, and 32-ounce sizes in this way.

It seems probable that carpenters built traditional houses on just such a system. We can never be sure of this, even in those Eastern Virginia counties where detailed investigations were carried out. Unlike soldiers, politicians, storekeepers, inventors or autobiographers, carpenters left few written records. They left no general plan explaining their system. Instead, a boy learned some basic principles of carpentry from an older man, usually his father or uncle. If he had a good teacher and was good at it himself, he might begin to specialize in building houses. He would not do this on a full-time, year-round basis. He would do other kinds of carpentry and would probably also be a farmer. But his reputation for building houses would grow. He would probably have a hand in building most of the new houses (or additions to houses) in his neighborhood. He would probably teach his sons the skills of carpentry. Possibly he would teach his nephews and his neighbors' sons also. Someday, one of them would be building houses just as he had. His system of building houses, then, did not grow out of a written plan. It came from experience which built up gradually. This experience was a store of knowledge that came from older people. And it was given to younger people in the same way - by word of mouth and by repeated example.

If the Eastern Virginia system was adopted by West Virginians, then here is what happened in building a house: The carpenter started out with a unit of measurement. Usually he started with a yard (3 feet or .9 meters) or a pace (2.5 feet or .75 meters). He used some multiple of this unit to establish the dimensions of the first room in the house. Other rooms in the house would be the same size. Their dimensions might differ from the first room's by one unit or a half unit or by some other multiple of the unit that the carpenter started with. The hallway dimensions would be determined in the same way. He would build as many rooms as the owner wanted or could afford. The relationship of the rooms to each other and to the overall shape of the house would grow out of that basic unit of measurement. This unit would probably be used over and over again in each house that the carpenter built. Other carpenters would build in the same general way, using the same principles of design, the same units of measurement and the same kinds of tools.

The unit of measurement a carpenter used would be represented by a thing - a yardstick, perhaps. The carpenter probably would have made this tool himself. He probably copied it from one owned by the man who taught him his skills. And he probably passed on similar measuring tools to the men he taught. It is important to realize that, for the folk carpenter, one yard was reckoned to be the length of his outstretched arm - from the tips of his fingers to the tip of his nose. Other units of measurement used in building were reckoned in similar ways. A cubit was half a yard. A span was half a cubit. But a span was also reckoned as the width of a man's hand stretched from the thumb to the little finger. A pace was reckoned as the length of a man's walking step. Thus, the dimensions that a traditional carpenter used to build a house were reckoned using the dimensions of the human body.

The principles of design that gave the house its appearance grew out of the cultural traditions of an ethnic group and the mixture of ethnic traditions in a region. The materials for building the house grew out of the very earth itself, as Julia Davis wrote of Media. The traditional housing of West Virginia was thus a product of both culture and environment. The precise mixture of culture and environment still needs to be investigated for West Virginia houses, particularly the middle-sized and smaller houses where most people lived. But whatever the mixture, it seems fairly sure that it grew out of the experience, the traditions and soil of the people who lived in them. The houses of a particular West Virginia place were very similar to one another. But they were never quite the same as the houses found in any other place.

14.5 The Industrialization of Housing

Industrialization changed this way of building houses completely. It brought four kinds of changes. First, industrialization made possible standardized building materials. Second, it enabled West Virginia builders to bring in materials - including human-made materials - from many other environments. Third, it created standardized house designs which were used all over the United States. Finally, it made possible housing that could be assembled in factories. At the beginning of the Industrial Period, the housing of West Virginia was unlike housing found in any other part of the country or the world. By the mid-twentieth century, the housing built in West Virginia was no different than housing built in any other part of the United States.

Standardized building materials began when sawmills started sawing timber into standard sizes of lumber. They also began turning out parts of a building according to standard patterns, rather than the individual needs of each customer. These components included window sashes, door frames, and the fancy machine-made wooden trim called "gingerbread." Brickmakers and glass manufacturers began making components according to standard patterns also. The sheet-metal manufacturers of West Virginia's Northern Panhandle led in the develop-

Topper Sherwood

Standardized building materials began with sawmills and developed with mass production and mass merchandizing. Compare these materials with the hand-hewn logs shown on page 250.

ment of steel and tin-plated roofing materials. All of these developments came about through mass production and mass merchandizing.

During the Frontier Period, West Virginia house builders hewed and sawed the lumber they needed for construction from trees on their own land. Statehood Period sawmills and brickyards produced materials for builders in their own neighborhoods. Slave owners in the Shenandoah, South Branch, Greenbrier and Kanawha regions frequently put slaves to work sawing lumber, cutting stone and making bricks for local use. By 1900, however, West Virginia building-material manufacturers were producing for a national market. They shipped hardwood lumber from Huntington, brick and tile from Newell and New Cumberland, roofing and ceiling materials from Wheeling and Follansbee, building glass from Clarksburg and Charleston, and softwood lumber for framing from Charleston, Richwood, Ronceverte, Davis and Cass.

In return, West Virginia builders could import materials from the rest of the nation. There was slate from Vermont, fir and pine lumber from the Great Lakes region, the deep South and Pacific Northwest, limestone from Indiana and marble from Georgia or Vermont. The heavy dark furniture that became popular in the early twentieth century was made from tropical woods imported from South America. Plumbing fixtures installed in newfangled bathrooms came from Midwest manufacturers. Electrical equipment for houses came from Pennsylvania or New York. It became possible for a West Virginian to build a house without using any local materials. Many homes did have locally obtained oak flooring and cherry or walnut paneling. But these would have been bought only because West Virginia was a leading supplier of these hardwoods to the national market.

The same was true of any West Virginia-made plumbing pipes and tiles or roofing materials which might have been used. During the 1920s, the United States Department of Commerce joined with manufacturers to promote more standardization. They adopted standard sizes and dimensions for such things as lumber planks and beams, nails, bricks, window sashes, copper wiring, building glass, pipes and tiles. They also reduced the number of sizes available for each product. The new standards were the same for the whole country, regardless of local building traditions.

Corporations and government agencies also conducted research into new types of building materials. Concrete and cinder blocks gradually replaced stone and brick in building foundations, sidewalks and driveways. Many more human-made materials became available after World War II. These included asphalt roofing materials, asbestos siding and shingles, aluminum and plastic siding and window sashes. Often these new materials were manufactured to look like traditional building materials. Asbestos sheeting was printed to look like bricks and was used to cover the wood siding on older and smaller frame houses. Aluminum and plastic siding is used on both old and new siding. But it is always manufactured to look like wood. The same practice was followed with man-made materials on the insides of houses. For example, linoleum "rugs" or plastic wall paneling are made to look natural by having color photographs of real wool carpets or real wood panels printed on the surface of the material. Such methods are as clever as the techniques that traditional carpenters and weavers and stone masons used. But this modern genius is something which can only be expressed with the aid of machines.

Another change was the use of standard housing designs. Books of house plans and blueprints for houses became available through lumber dealers during the 1870s. By 1920, most urban and town houses were built according to blueprints. These blueprints were published by companies that sold them nationwide. They were designed to use standardized building materials. The houses built in this way have a basically square or rectangular shape. The differences among these houses come from ornaments on the outside. Styles of housing ornamentation have changed frequently sinced the 1880s. But they have changed much in the same way that fashions change in clothing. Beneath the ornaments, the basic box shape of middle-class housing remained the same.

Three versions of the box-shaped house were especially popular in West Virginia between 1900 and 1930. One was square, usually 28 or 32 feet on each side. It had four rooms downstairs and four upstairs. It was built with the roof sloping up from four sides toward a central point. This gave the house a pyramid-shaped roof. Sometimes it was called a "pyramid house." Another popular style was rectangular in shape. Usually it had three rooms downstairs and four upstairs. Its roof was steeply sloped and ended in the triangular gable facing the front. This

National Park Service

"Pyramid" house.

Library of Congress

A temple house.

Library of Congress

A bungalow.

gable gave the house a vaguely classical Greek appearance. So it was called a "temple house." The third popular style was called a "bungalow." It was a one-story house with four or six pairs of rooms in a rectangular shape. Like the pyramid and temple house, the bungalow was usually built with a porch stretching almost across the entire front of the house. This porch provided a pleasant place to sit during rainy days or hot summer evenings. It shaded the first floor and provided a place to sit in public view but not far from the family's private quarters. This was probably important since, unlike farm houses, these houses were usually built close to roads and streets.

After World War II, one-story houses became popular. They were called "ranch houses." They were inspired by the traditional housing of the southwestern states. The most popular two-story style was called "colonial." It was modeled on the traditional housing of New England. Neither of these styles reflected the traditional housing of West Virginia. But their popularity showed how completely local housing traditions had given way to national trends.

Actually, the style of post-war housing was apparent only on the surface. Underneath the outside ranch or colonial ornament was a basic rectangle or square of one or two stories. Both the ranch and colonial styles were generally placed further from streets or roads. They were designed to be approached by automobiles. This type of house usually included a garage. In some suburban districts, sidewalks were completely left out.

Porches also tended to disappear. Instead, builders and home owners built "patios." A patio is an outdoor living space developed first in North Africa and Spain. It was brought to America by Spanish colonists in Mexico and California. Thus, the patio was originally intended for dry, sunny climates. It is too rainy or cold to use patios much of the time in West Virginia. Still they are very popular, although not with everyone. A Lincoln County man whose wife wanted a new house with a patio failed to see any great improvement. In the old days, he explained, his family ate indoors and used an outdoor toilet - a privy. Now, in the new house, they had an inside bathroom and ate outside on the patio. "What's the difference?" he asked. One difference was privacy. Porches generally face the public road or street. Patios, like privies, are generally hidden behind the house.

Wealthy West Virginians hired architects and built one-of-a-kind houses. But they, too, used standardized building materials. They, too, were subject to changing fashions in housing styles. Along Huntington's Fifth Avenue or Wheeling's National Pike, businessmen built houses in the style of English Gothic estates, Moorish palaces, Scottish castles, and French or Italian town houses. The oil barons of Sistersville and the coal barons of Bramwell did the same. Later, during the 1920s and '30s and after World War II, rich people tended to favor quieter styles, especially the New England colonial style and the classical style of the Deep South. The style of the exterior tended to be repeated in the interior design and furnishing.

Topper Sherwood

This house was completed in 1852 for a wealthy Kanawha Valley businessman, who hired an English-born architect to build it. The house was sold in 1857 to pro-Union politician George Summers.

The most drastic effects of standardized housing design could be seen in the coal camps. The builders of company towns usually built twenty or more houses at a time. They rarely used more than one or two styles. If the mine owner or superintendent came from eastern Pennsylvania, he might build barracks-style housing, with apartments for several miners and their families. If he came from western Pennsylvania, he might build two-family double houses. If he hired a local carpenter who was trained in traditional house building, he might get a camp full of little frame I- or L-houses. Or he might get two-room "miners' cabins," such as the ones Fred Mooney lived in after he started work in the mines. There were also coal camps full of pyramid, temple and bungalow houses, although these were rarely as large as town or city houses of the same style. The temple house was particularly

common in lumber mill and tannery towns. This was because many of the managers of this industry had started out in New England, where the temple-house style started. Temple houses were the most common style of workingman's house in the Pocahontas County lumber town of Cass, for example.

The first town in West Virginia to be built out of **prefabricated** houses was a coal camp. Prefabricated means made in a factory instead of assembled on the building site. Traditional housing was assembled from materials which were often created at the site, such as the hewn logs for log houses. Industrialization brought the production of more and more housing components into factories. The stamped metal ceilings that Wheeling Steel Corporation made is an example of a prefabricated building component that formerly had been made at a building site.

In order to attract and hold workers in isolated locations, coal companies often built houses - and sometimes entire towns. These company houses were built at Monongah, in Marion County.

Throughout the twentieth century, housing researchers have studied ways of building entire houses in factories. But generally such products have not been popular with consumers. No one is quite sure why. But consumers have resisted factory-made housing while accepting factory-made clothing or factory-processed food. Thus, prefabricated housing has generally been successful only where consumers had no other housing choice. The miners who lived in a company town had no choice about where to live. And so when one coal company decided to build a town of prefabricated houses, it was quite a success. The town is Itmann, in Wyoming County. The houses were built by the

Ritter Lumber Company of Huntington and shipped to Itmann in sections by railroad. The town was built in 1918-1919, and the houses continued to be in use for many years.

Some prefabricated housing was built for needy people during the Great Depression and for workers in weapons factories during World War II. Prefabricated barracks were used to house German prisoners of war at White Sulphur Springs during the war. They were later used as temporary structures in various Greenbrier County schools. Structures made entirely from prefabricated units became common for business or farm use after the war. These were usually made of steel or aluminum. They were particularly useful as barns, garages, warehouses and other large open structures with few or no internal walls. Most of the restaurants built by the fast-food industry during the 1960s and '70s were prefabricated. Prefabricated units were also used to build motels, even small libraries.

The great breakthrough in prefabricated housing came with the emergence of the house trailer or mobile home. Originally trailers were small. They were meant only for recreation or other temporary uses. After World War II, they began to be used as permanent residences. They have been especially popular in rural West Virginia. This is partly due to serious shortages of other types of housing. Very little housing was built during the Great Depression and World War II. During the Depression, people were too poor to afford new housing. During the war, building materials were needed for military use. After World War II, a great housing boom developed in the United States. But West Virginia's economy was deeply depressed between 1953 and 1969. Its stock of housing therefore did not expand as rapidly as the nation's did. Moreover, houses built during the last housing boom of the 1920s had begun to decay. This was especially true of the coal camps whose housing had been cheap and hastily built in the first place. In 1966, a special state government agency studied the housing situation. This agency said that "perhaps no more than one family out of three lives in decent, comfortable housing." It said that one-third of the houses in West Virginia were unsound.

In these conditions, mobile homes provided one way for people to acquire new housing that they could afford. The number of mobile homes increased greatly during the 1960s. By 1970, 6 percent of the dwellings in West Virginia were mobile homes. In rural areas the percentage was even higher. Prosperous rural counties that are close to big cities, such as Jefferson

Topper Sherwood

Mobile homes created a boom in the prefabricated housing market. Their popularity increased during the 1960s. By 1970, 6 percent of West Virginia's dwellings were mobile homes.

and Putnam counties, had the highest number of mobile homes in 1970. During the 1970s and '80s, the number of mobile homes in coal field counties grew. This was almost the only type of new housing available in some coal-mining districts.

Mobile homes are truly prefabricated houses. They are made entirely in factories. The oldest concentration of mobile home factories is in northern Indiana. But such factories are found all over the country. Mobile homes are distributed much like automobiles. They are brought from the factories with special trucks to dealers who, in turn, sell them to consumers. Once in place at the building site, a mobile home is rarely moved. They are mobile only from factory to consumer. Because they have to be pulled along public highways and roads, mobile homes are long and narrow. Essentially they are long metal rectangles, with interior portions arranged like rooms in modern one-story conventional houses. They can look rather strange parked in a West Virginia environment. But mobile homes are really no stranger in West Virginia than Scottish castles or Mexican patios. Their long narrow shape and metallic appearance blends into the landscape as well as traditional rural housing does. They are simply another example of how industrialization has altered the way that West Virginians live.

14.6 Conclusion

What is true of food, clothing and housing could also be said of other areas of everyday life in West Virginia. Consider the basic activities of working, playing and learning. Work in the Frontier and Statehood periods was carried out on an individual basis or in small family groups. People began to work in teams or gangs during the Industrial Period. Today they are likely to work as part of large organizations with thousands of employees.

Sports in Joseph Doddridge's day involved hunting, fishing, wrestling, and foot and horse racing. These activities were enjoyed in groups. But they all involved individual efforts. During the Industrial Period, team sports such as basketball, baseball, and football became popular. During the Bureaucratic Period, sports became multimillion-dollar businesses with professional coaches and athletes paid to perform on a full-time basis. Even at the level of small boys and girls, as in Little League baseball, games are played under rules enforced by bureaucratic organizations which operate all over the nation. The same pattern can be seen in the growth of schools from one-room log schools to consolidated high schools that draw students from an entire county.

Today there are some people who think these changes have gone too far. They say that life has become too impersonal, that it has become too cut-off from nature, that it is dominated too much by large organizations. What do you think? Would you rather have oranges and junk food every day, or no junk food and oranges only at Christmas? Would you rather go to a small school with just your relatives and friends or do you want a school with a large library, science labs and gymnasium? Would you rather live in a small house built out of local materials or in a large mobile home with electric kitchen appliances? Would you prefer one really splendid silk dress or a half-dozen dresses made from polyester? Which keeps you warmer at night, an electric blanket or a quilt? Would you be willing to give up your television set if you could swim every summer in an unpolluted river near your home?

These may seem like silly questions today. But the values which such questions involve are important. Recently, West Virginia has become known as a beautiful place where people may live quiet, simple lives close to nature. There is much truth in this idea. But West Virginia can also be a noisy, active and complex place. Most of its people live just like other Americans do. The majority of them live in towns and cities. Some of these places are beautiful, others are not. But in all of them, nature is something that people experience in their back yards, in parks or on weekend retreats. Within the mountains and hills of our state are highways, factories, mines, office buildings, apartment buildings, shopping centers and schools.

Which West Virginia do you live in? Which one do you want to live in when you grow up? Certainly, you don't have to answer these questions now. But maybe you will someday.

Study Questions - Chapter 14

1. Has standardization affected housing more than food and clothing today or has it affected housing less? What are some of the advantages of standardization of products in each of these areas? What are some of the disadvantages?

2. Find an I-house, a pyramid house, and a temple house in the historic photo of Smithers, West Virginia, shown on page 214.

3. How does the principle of **symmetry** apply to buildings as different as Harewood (page 255) and the miner's house (page 264).

ANALYSIS - An explanation. In history, an analysis tries to explain why an event happened or why a person behaved as she or he did. See also NARRATION.

APPORTIONMENT - Dividing something up into shares. In a political system, apportionment usually means the way seats are divided up in a legislature.

ARCHAEOLOGY - A method of studying societies by searching for and analyzing physical remains, such as objects, bones and structures.

ARISTOCRACY - A political system in which an upper class made up of rich families and their followers have most of the power.

AUTOBIOGRAPHY - The story of a person's life, written by himself or herself.

BARTER - A way of exchanging goods and services without using cash. When something is bartered, it is traded for another thing or service of roughly equal value.

BIOGRAPHY - The story of a person's life, written by another person.

BUREAUCRACY - A large and complex organization, organized according to some rational plan.

BUSINESS CYCLES - A pattern of changes in business activity which occurs over and over again. At the high point of a cycle, business is good and the economy is growing. At the low point, business is bad and the economy is contracting. The low point is called a depression.

CAPITAL - The money which is needed to produce goods and services in an economic system. It has bo be combined with other economic resources, such as HUMAN RESOURCES, NATURAL RESOURCES and MANAGEMENT.

CLASS CONSCIOUSNESS - A feeling of group identity and of mutual support among members of a social class.

CLASSIFY - Sorting out things or observations into categories or groups. The categories are arranged so that different types of things or observations will fall into different groups.

COMMERCIAL FARMERS - Farmers who produce crops or herds which they can sell in a market for cash.

CRAFT UNION - A labor union whose membership is limited to workers who practice a particular trade or set of skills. Carpenters, electricians, plumbers, railroad engineers and glass blowers are a few of the types of workers who have formed craft unions.

CULTURE - The patterns of beliefs, customs, values and behavior which a society practices and teaches to its children. See also MATERIAL CULTURE.

CULTURAL CONFLICT - Conflict which grows out of the differences between the cultures of different groups or societies.

CULTURAL EXCHANGE - The exchange of objects, values or behavior patterns between groups or societies which have different cultures.

CULTURAL TRAIT - A repeated pattern of behavior which helps to distinguish people of a particular culture from groups or societies with different cultures. Archaeologists observe cultural traits through the way that societies make and use objects or through customs such as burial practices.

DEMOCRACY - A political system in which power is shared equally by all the people in the system and the government is chosen in such a way as to represent all the people.

DEPRESSION - An extreme slowing down of economic growth. See also BUSINESS CYCLES and UNEMPLOYMENT.

DESIGN - The way the parts of something - a house for example - fit together.

DIRECT ACTION - An attempt to cause social change through such methods as strikes, demonstrations and disobeying laws that are thought to be bad.

ECONOMIC GROWTH - An increase in the

amount of goods and services produced by an economic system. This means increases in the number of jobs and businesses in the system.

ECONOMIC SYSTEM - A society's system for the production of goods and services.

ENTREPRENEURSHIP - The array of skills that are needed to manage businesses and economic activities generally.

ENVIRONMENT - The natural resources and natural forces (such as climate) which affect the way a society operates. Environmental influences within a society come from nature, while cultural influences come from human beings.

EQUAL APPORTIONMENT - The creation of political districts that encompass about the same number of people. During the Statehood Period, equal apportionment had the effect of increasing the political power of slave-holding districts and was, therefore, undemocratic.

ETHNIC GROUP - A large group of people whose culture differs in important ways from the society the group belongs to. Ethnic groups can differ in the language they speak or in their racial backgroud or both. Members of ethic groups share a sense of society or belonging together. This also serves to set them apart within the larger society.

EVALUATE - A way of comparing historical historical evidence and interpretations in order to see how good they are.

EVIDENCE - Information that furnishes clues about behavior which the investigator has not observed directly. Both historians and detectives need evidence to solve mysteries about past behavior.

EXTRACTIVE INDUSTRY - An industry which produces goods by taking (or extracting) them from the natural environment. Farming, mining, fishing and lumbering are all extractive industries. The products of extractive industries are usually processed before being sold. (See also PROCESSING.)

FAMILY - The basic group in a social system,

consisting of the parents, children and people to whom they are related by birth or marriage.

FEDERAL GUIDELINES - The rules which state and local governments have to follow in order to operate programs that are paid for by the federal government.

FEDERAL NUMBER - A population count that included slaves and was used in assigning (or apportioning) delegates to the Virginia state legislature.

FRONTIER - A border zone. In American history, this was the overlapping zone of white and Indian settlements.

HISTORICAL METHODS - The ways in which historians use EVIDENCE and INTERPRETATION to create historical judgements.

HUMAN RESOURCES - The human thought and energy which is needed to produce goods and services in an economic system.

HYDROELECTRIC POWER - Electricity which is produced from the energy of falling water.

INDUSTRIALIZATION - The process by which the economic system of a society is converted to producing goods and services with machines run by fuels or water power instead of muscle power.

INDUSTRIAL DISCIPLINE - The kind of steady, predictable behavior that is most efficient among workers who work with machines.

INDUSTRIAL UNION - A labor union which takes in all of the workers who work in a particular industry, regardless of the kind of skills they use in their jobs.

INTERPRETATION - An analysis of an historical event which identifies the most important evidence and theories about the event, and explains how and why the event took place.

LAND SPECULATION - The practice of obtaining land in order to sell it rather than use it. Speculators tried to sell their land as quickly as they could at a high profit, but wer not often success ful. However, their activities often kept land from being used normally by settlers.

LAND TITLE - The legal record of deed which proves that a particular owner owns a particular piece of land.

LAND USE - The ways in which a society uses land as a NATURAL RESOURCE in its economic system.

LOBBYIST - A person who volunteers or is hired to try to influence government actions on behalf of a PRESSURE GROUP. The name comes from the old-fashioned practice of hanging around in the lobbies of government buildings.

MANAGEMENT - The activities which organize and direct economic activity.

MASS COMMUNICATION - Communications methods which allow large numbers of people to exchange information and messages quickly. Telephones, telegraphs, postal systems, satellites and MASS MEDIA are types of mass-communication methods.

MASS MEDIA - Systems for distribting information to large numbers of people. Newspapers, magazines, telelvision, radio, films and recordings are examples of mass media.

MASS MERCHANDISING - Systems for selling large amounts of goods to large numbers of consumers. Department and chain stores, mail-order systems, advertising and credit cards are all systems of mass merchandising.

MASS PRODUCTION - The system of producing large quantities of standardized goods with machines.

MATCHING GRANTS - A way of financing programs operated by two levels of government. In this method, the larger government (usually the federal government) puts of a certain amount of money to match each amount put up by the smaller government (usually a state).

MATERIAL CULTURE - The part of a society's culture which consists of objects.

MECHANIZATION - Changing a production pro-cess so that all of most of the work is done by machines rather than by the muscles of animals or human beings.

MEMOIRS - A form of autobiography in which the writer discusses only parts of his or her life. Usually memoirs focus on well-known people or events.

MERGER - The combination of two or more business corporations. Usually one buys control of the other.

MERIT APPOINTMENT - The practice of giving government jobs to people who have demonstrated, in some formal way, their ability to do the job. See also PATRONAGE.

NARRATION - Telling a story. In history, narration describes an event or the behavior of a person or group. See also ANALYSIS.

NATURAL RESOURCES - Raw materials and other forces (such as climate or land) which are needed to produce goods and services in an economic system.

PATRONAGE - The practice of giving government jobs to people who have performed services for a political party or leader. See also MERIT APPOINTMENT.

PERIOD - A length of time (years, decades or centuries) which can be identified by its historical features.

POLITICAL CULTURE - A part of a political system which consists of practices or values which are not formally organized or written down, but which are used regularly by the system.

POLITICAL INSTITUTIONS - The parts of a political system which are well-organized and well-defined. Formal institutions include things like courts, laws, legislatures and voting practices. Informal institutions include well-established political customs and habits.

POPULAR ELECTION - The choosing of government officials by the voters, as opposed to their selection by others in office.

PRESSURE GROUP - A group of people, organized to bring pressure on government officials. The goal of such a group is to influence government actions in favor of itself or its members. See also LOBBYIST.

PRINCIPLE OF INTERCHANGEABLE PARTS - The practice of assembling parts which are designed to be identical with each other. Thus a part from one item can replace the same part from another item of the same time. This makes it possible to repair products more efficiently and cheaply, and it requires producing the parts with machines.

PRODUCTIVITY - The efficiency with which resources are used in producing goods and services. Increasing productivity is done by using a certain amount of resources to produce more than was done before, or using fewer resources to produce the same amount.

PROPERTY - Goods and resources (such as land) which are owned by individuals or by groups such as families, corporations or governments.

PERSONAL PROPERTY - Goods and resources which are not attached in some way to the earth. This includes such things as equipment, jewelry, furniture and stocks and bonds. For tax purposes, personal property is treated differently from REAL PROPERTY.

PRVIATE PROPERTY - Goods or resources which are owned by individuals or groups, as opposed to governments.

PROPORTIONATE - A relationship between the sizes of two or more objects or quantities. When the size of something is determined so that it will be a certain amount larger or smaller than the size of something else, then the two sizes are said to be proportionate to one another.

REGION - An area or part of the earth's surface which has features that set it apart from other areas.

SECESSION - The attempt by the Southern states to secede, or withdraw, from the United States at the start of the Civil War.

SECTIONALISM - Political activities inspired or caused by geographic differences between two or more regions or sections within the same political system.

SEQUENCE - The order in which things occur. In archaeology, the order in which objects are found, as a particular site is dig up and carefully recorded, so that the objects can be compared with other objects found in the same sequence or level.

SOCIAL CHANGE - Changes which affect an entire society. Usually social change takes place slowly over long periods of time, but sometimes it can occur rapidly.

SOCIAL CLASS - People who are set apart from other people in their society by similarities in the amount of wealth, power or prestige they have (or lack).

SOCIAL SYSTEM - The way in which a society is organized into groups. The social system determines how people become members of groups and which groups are most important in the society.

SOCIETY - A large number of people who live together in an organized way. Usually they share the same territory and often (though not always) they share the same culture. A society can be very large, as a nation, or very small, as in a tribe.

STANDARDIZE - To organize or make objects so that each one meets or fits a certain standard. The standard usually is set up to make sure that the size, weight, shape or content is the same for each object to which the standard applies.

STRUCTURE - The way in which a building is built.

SUBSISTENCE FARMER - A farmer whose crops and herds are used to feed the farm's people and animals, instead of being sold in the market for cash. See also COMMERCIAL FARMER.

SUFFRAGE - The right or privilege of voting. See also WHITE MANHOOD SUFFRAGE.

SYNTHETIC - Something which is artificially combined together. Synthetic textiles are made from chemical fibers developed from coal, wood, petroleum and other materials.

TERRITORY - Land which belongs to an entire society and is usually controlled by the society's government.

TEXTILE - A woven fabric or cloth.

UNEMPLOYMENT - The situation that occurs when workers lose their jobs because of economic DEPRESSIONS or through other types of changes, such as MECHANIZATION. The term is also used when there are not enough jobs for all the people who need them.

VOLUNTARY ASSOCIATION - A group formed when people join together to pursue or promote some common interest.

WHITE MANHOOD SUFFRAGE - The right or privilege of white men to vote. See also SUFFRAGE.

WHITE BASIS OF EQUAL APPORTIONMENT - The design of election districts so that they contain about the same number of white people, as opposed to all people, including slaves. The white basis was more democratic because slaves had no real political power.